PRAISE FOR *THE BABY BOMBERS*

"A number of books likely will be written about the Yankees' renaissance, but Bryan Hoch has beaten everyone to the punch with *The Baby Bombers*, a compelling look at the team's past, present, and future. Hoch is around the team every day, and he masterfully demonstrates the connections between the Core Four and the current group. *The Baby Bombers* is a must-read for anyone who wants to understand who these new Yankees are, and where they are going."

　　—KEN ROSENTHAL, baseball writer and columnist for *The Athletic*, and Emmy Award-winning field reporter for MLB Network and FOX Sports

"The Core Four is impossible to replicate, but this young group of studs is special and unique. It will be exciting to see what mark they make in Yankees history, and Bryan Hoch is the perfect person to tell this story. His knowledge and understanding of baseball and Yankee culture offer readers an insider's perspective into New York's bright future!"

　　—NICK SWISHER, New York Yankees 2009–2012, 2009 World Series Champion

"It was only natural the first book on the Baby Bombers should be written by Bryan Hoch, the respected veteran Yankees beat writer who has chronicled their development all through the minors to their fruition as stars in 2017–18. Nobody knows them better than Hoch and nobody tells their story better."

　　—BILL MADDEN, 2010 J.G. Taylor Spink Award winner and author of the *New York Times* bestseller *Steinbrenner: The Last Lion of Baseball*

"Having been around Bryan Hoch for a number of years, I could always tell his passion for creating something special through his stories. *The Baby Bombers* is a beautiful work of art in so many ways. As a Yankees fan or— for that matter—simply a baseball fan, this is a must read!"

　　—JOBA CHAMBERLAIN, former Major League pitcher and 2009 World Series Champion for the New York Yankees

"Few people have a better feel for a team than a beat writer like Bryan Hoch, who takes readers inside the Yankees' front office and clubhouse to experience the emergence of the franchise's next great dynasty. Thoroughly reported and written through the keen lens of an insider, Hoch's great work shines through in a remarkable story that seemingly belongs on a Broadway stage rather than a ballpark in the South Bronx."
— MARK FEINSAND, executive reporter for MLB.com, long-time New York Yankees beat writer, and author of *The New York Yankees Fans' Bucket List*

"With *The Baby Bombers*, Bryan Hoch dives into the many origins of what the Yankees hope is their next great run. You'll learn plenty about these guys and how they got here. A very enjoyable read."
— KEN DAVIDOFF, baseball columnist for the *New York Post*

"The 2017 and '18 seasons were two of the most exciting for Yankees fans in recent years. It wasn't just lightning in a bottle—it was built with a lot of hard work and attention to detail. No one can tell that story better than Bryan Hoch, who employs the same efforts in *The Baby Bombers*. Bryan takes you inside the process of how prospects became stars and planted the seeds of what could be the next Yankees dynasty. If you loved watching that magical run last October, you need to read this book."
— SWEENY MURTI, New York Yankees beat reporter for WFAN

"There's no shortage of interest in where the Yankees are headed in 2019 and beyond. Bryan Hoch delivers a detailed, richly-reported road map that makes for essential reading for fans."
— BOB KLAPISCH, veteran baseball columnist and author

THE BABY BOMBERS

THE INSIDE STORY OF THE NEXT YANKEES DYNASTY

BRYAN HOCH

FOREWORD BY MARK TEIXEIRA

DIVERSIONBOOKS

For Connie
As George McFly said, "You're my density."

And for Penny and Maddie
May you always swing for the fences.

Diversion Books
A Division of Diversion Publishing Corp.
443 Park Avenue South, Suite 1004
New York, New York 10016
www.DiversionBooks.com

For more information, email info@diversionbooks.com

Front cover images: Top, Aaron Judge © Rob Cuni; Middle, Gary Sanchez
© Rob Cuni; Bottom, Luis Severino © Arturo Pardavila III

Image credits: 2, 5, 102, 114, 159, 131 © Arturo Pardavila III; 52, 241 © Bryan
Green; 120 © Buck Davidson / Pro Sports Media, Inc.; 114 © David Monseur,
MiLB; XII, XV © David Richard-USA TODAY Sports; 129 © Fredrik Bouw/
Phrake Photography; 144, 147 © Jasen Vinlove-USA TODAY Sports; 23, 25, 30,
48, 69, 87, 178, 190, 202, 213, 232 © Keith Allison; 76 © Laura Nawrocik; 8, 8,
12 © Lawrence Fung; 241 © Lianna Holub; 56, 105, 224 © Rich L. Wang; 188
© Rick Osentoski-USA TODAY Sports; 147 © Steve Mitchell-USA TODAY
Sports; 229 © Troy Taormina-USA TODAY Sports; 43, 95, 144 Courtesy of
Fresno State Athletics; 65, 65, 153 Courtesy of the Charleston RiverDogs; 237, 239
Photo by Bryan Hoch; 123, 166 Photo Credit: Hayden Schiff, CC BY 2.0 license

First Diversion Books paperback edition March 2019.
Paperback ISBN: 978-1-63576-604-2
eBook ISBN: 978-1-63576-418-5

Printed in the U.S.A.
1 3 5 7 9 10 8 6 4 2

CONTENTS

CONTENTS

FOREWORD

If there is one thing I learned during my career in Major League Baseball, it's that a championship roster requires a blend of experience and youth. The last Yankee dynasty ended with five World Series rings for the "Core Four." I was lucky enough to join Jorge Posada, Andy Pettitte, Mariano Rivera, and Derek Jeter for their last title in 2009. In the years following that 2009 World Championship, our Yankee teams became more reliant than ever on veterans, and were short on the energy and talent that young players bring to the field. Yankee Universe was looking for the next Core Four to bring a winning dynasty back to the Bronx. Even better, if these young players were homegrown.

Enter the "Baby Bombers."

I first met Gary Sanchez, Luis Severino, Greg Bird, and Aaron Judge years ago in early spring training when major and minor leaguers worked out together. I saw their individual talents right away, but more importantly, I could confidently say about any of them, "Hey, this guy *gets it*." For those unfamiliar with the term, when a prospect not only has talent, but also the intangibles and work ethic to want to be a great major leaguer, he "gets it." And I knew it wouldn't be long before these kids who *got it* were called up to the parent club.

When I played with those guys during their big league stints in the 2015 and 2016 seasons, everybody in the clubhouse realized that what we were seeing then in small samples, we had the potential to see for a long time as their careers developed: Sanchez's throwing arm and bat control, Severino's electric stuff, Bird's sweet swing, and Judge's immense power.

All of these tools were on display in the 2017 season, a campaign that ended one win shy of a World Series berth. While watching the 2017 play-offs, what jumped out at me wasn't that the Baby Bombers were making key plays every game, it was that these ballplayers who were so amazingly good, were going to get even better. Sanchez will improve behind the plate, Severino will perfect his changeup and add another devastating pitch to his arsenal, Bird will put up monster numbers when healthy for a full year, and Judge will continue to learn better plate discipline to complement his power.

When I think of the groundwork that has been laid with these Baby Bombers, I can't help but get excited (almost giddy) to watch them grow up in pinstripes. I tell Yankee fans to get ready for another run of championships because this roster will be full of talented players for a very long time. Yankees general manager Brian Cashman has done an unbelievable job of stockpiling talent in the major and minor leagues, and he'll have the payroll flexibility to add in free agency as well as minor league depth to make key deadline trades for years to come.

I am so happy that Bryan Hoch is telling the story of the Baby Bombers, a story that I was lucky enough to witness up close and personal for the first few chapters. Bryan is in the Yankee clubhouse every day and understands the highs and lows of a young baseball player becoming a star. Even better, he understands the science and art of scouting, development, and front-office strategy.

I hope that you enjoy reading about the Baby Bombers as much as watching them. As you know, these guys never seem to disappoint!

Mark Teixeira
ESPN Baseball Analyst
New York Yankees 2009-2016
2009 World Series Champion

PROLOGUE

AMERICAN LEAGUE DIVISION SERIES, GAME 5

October 11, 2017

The hardest thrower in the history of baseball placed his left foot along the rubber on the mound of Cleveland's Progressive Field, oblivious to the roars being unleashed by a frenzied, towel-waving crowd of 37,802 attempting to will their hometown Indians into extending their season for a few more precious minutes. Aroldis Chapman trained his eyes upon catcher Gary Sanchez as he looked for a sign, his New York Yankees one strike away from completing a historic and unlikely comeback in the American League Division Series.

Fastball, Sanchez suggested. His fingers flashed the sequence quickly, so as to conceal them from Carlos Santana, the runner at second base. Cradling the baseball in his left hand, Chapman nodded, rotating his digits expertly around the seams and bringing his glove to a high set in front of his face. Chapman's fluid motion brought his right knee into his chest, generating immense torque before the baseball was released from his hand, hissing toward home plate.

A radar gun clocked the ball's velocity at 101 mph, remarkable for most pitchers but another day at the office for Chapman, as the hurler's thirty-second offering of that sixty-one-degree, overcast evening buzzed up and in toward Austin Jackson. The outfielder flinched, jerking his body toward the third-base dugout as the ball smacked into Sanchez's glove.

Jeff Nelson, the home plate umpire, raised his right hand and jabbed the air with his left, signaling a third strike. Chapman clenched his fists and screamed toward the sky, addressing no one and everyone all at once. Sanchez tucked the ball into the back right pocket of his uniform pants, trotted to the mound and was the first to embrace Chapman. The battery was quickly surrounded by their teammates, as they hugged and shook hands to celebrate their advance to the AL Championship Series.

As the Yankees charged off the diamond and through the dugout runway that led to the visiting clubhouse, they seemed to be drawn magnetically toward the dozens of champagne bottles that waited on ice in the center of their dressing area, and their hoots and hollers echoed in the concrete corridor. Plastic sheeting had been tacked over their belongings and the industrial-strength gray carpet, creating the appearance of a boozy backyard Slip 'N Slide.

Goggles were strapped on and corks were popped as the team enjoyed their third—and ultimately, final—celebration of the year. They had also doused each other with bubbly after clinching a postseason berth with a September 23 victory over the Blue Jays in Toronto, and again after prevailing over the Twins in the American League Wild Card game on October 3

The 2017 Yankees exceeded expectations all season long, highlighted by their comeback to defeat the Indians in the ALDS. New York was the tenth team to recover from an 0-2 deficit in a best-of-five postseason series.

at Yankee Stadium. Considering the stakes, the stage, and the opponent, this Cleveland edition of the ongoing party seemed to signal that great things were in the very near future. Not bad for a young team that had been widely expected to endure a rebuilding season.

"They just keep getting better and better, to be honest," power-hitting phenom Aaron Judge said, squinting through the droplets while pitcher Luis Severino attacked him with an overflowing bottle of Napa Valley sparkling wine. "This was a pretty huge win against an incredible Indians team."

The Yanks had come out swinging to win three straight games and upend Cleveland—a 102-win force during the regular season—in an epic ALDS. By doing so, the Yankees became the tenth team to recover from an 0–2 deficit in a best-of-five postseason series, and all of the "Baby Bombers" had been smack dab in the middle of the action.

First baseman Greg Bird connected for what may have been the team's most important home run of the postseason in Game 3 of the ALDS, backing a dominant Masahiro Tanaka outing with a seventh-inning drive to right field off Andrew Miller—an intimidating left-hander who'd surrendered five homers to left-handed hitters since the beginning of the 2015 season. Bird's deep drive represented the only run of that game.

No less important had been the contributions from the talented young duo of Judge and Gary Sanchez. They had been key cogs in the offense all season long, combining to belt 85 homers, but it was the young stars' defense that earned plaudits that night. Sanchez made several blocks on Tanaka's hellacious splitter that saved runs, including a fourth-inning sequence that froze Jason Kipnis at third base after a one-out triple. The welts that Sanchez absorbed allowed Tanaka to keep his pitches diving out of the strike zone, and the Indians' lineup flailed helplessly.

Bird's homer came one inning after Judge's six-foot-seven, 282-pound frame crashed into the ten-foot wall in right field, his leaping grab bringing back what could have been a two-run homer off the bat of shortstop Francisco Lindor. Chants of "M-V-P!" echoed throughout the crowd, as they had all season for the rookie standout, and they spilled into the continuation of action as the Bronx faithful applauded their new favorite.

"That's what it's all about," Judge said. "That's what this team loves. Our backs are up against the wall, and then we come out swinging. That's what we do."

Pitching in front of a raucous crowd at Yankee Stadium, Severino rewarded the team's confidence in Game 4 of the ALDS, bouncing back from an awful outing in the Wild Card game to pick up the win with a nine-strikeout performance. Showing off a thick gold chain that jangled out of his uniform shirt, Severino's right hand unleashed fastballs that buzzed between 97 and 100 mph all evening. No Tribe hitter was rushing to the bat rack in order to face him.

His bat silenced to that point by Cleveland's pitching staff, Judge broke through with his first hit of the ALDS, raking a two-run double that capped a five-run second inning and sent right-hander Trevor Bauer to an early exit. Sanchez completed the scoring in the sixth with his second homer of the postseason, an opposite-field bash that put the game out of reach.

In the series opener, the Indians had blanked New York before dealing them a gut-punch for the ages in Game 2, when manager Joe Girardi failed to challenge a hit-by-pitch on Lonnie Chisenhall. That set up Lindor's sixth-inning grand slam off Chad Green, bringing the Indians back to life in a game that the Yanks believed had been put away.

"It was tough, but I feel like the guys were in good spirits, as good as we could be," Bird said. "We knew we still had work to do and we weren't out of it yet."

So, they were here again in Cleveland, the home of the Rock & Roll Hall of Fame, a river that once caught fire, and where a ten-story banner of NBA superstar LeBron James was proudly displayed in the shadows of their baseball stadium. At age twenty-seven, shortstop Didi Gregorius was a few years too old for the Bomber to be considered a "Baby," but he had represented a key figure in the team's roster turnaround. Now, he was about to take a boisterous Game 5 crowd out of the game, mashing a first-inning homer that stunned ace Corey Kluber.

When Gregorius doubled his fun by crushing a hanging curveball out of the yard two innings later, Kluber was on his way to the showers and the Yankees were rolling. As David Robertson completed 2⅔ scoreless innings and Gardner worked an epic twelve-pitch at-bat that produced a hit and two more runs, the "Big Buck Hunter Pro" cabinet arcade machine that had been shared by members of every American League club was being wheeled out of the visiting clubhouse, with workers behind the scenes preparing for the bubbly precipitation that seemed certain to come.

On the stadium's suite level, Hal Steinbrenner sported a blue blazer

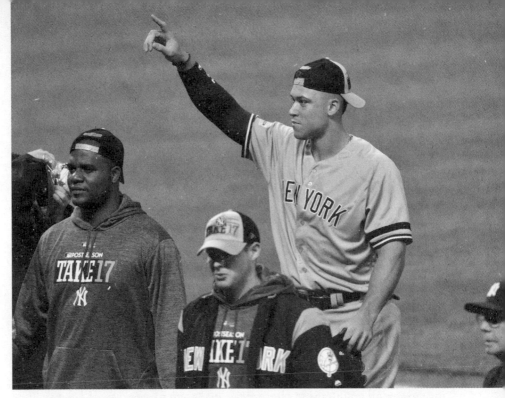

No one hit baseballs harder in 2017 than Aaron Judge, who was unanimously selected as the American League's Rookie of the Year. He led the AL in runs scored (128), home runs (52), and walks (127).

across his shoulders and a satisfied grin on his face while he playfully jockeyed for position in a crowded elevator with his sister, Jennifer. The youngest son of George and Joan Steinbrenner, the forty-seven-year-old was handsome with a thick head of perfectly coiffed brown hair, and he preferred to steer the Yankees in a much different fashion than his bombastic father had.

After taking over as the team's managing general partner and day-to-day control person in 2008, Steinbrenner had been among the most vocal proponents in directing the organization toward a future that could be both exciting and cost-effective. As Steinbrenner made his way toward the celebration on the stadium's basement level, he was aware of the outside perception that this Yankees team had overachieved. It was a sentiment that he had vehemently disagreed with.

"That clubhouse is one of the best we've ever had," Steinbrenner said. "You saw it during the season, even in the times that they weren't playing well. Every time I would go down to the clubhouse during a homestand, it just seemed like it was always the same. You wouldn't be able to tell if they won twenty in a row or lost twenty in a row. They're always loose, they're always confident, they've always got each other's back. And I don't think [their success] is a surprise to them at all."

As they bounced and splashed joyously in that room, Judge called the experience "a dream come true," but he wasn't shocked that the Yankees had been able to overcome Cleveland. It was a story that Judge had seen and participated in many times before. Those off-Broadway performances in places like Charleston, Tampa, Trenton, and Scranton/Wilkes-Barre had prepared Judge and his teammates for moments like this.

"There's a lot of fight. We fight and we fight and we fight," Judge said. "It's incredible to watch. A lot of these guys I've gone through the minor leagues with. To see them develop and turn into what they have now, it's amazing."

As the revelry tapered off, a charter plane sat at one of the gates of Hopkins International Airport, waiting to ferry the Yankees to their next destination: a showdown with the Astros to decide which team would have the honor of representing the American League in the World Series. For everyone who had set foot in that room on that gleeful night in Cleveland, there was an overwhelming sense that the Baby Bombers' journey was only beginning.

CHAPTER 1

CHANGING OF THE GUARD

Two years, seven months, and nineteen days had passed since Derek Jeter's final Yankee Stadium at-bat, and as the longtime captain tugged on a three-piece royal blue suit and walked the hallways of his baseball alma mater, retirement seemed even more enjoyable than he had anticipated. No longer was he forced to check into a Rust Belt hotel at 4:00 a.m. or to keep an eye on the weather forecast, unless it was to check on a tee time. Your calendar opens to a great number of possibilities when you no longer have to try to win the World Series each and every year.

Jeter scaled the steps leading to the first-base dugout and found himself surrounded by players nearly half his age, milling about in a set of pink pin-striped uniforms that the team had been issued in observance of Mother's Day. Offering a friendly grin, Jeter watched as his outstretched right hand was swallowed into the meaty palm of twenty-five-year-old right fielder Aaron Judge, who held a good four-inch, eighty-seven-pound advantage over Jeter's final listed playing measurements.

Now forty-three, Jeter said he had not watched much baseball immediately following his retirement, eager to create some distance from the sport that had dictated his every action from February to October (and occasionally November) for more than two decades. Of late, he had found himself flipping on the TV in his Tampa, Florida, home more often, checking in on the only organization he had ever played for. As a child, Jeter's favorite Yankee had been Dave Winfield, a towering right fielder with power. Now, all these years later, Jeter was becoming an Aaron Judge fan.

"He's had a tremendous start to his career, but more importantly, he handles himself well," Jeter had said two days earlier in Rockefeller Center's Studio 6-B, where he taped an interview segment with Jimmy Fallon for *The Tonight Show*. "He's a good person, he works hard, he has the right demeanor and attitude, and hopefully he has a long career."

Judge said he was humbled by the comment, calling it "incredible." Their careers had hardly intersected to that point; Jeter had been on the disabled list for most of the 2013 season, including the day that Judge signed his first professional contract and was rewarded with an invitation to the Oakland Coliseum, where he whacked batting practice homers with the big league team. Judge was across the street in minor league camp while Jeter went through the paces of his final spring training in 2014, but the parallels between the stars seemed to be evident on this May afternoon in 2017.

"He's a little bit like Derek, to me," manager Joe Girardi said. "He's got a smile all the time. He loves to play the game. You always think that he's going to do the right thing on the field and off the field when you look at him. He's got a presence about him. He plays the game to win all the time. That's the most important thing, it's not about what you did that day.

"I understand that's a big comparison, but I remember Derek when he

Derek Jeter poses with his Monument Park plaque prior to the Yankees' game on May 14, 2017. Jeter specifically selected Mother's Day for the event to honor his mom, Dorothy. Jeter's uniform No. 2 was the final remaining single digit to be retired by the Yankees.

was young. He grew into that leadership role, but that was Derek. Derek loved to have fun, loved to laugh, and loved to play the game. Always had a smile on his face and was energetic, and that's what I see from this kid."

As the Yankees celebrated Jeter's accomplishments, retiring his uniform No. 2 while dedicating a Monument Park plaque in his honor, the current players lined the top step of the dugout to absorb a picturesque moment that promised to be recalled as their generation's Mickey Mantle Day. Jorge Posada called the afternoon "the end of an era," but it felt like another had already begun; Judge was even deployed in a supporting role, escorting Don Zimmer's widow, Soot, to home plate.

To an incredible ovation, Jeter and his family were driven onto the field in golf carts, with a recording of Frank Sinatra's "My Way" playing through the stadium's loudspeakers. That same track had been heard on the night when Jeter notched a walk-off hit in his final Yankee Stadium at-bat, accompanying him as he strode alone to his shortstop position to crouch and say a prayer. Posada was correct in stating that this Derek Jeter Day represented a turning point for the organization, but a better place to pinpoint the milestone was September 25, 2014, Jeter's final day in pinstripes.

There had been gray skies reflecting off the roof of Jeter's late-model sport utility vehicle as it rumbled underneath the elevated tracks of the 4 train that afternoon, its wipers rhythmically dismissing precipitation. Unbeknownst to anyone walking along River Avenue, one of New York City's most recognizable celebrities was behind the wheel, approaching the finish line of a celebrated twenty-year journey.

Slowing to a crawl with Yankee Stadium towering above his left shoulder, Jeter descended the ramp that leads into the players' parking garage. It was a commute that Jeter had made dozens of times that season, motoring from his swanky apartment in Manhattan's West Village, and this time he was grateful for the privacy that his ride's tinted glass provided. Choking back tears on the way to his final home game, the outpouring of love and appreciation in a season's worth of plaudits and celebrations had finally cracked the coolest Yankee.

"You almost feel as if you're watching your own funeral," Jeter said. "People are telling you great things, and they're showing highlights and reflecting. I understand that my baseball career is over with. But people are giving you well wishes like you're about to die. I've appreciated it all, but internally it feels like part of you is dying, and I guess that's true because the baseball side, it's over with."

Jeter detested the term "farewell tour," believing that it made his final pass through the schedule somehow more important than the outcome of the games, but in this case, that was true. The Yankees had been officially eliminated from contention one day earlier, so this would mark the second time in 2,745 career games that Jeter took the field with his club mathematically eliminated from the postseason. Once Jeter cleaned out his locker for the final time, it would mark the official end of the "Core Four," a vaunted group that celebrated World Series titles in 1996, 1998, 1999, 2000, and then again in 2009 after helping to open the glittering $2.3 billion cathedral that sat across East 161st Street from the original.

The phrase "Core Four" always struck Jeter as discordant. Bernie Williams had been as important to the success of the 1996–2000 dynasty, Jeter would argue, arriving before the celebrated quartet of Jeter, left-hander Andy Pettitte, catcher Jorge Posada, and right-hander Mariano Rivera. Williams made his big-league debut in 1991, and the sensitive, guitar-strumming switch-hitter had been seemingly excluded from the catch-phrase only because his playing career ended three years before the Core scored their rings for the thumb by defeating the Philadelphia Phillies in the 2009 World Series.

The intensely passionate Posada had been the first of the Core to hang up his gear, announcing his retirement after a trying 2011 season when he lost his job as the starting catcher and was transitioned into a designated hitter while occasionally clashing with Girardi. Rivera's exit had been a league-wide source of celebration during the 2013 campaign, with the all-time saves leader returning from a catastrophic knee injury sustained while shagging batting practice fly balls at Kansas City's Kauffman Stadium.

It had been Girardi's idea to send Jeter and Pettitte to the mound on the evening of September 26, 2013, retrieving the baseball from Rivera for the final time. When Jeter told his longtime teammate, "Time to go," Rivera hid his tears by burying his face into Pettitte's right shoulder. Pettitte could sympathize with those emotions. He had recently announced his retirement for the second time and ended his career two days later with a complete game victory over the Astros in Houston, about a half hour from his home in Deer Park, Texas.

In May 2015, the Yankees' Fab Five reunited for Bernie Williams Day in the Bronx. From left: Andy Pettitte, Jorge Posada, Mariano Rivera, Williams, and Derek Jeter.

Because those two exits stood as the most memorable moments of an otherwise unremarkable 2013 Yankees season, Jeter sensed that his departure was approaching. Jeter had dealt with a catastrophic injury of his own, having shattered his left ankle while chasing a ground ball in the 12th inning of Game 1 of the 2012 American League Championship Series. It was an injury attributed to the repeated cortisone injections that had kept the captain on the field in the second half of that season.

Though Jeter could not have suspected it at the time, that 6–4 loss to the Tigers marked the final game of his illustrious postseason career. He had spent an entire extra season in October: 158 playoff games against the sport's best teams and pitchers, in which Jeter batted .308 with a .374 on-base percentage and a .465 slugging percentage, collecting 200 hits, 20 homers, 61 RBIs and 18 steals—and those numbers don't even quantify feats like the iconic "Flip Play" that turned around Game 3 of the 2001 American League Division Series, helping the Yanks recover from an 0–2 series deficit against the Athletics.

In a hint of the publishing aspirations that would mark the beginning of his post-playing career, Jeter bypassed the traditional media in order to announce his own retirement on a Wednesday afternoon in February 2014.

Having spent the previous evening personally crafting his message, Jeter clicked the "post" button on a 735-word Facebook announcement that created a seismic ripple throughout the game.

"The one thing I always said to myself was that when baseball started to feel more like a job, it would be time to move forward," Jeter wrote.

Playing shortstop for the Yankees had been Jeter's dream since his days as a Little Leaguer in Kalamazoo, Michigan—he'd announced as much to his fourth-grade classmates—and he had achieved close to every personal and professional goal that he had set. Other thoughts were beginning to enter Jeter's mind. His sister, Sharlee, had recently given birth to a son, Jalen, who would steal the show of Jeter's final home game when television cameras caught the adorable toddler tipping his "RE2PECT" cap in his uncle's direction.

That introduction to family life stirred new aspirations for a man who was perennially regarded as one of Manhattan's most eligible bachelors. To the approval of his longtime teammates, the idea of marriage was finally on the table. "There was always hope," Rivera had joked. By the summer of 2016, Jeter had tied the knot with *Sports Illustrated* supermodel Hannah Davis; the couple would welcome a daughter, Bella Raine, in August 2017.

Throughout his playing career, Jeter frequently voiced his desire to secure an ownership role with a Major League Baseball team. His years playing under the late George M. Steinbrenner had instilled a desire to be the one calling the shots; if and when that opportunity ever came, Jeter said he intended to use some (but not all) of the leadership traits employed by "The Boss" during his tumultuous reign over the game's most valuable franchise.

In a twist, Marlins owner Jeffrey Loria—a New York art dealer who, less than three years later, would agree to sell his franchise to a group involving Jeter for $1.2 billion—happened to be among the 48,613 clutching tickets for that final Yankees home game of the 2014 season, with the playoff-bound Orioles in town to wrap the regular season. South Florida was a dream for another day; for now, Jeter needed to get through nine more innings without his frazzled nerves going completely haywire.

Jeter made his way through the clubhouse, which was hidden underneath the field level seats on the first-base side. At 30,000 square feet, it is the largest in all of baseball—2½ times larger than its predecessor across the street—so massive that Jeter once got lost in April 2009 while trying to return to his locker from the dining area. In the players' plush dressing area, Jeter's assigned locker sat on prime real estate, to the right of a double-doored exit that was off limits to the reporters covering the team. That allowed for a quick escape whenever necessary.

The Yankees are perhaps the most closely chronicled team in baseball, with numerous "beat" reporters attached to their home and road games. In Jeter's final season, outlets regularly covering the team included the *Bergen Record*, *Journal News*, *Newsday*, *New York Daily News*, *New York Post*, *The New York Times*, and *The Wall Street Journal*, plus representatives from *ESPNDeportes.com*, *ESPNNewYork.com*, *MLB.com*, and *WFAN* radio. That did not even include the host of Japanese outlets tracking the careers of outfielder Ichiro Suzuki and right-handed pitcher Hiroki Kuroda, both of whom were on the team at that time.

Suffice it to say that Jeter was accustomed to being interrupted by an eager questioner at some point during his daily ritual. Entering the clubhouse, he would usually set a venti Red Eye—black coffee with an extra shot of espresso and two sugars—on a shelf of his locker, then dole out a few minutes of his time to the press. Jeter had started his Starbucks addiction a few years prior with sugary Frappuccinos, and now joked that he was slowly but surely turning into his father, Charles. He'd then sling a pair of athletic socks over his shoulder and begin the task of getting dressed for batting practice.

Jeter believed that he had seen it all by this time, but even he was taken aback when he turned the corner from the team's kitchenette and was greeted by a pack of more than 100 media members, all there to chronicle his every move. Dealing out an assortment of clichés with an extremely short shelf life—"My feelings are, I hope the rain stops," was one—proved a simple task compared to what took place when the media was finally booted from the clubhouse two hours before game time. On behalf of the players, pitcher CC Sabathia presented Jeter with a painting and a gold watch. Jeter had to shift his gaze toward the ceiling, so overcome with emotion that he dared not make eye contact.

"Again, I almost lost it, and I had to turn away from them in order not to," Jeter said. "At that point, I wasn't sure how effective I was going to be in the game."

Despite threatening forecasts, the dark skies gave way to a blue and

The end of an era. Derek Jeter, Jorge Posada, and Mariano Rivera were the first trio of teammates in MLB, NFL, NBA, or NHL history to have played together in sixteen seasons.

A season of league-wide tributes to retiring shortstop Derek Jeter culminated with the longtime Yankees captain's final home game on Sept. 25, 2014.

orange panorama, setting up a crisp and clear evening that reminded of October—and that was an atmosphere in which Jeter was right at home. Taking the field for the top of the first inning, chants of "DE-REK JE-TER" rang out at deafening decibels, prompting Jeter to take a deep breath and stare into his glove—a future Hall of Famer transformed into a frightened Little Leaguer.

"I was honestly out there saying, 'Please don't hit it to me, because I don't know what's going to happen,'" Jeter said. "To be honest with you, I don't know how I played this game. I went up my first at-bat, I forgot my elbow guard. I was throwing balls away. I was giving signs to [infielder Stephen] Drew on who should cover second base on a steal, and there was no runner on first. I was all messed up."

Jeter's muscle memory responded. He turned on a 95-mph fastball from Baltimore right-hander Kevin Gausman in the first inning, pelting the left-field wall for a double, and knocked home a go-ahead run in the seventh inning on a broken-bat ground ball that shortstop J.J. Hardy threw away for an error. As far as Jeter was concerned, he would have been satisfied if the story ended right there. The top of the eighth produced another chant from the bleachers: "THANK YOU, JE-TER," which was acknowledged with a wave of the shortstop's glove. Jeter's eyes moistened.

"I'm thinking to myself, 'What are you thanking me for? I was just trying to do my job,'" Jeter said. "Really, they're the ones I want to thank. They're the ones that have made this special."

There had been a healthy amount of discussion amongst team employees about how to best orchestrate Jeter's departure from the field, and in fact, there was a plan in place. Longtime equipment manager Rob Cucuzza produced the winner, suggesting that Jeter take a celebratory lap around the stadium's warning track. In the final turn, he would have been joined by Pettitte, Posada, Rivera, Williams, Tino Martinez, Gerald Williams, and Joe Torre, who would have escorted Jeter down the dugout steps and into retirement.

"We were going to make him walk around the whole field," Girardi said. "And then when he got to the left-field corner, that group was going to walk out—the Posadas, the Torres, the Mos. They were going to wait for him at home plate, let him walk off into the tunnel—basically saying, 'It's time to join us.'"

Relief pitcher David Robertson altered the blueprint in the ninth inning, surrendering long home runs to Adam Jones and Steve Pearce that erased what had been a 5–2 Yankees lead. Standing at shortstop, Jeter slumped his head ever so briefly in disbelief, and the scramble was on to complete Jeter's Bronx tale on a more appropriate note.

"Pretty much the all-time low to all-time high," Robertson said. "I think back to when Derek got his 3,000th hit [on July 9, 2011]; I came in in the eighth inning and gave up the lead, and then he came up in the eighth inning and drove in a run to take the lead. So jokingly, Mo slaps me on the back and says, 'Hey, you're the best setup man in the league, you set him up again.' That's what kind of guy he is. But it was a really hard outing to take at first."

In the visiting dugout, Orioles manager Buck Showalter summoned Evan Meek, a right-handed reliever who had been selected as a National League All-Star with the Pirates in 2011. Meek had managed a 5.48 ERA through his first twenty-two games for Baltimore, and he was unwittingly making the final appearance of a six-year career in the majors.

Jose Pirela, a twenty-four-year-old utility man playing in one of his seven games for New York that season, greeted Meek with a line drive to left field that found turf for a single. With rosters swelled to forty players by September call-ups, Girardi signaled for the speedy Antoan Richardson to run for Pirela. In an indication of the state of the Yanks' farm system, Richardson was a thirty-year-old non-prospect who would not appear in the majors after 2014.

Brett Gardner dropped a sacrifice bunt that advanced Richardson to second base, and the crowd voiced an ecstatic roar as the late Bob Sheppard's voice echoed throughout Yankee Stadium for the final time in a game situation. Through the magic of a recording loaded into the facility's state-of-the-art soundboard, Sheppard intoned in his clear, concise, and correct manner: "*Now batting for the Yankees, Number 2, Derek Jeter. Number 2.*"

Jeter crouched near the dugout, removed the weight from his black Louisville Slugger P72 and applied a healthy slick of pine tar to the handle. It was the same model of bat he'd once selected in Florida as a lanky, homesick eighteen-year-old, believing that the thirty-four-inch, thirty-two-ounce build of northern white ash was similar to the aluminum bats he'd been swinging a few months earlier at Kalamazoo Central High School. Jeter never used a different model in a big-league game, and the appreciative company had renamed the P72 in his honor one day prior.

As Jeter took a practice cut outside the batter's box, fidgeting with the protective guard on his left elbow, Showalter surveyed the scene. With one out and slow-footed catcher Brian McCann waiting on deck, the Orioles could have walked Jeter to set up a potential double play. Showalter sniffed at the idea. How could he take the bat out of Jeter's hands? Showalter had been Jeter's first major league manager in 1995, inviting the twenty-one-year-old to travel with the team as a non-active player for the postseason, allowing Jeter and Posada to gain valuable experience by watching from the bench for that year's epic five-game American League Division Series against the Mariners.

"We said, 'They can go back to instructional league or whatever, or they can stay here with us, but we don't want to hear about them running the streets and not taking this real seriously, not soaking up everything,'" Showalter said. "I found out later that they basically didn't leave the hotel for three weeks. They were scared to death."

Showalter had settled for watching the dynasty develop from the outside, having been dismissed by George Steinbrenner shortly after surly veteran Jack McDowell surrendered a season-ending hit to Edgar Martinez. Maybe history would have played out differently had Showalter known that Rivera, his twenty-five-year-old Panamanian right-hander, would eventually become the game's all-time saves leader. Showalter had pondered that alternate outcome many times over the years since.

Now, with no instructions coming from the dugout, Meek fired an 86-mph cut fastball on which Jeter deployed his trademark inside-out swing, slashing a hard grounder that rocketed past first baseman Steve Pearce. Richardson took off, digging as quickly as his legs could carry him. A product of the Bahamas who scored a grand total of four runs in the big leagues, he was about to become the answer to a trivia question. Right fielder Nick Markakis scooped the ball and launched a rocket to catcher Caleb Joseph, who couldn't handle the throw as Richardson swiped his left hand across home plate.

"The crowd went nuts," Meek said. "In that situation, you just can't be upset about that kind of thing. It's bigger than all of us. It was just a great moment. A great moment for the game and him. There's no better way for him to go out. It was just an amazing moment."

Miles upon miles away, as he enjoyed some downtime before reporting to an upcoming assignment in the Arizona Fall League, Aaron Judge sat up and cheered.

"I was watching it in bed," Judge said. "I got goosebumps, I remember, watching that game. Seeing how it unfolded, and of course it would just so happen to be that he's coming up with a guy on second base. His signature hit to right field. It was crazy."

Jeter raised his fists toward the sky and leapt, in what he'd later describe as "an out of body experience." It created a magnificent photograph that would be reproduced thousands of times to appear in living rooms, studies, and bedrooms across the tri-state area, peddled with Jeter's swirling signature in silver Sharpie for the low, low price of $799.99 (plus $165 if you wanted it framed).

The Orioles remained in their dugout to watch as the crowd serenaded Jeter, who embraced family members, former teammates, and others before making a slow solo walk to his position. While Sinatra crooned, Jeter's spikes nestled into the soft lip of the outfield grass and he stole a moment.

"I wanted to take one last view from short," Jeter said. "I say a little prayer before every game, and I basically just said thank you, because this is all I've ever wanted to do and not too many people get an opportunity

Derek Jeter was a fourteen-time AL All-Star, a five-time Gold Glover, a five-time Silver Slugger, and a two-time Hank Aaron Award honoree, among other plaudits. Yet Jeter was most proud of his five World Series rings with the Yankees.

to do it. It was above and beyond anything I'd ever dreamt of. I mean, I've lived a dream."

That marked Jeter's final game playing shortstop, though he would bat in two more games before ending his career with 3,465 hits, sixth all-time and the most ever by a Yankee. Jeter finished as a lifetime .310 hitter, the last at-bat yielding a dribbler of an infield single at Fenway Park that third baseman Garin Cecchini couldn't pick cleanly.

"He didn't say anything; he just tipped his cap at me," Cecchini said. "I tipped my cap right back at him. I'll always remember that for the rest of my life. I wasn't trying to give him a hit. I was trying to make a play, because you don't think about that. But after the fact of what happened, you think, 'Oh man—that was the last hit of Jeter's career.'"

• • •

The Yankees faced an identity crisis as they headed into the 2014–15 off-season. For two decades, they had been synonymous with Jeter, a marriage that began in a more innocent time when Jeter could still comfortably ride on a New York City subway without being noticed. Their impressive string of winning seasons dating to 1993 remained intact, and Gardner, Robertson, Sabathia, and Teixeira were still around to represent the last World Series-winning club. Alex Rodriguez was also set to return to the lineup after serving a historic 162-game suspension for performance-enhancing drug use.

The Steinbrenner family had authorized the expenditure of nearly a half-billion dollars on star power, pursuing right fielder Carlos Beltran, center fielder Jacoby Ellsbury, catcher Brian McCann, and right-hander Masahiro Tanaka. Those fresh faces had the potential to add sizzle and help the turnstiles click, but who were the Yankees without Derek Jeter?

They were about to figure that out.

"Who's going to become the next great Yankee that people really latch onto?" Girardi said then. "I'm curious to see how it develops."

CHAPTER 2

THE KNIGHTED SUCCESSOR

The Landmark Building is a commercial office tower that rises twenty-one stories above the city of Stamford, Connecticut, and on a clear day, the southwestern corner of its roof provides a panoramic vista of the Manhattan skyline. Each December, the facility's management team hosts a "Heights and Lights" holiday festival where Santa Claus and his celebrity helpers make a rappelling descent to street level as the prelude to fireworks and a tree lighting ceremony.

It was a blustery, gray morning as Brian Cashman yanked down on the elf cap covering his head and peered at the passing traffic below, preparing to attach a rope to his belt and dangle off the side of the structure once again. Having been somewhat reluctantly named the Yankees' general manager in February 1998, Cashman had outlasted his competition and now held the title of baseball's longest-tenured person in that position. He had recently discovered that these types of adrenaline-inducing adventures provided a welcome release from one of the most demanding day jobs in all of professional sports, once saying, "I call it living."

During spring training in 2013, Cashman had tried skydiving with the Army Golden Knights, flawlessly executing a tandem freefall from 12,500 feet. He had accepted when offered a second jump that afternoon, and that one did not go as well; thanks to a landing that Cashman jokingly compared to one of Paul O'Neill's ugly slides into second base, Cashman sustained a broken fibula and a dislocated ankle. The injury required the installation of a plate and eight screws.

While being transported to the hospital, Cashman said that he could hear the late George Steinbrenner's voice barking in an inimitable staccato: "You've got to get back to Tampa." He had no regrets about the experience, saying that he was pleased the jumps had generated additional publicity for the Wounded Warrior Project. Cashman has thus far declined to open another parachute, preferring his death-defying activities to at least include some sort of anchor.

A momentary escape was welcome now. Cashman was being tasked with restoring the Yankees' luster after missing the postseason for a second consecutive season—the first time they had done so in a non-strike season since 1992 and 1993, the conclusion of a twelve-year playoff drought. Compared to the challenges that waited in the Bronx, spending a few hours this 2014 holiday season helping Jolly Old Saint Nick liberate a bag of toys from the Grinch seemed to be a pleasant diversion.

In previous years, Cashman had welcomed any media members hardy enough to wake up in time for his 6:00 a.m. practice rappels, rewarding guests with a stream of quotes that served to warm baseball's often dormant Hot Stove season. This time, however, the building's public relations department issued a tersely-worded e-mail that indicated Cashman's only availability would be following the event on Sunday evening. By then, most of the reporters covering the team would already be on their way to the Winter Meetings, an annual gathering of the sport's decision-makers that was being held at the stylish Manchester Grand Hyatt resort in San Diego.

Though Cashman would acquiesce and offer public comments of little consequence that morning, he had a good reason for not wanting to be quoted on the record, preferring radio silence to dodges and fibs. Over the past several weeks, Cashman had been attempting to orchestrate a trade to pluck shortstop Didi Gregorius from the Arizona Diamondbacks, and the tea leaves indicated that he was finally nearing the finish line on a three-team deal that would deliver Derek Jeter's replacement.

Regarded as an excellent defender with a strong throwing arm, Gregorius was available this trade season due in part to some lingering questions about his offense. As a twenty-four-year-old, Gregorius had batted .226 with six home runs and 27 RBIs in 80 games for Arizona, which on its face did not exactly make him the prime candidate to claim Jeter's place in the field. The Yankees' scouting and analytics departments looked past those raw digits, believing that Gregorius was capable of more than he had shown.

Cashman said that he had several trusted voices encouraging the pursuit of Gregorius, who had been seen and touted by at least six Yankees scouts in recent months. The most vociferous supporter was Tim Naehring, who had enjoyed a solid eight-year run as a Red Sox infielder before a torn right elbow ligament ended his playing career in the summer of 1997. Even as the input of Ivy League-educated numbers crunchers increasingly influenced front office decisions, Cashman seldom made a move without seeking Naehring's input.

A Cincinnati native, Naehring found a comfortable landing spot in the Reds' front office in 1999 before the sale of the team prompted a house-cleaning purge in late 2005. Naehring landed with the Yankees in 2007 and was primarily tasked with scouting players in the National League. His accounts of Gregorius had been overwhelmingly positive.

"I saw some things offensively that I thought were untapped," said Naehring, who was promoted to a role as the Yankees' vice president of baseball operations in 2016. "There were times where I saw the actual swing, he was making a bunch of adjustments with the setup of his swing. There was some late bat movement. There were some things where I thought if we could assist him and get him into a little better position to hit, I thought there was upside with hitting for average."

Naehring said that as the Yankees dug deeper on Gregorius, they uncovered convincing reports about him as a person, while his work ethic had been evident in watching him play. Eric Chavez, a six-time Gold Glove Award winner with the Athletics who played third base for the Yankees in 2011–2012, had been one of Gregorius' teammates for two seasons in Arizona near the end of his playing career. During a brief stint as one of Cashman's special assistants, Chavez also opined that the Yankees should take a crack at acquiring Gregorius.

"I was really high on him," Chavez said. "His defense is unbelievable, and hitting-wise he has the potential to be a good hitter—[I saw] a good .275, .280 hitter, 12 to 15 home runs. His swing plays perfect for Yankee Stadium; he's kind of got that pull swing."

It would turn out that Chavez had actually underestimated Gregorius' power, but Cashman was sold. He recalls making at least ten different pitches to Arizona general manager Dave Stewart, a former star right-hander who carried the nickname "Smoke" and was the MVP of the 1989 World Series with the A's. Each offer was rebuffed, as Stewart scanned the Yankees' farm system and told Cashman that he could not find a match between the clubs. Frustrated, Cashman changed course, recalling that the Tigers had contacted the Yankees earlier that winter as part of their quest to secure a young starting pitcher.

Detroit general manager Dave Dombrowski had been particularly interested in Shane Greene. A twenty-five-year-old right-hander from Daytona Beach, Florida, who had compiled a seemingly ordinary minor league career, Greene emerged from the 15th round of the 2009 draft to become a surprise contributor down the stretch for the Yankees in 2014, leaning on a power sinker to go 5-4 with a 3.78 ERA in 15 games (14 starts) at the big-league level. Two of those starts had come against the Tigers, in which Greene permitted two runs in fifteen innings.

"They called us a couple of times," Dombrowski said. "[Cashman] said, 'If you have any way to get Gregorius from Arizona, we would trade Greene for him.' So, I made contact with Arizona at that point to see if we could make anything work."

Though the Yankees were reluctant to part with Greene, cognizant of the inflated value of starting pitching in the open market, Cashman decided that Gregorius was worth the gamble. During his days as the team's assistant farm director, Cashman had absorbed the advice of front office mentors like Gene Michael, Bill Livesey, and Brian Sabean, all of whom stressed that championship teams needed to have a "strong spine" up the middle. That phrase kept running through Cashman's mind while he pursued the Gregorius deal.

"Everything needs to be working—from the catcher to the middle of the infield and center field," Cashman said. "With Jeter, toward the back end of his career, he wasn't the same player. No one is. So now we had a void at shortstop to fill. I didn't have a shortstop, bottom line. Unfortunately, it wasn't going to come from within; we didn't have somebody waiting in the wings ready to go. It's not like we hadn't tried—we failed in that category, so now we were forced to go to the market and trade for somebody if we could."

The Tigers accepted Greene from the Yankees, then flipped left-handed pitcher Robbie Ray and infielder Domingo Lebya to Arizona, a sequence that delivered Gregorius to New York. Stewart said at the time that Gregorius had been one of the D-backs' most requested trade chips, but Arizona was comfortable drawing from their middle infield depth in exchange for Ray, who would struggle in his first two seasons in the desert before going 15-5 with a 2.89 ERA as a National League All-Star in 2017.

Baseball executives often say that trades can only be properly evaluated in years, not days or months, and Greene's introduction to Detroit served as a perfect example of that axiom. Greene won his first three starts in a Tigers uniform, compiling a 0.39 ERA which invited suggestions that the Yankees might have made a costly mistake. When hitters adjusted, Greene tumbled hard. He finished 2015 with a 4-8 record and 6.88 ERA, and Detroit moved him to the bullpen for the following season. He remained there in 2017, finishing 71 games with a solid 2.66 ERA and nine saves for the last place Tigers.

"The tough decision-making in that process was that we were pitching deficient, especially starting pitching," Cashman said. "It was going to cost us a guy that we did like in Shane Greene, who was a young, under-control starter. You're robbing Peter to pay Paul, but it speaks to how important the shortstop position is. We held our breath and made the decision to do so."

When Cashman called his manager to tell him that the deal had been completed, a highlight popped into Joe Girardi's mind. Gregorius had hit his first big league homer against the Yankees in April 2013, jumping on a fastball to take right-hander Phil Hughes deep over Yankee Stadium's right-field wall. It was Gregorius' first at-bat as a Diamondback and at the time, Girardi said that he had wondered, "Who's this kid?"

Had Girardi dug into the wiry athlete's background that evening, an intriguing story would have emerged. While fans often spoke of Jeter as though he were royalty, Gregorius actually had the credentials, proudly carrying the title of "Sir Didi." In 2011, Gregorius and most of his teammates were called to a state building in Curacao for a formal ceremony in which they would be knighted as members of Order of Orange-Nassau, their reward for being part of the Netherlands club that defeated Cuba in the IBAF Baseball World Cup.

"Instead of giving us money, they decided to just knight us, all the guys that had a clean record," Gregorius said. "I'm happy to say it out loud every day."

Born in the Netherlands, Mariekson Julius Gregorius moved to Curacao at age five and began answering to the nickname "Didi," which created some confusion in his household. Gregorius's father, Johannes, and his older brother, Johnny, also favored the nickname, which necessitated qualifiers like "Didi Dad" or "Didi Son" at family gatherings. The three even played on the same semi-pro baseball team for two summers in the early 2000s, where they were referred to as "Didi Sr.," "Didi Jr.," and "Didi Little."

Didi Sr.'s trade was carpentry, but he had also been a top pitcher for more than two decades in Curacao and the Netherlands. Gregorius' mother, Sheritsa, played for the Dutch national softball team, and the couple has a treasured photo that shows the future shortstop, probably two years of age, wandering on a ball field with a bat in his hand. Around age seven, he'd comprised one half of a stellar Little League double play combination with Andrelton Simmons, who'd go on to win Gold Glove Awards with the Braves and Angels. Gregorius also played basketball and soccer, and swam competitively as a youth, even dabbling in speed skating at one point, but baseball powered the Gregorius household.

An accomplished artist and computer whiz who regularly edits videos and paints on road trips, Gregorius quickly earned a reputation as the go-to person in the Yankees' universe for tech support. Alex Rodriguez often asked Gregorius to tweak his iPad and once referred to him as "the modern-day Bill Gates who plays shortstop."

Carrying a polymath background scarcely found in big league clubhouses, Gregorius speaks four languages—English, Spanish, Dutch, and his native Papiamento, plus fluent "emoji." In a move that would endear him to the fan base, Gregorius soon composed celebratory tweets after each team victory, representing each contributor with a different cartoon graphic while adding the hashtag #StartSpreadingTheNews.

Years before he'd tag his teammates with hieroglyphics like clown face (Brett Gardner), bow and arrow (Jacoby Ellsbury), and boxing glove/carrot (Clint Frazier), Gregorius said that his earliest sketches began appearing in the margins of his school notebooks around age 10, occasionally drawing the ire of his teachers.

Even from afar, Gregorius had been touched by the drama of Jeter's retirement, experiencing a rush of inspiration late in 2014 that prompted him to pull out his charcoal pencils. In one six-hour session, Gregorius painstakingly sketched Jeter doffing his batting helmet to a Yankee Stadium crowd. He posted the results of his effort on Twitter.

"That's one thing that I really like," Gregorius said. "When you sit down for an hour without the TV on, see what you're going to do in those situations. I always get the drawing book."

The Reds signed Gregorius out of Curaçao for $50,000 in 2007, the same year that Cincinnati drafted infielder Todd Frazier in the first round from Rutgers University. Frazier, who would be reunited with Gregorius on the Yankees in 2017, recalled that the lithe Gregorius had been a "skin and bones" teenager who had yet to discover the benefits of weight lifting. His minor league high in home runs had been seven, which he reached twice.

Gregorius made his big-league debut with the Reds in September 2012, notching his first hit with an infield single off the Astros' Wesley Wright. Cincinnati traded Gregorius as part of a three-team deal with the D-backs and Indians three months later, and Arizona general manager Kevin Towers did not attempt to conceal his high hopes for the young shortstop.

"When I saw him, he reminded me of a young Derek Jeter," Towers said at the time. "I was fortunate enough to see Jeter when he was in high school in Michigan and [Didi has] got that type of range. He's got speed. He's more of a line drive-type hitter, but I think he's got the type of approach at the plate where I think there's going to be power there as well."

If there was one consistent knock on Gregorius' game, it was a perceived inability to hit left-handed pitching. That had relegated him into something of a part-time player with Arizona, and Gregorius arrived in New York carrying a .243 average over his three seasons in the majors. He had batted .184 with a .490 OPS (on-base percentage plus slugging percentage) against lefties.

Three years later, while savoring his two homers off Indians ace Corey Kluber in the deciding Game 5 of the AL Division Series, Gregorius said that his confidence had never been shaken—even if it took others longer to come around on his potential.

"A lot of times, guys put a label on a person without letting the person develop," Gregorius said. "They always predict something, like, 'This guy can only play defense or this guy can only play offense.' But you don't know how hard a guy works to get where he wants to be, to stay where he wants to be, and to keep making adjustments every year to try to get better. For me, I always believed in myself. There's always people that are going to doubt you. At the end, it's up to you how hard you want to work."

Girardi had made the point shortly after the trade that Gregorius seemed to have been stuck with a reputation based upon a small sample size, noticing that the D-backs only gave Gregorius fifty-one at-bats against lefties in 2014, in which Gregorius managed seven hits (.137). The Yankees hedged their bet by keeping the light-hitting defensive whiz Brendan Ryan around, believing that they could have the right-handed hitting Ryan face all of the lefties if necessary.

It was an issue that never presented itself. Jeff Pentland and Alan Cockrell, the team's hitting coaches that season, said that they discovered Gregorius had been taught to hit the ball on the ground up the middle or to the opposite field in his previous big-league stops. They wanted Gregorius to embrace his latent power, encouraging him to pull the ball to right field more often.

"I think he's always had bat speed and leverage, God-given," Cockrell said. "He was able to kind of shorten his swing and more efficiently get the barrel to where it needed to be, and he's always behind the baseball. He puts himself in a good position to hit, so I saw that coming before I think Didi saw it."

Hensley Meulens also deserves some credit for helping Gregorius take his swing to the next level. Once a touted Yankees prospect nicknamed "Bam-Bam" who played parts of five seasons in the Bronx from 1989–1993, Meulens operates a camp for professional ballplayers in Curacao during the offseason, where some three dozen athletes gather on Mondays, Wednesdays, and Thursdays for morning workouts.

A highly-regarded coach on the Giants' big league staff who would be one of the six men to interview for the Yankees' managerial vacancy after the 2017 season, Meulens observed Gregorius in the batting cage and remarked that he had recently helped left-handed hitting shortstop Brandon Crawford improve his performance against lefties. Crawford had batted .199 against lefties in 2013, improving that mark to .320 in 2014.

"We had closed Brandon Crawford off a little bit from leaking in the front side against lefties, and he had great success," Meulens said. "I told him, 'What I would try to do is stay in there and hit a line drive toward the shortstop.' I'm not saying that triggered Didi to hit better against lefties the last few years, but he is a hard-working guy. He knows what information to take from whom and put it into the game."

By 2016, Gregorius was batting .324 against left-handed pitching, the third highest such average by a lefty batter in the big leagues. Naehring was not surprised that Gregorius had been able to make the necessary adjustments to succeed against all pitchers.

"I was never in the camp of, 'He's going to be tremendously exposed by left-handed pitching,'" Naehring said. "I thought he had the ability to manipulate the bat barrel and I thought he showed raw power, especially to the pull side, that I thought would play up at Yankee Stadium."

Gregorius also showed a knack for handling the demands of the post-Jeter era, often deflecting questions about his predecessor. While some feared that the weight of Jeter's legacy could overwhelm Gregorius, Cashman articulated it another way. In his final season, Jeter had batted .256 with four homers and 50 RBIs in 145 games, and Cashman suggested that Gregorius wouldn't have to do much to represent an improvement over that diminished version of the captain.

"It's never going to go away," Gregorius said. "It's a game of comparisons. No matter what you do, you're always going to get compared. Maybe when he played, he got compared to somebody else."

As the 2015 season dawned, Gregorius was the only player in the Yankees' starting lineup under the age of thirty, and his inexperience showed. On Opening Day against the Blue Jays, he committed a cardinal sin by being thrown out attempting to steal third base with his team down by five runs, one example in a series of routine fielding errors and baserunning miscues. After getting those initial jitters out of the way, Gregorius steadily improved. A .206 hitter in April, Gregorius batted .232 in May, .258 in June, and .317 in July.

One afternoon in late April, infield coach Joe Espada summoned A-Rod as a guest tutor, with Espada saying that they wanted to help Gregorius anticipate plays better, remain aware of outs, and know when to charge the ball and when to stay back. Once the game's premier shortstop before agreeing to shift to third base following his 2004 trade to New York, Rodriguez conveyed the importance of a shortstop's positioning, cadence, and internal clock, predicting that Gregorius would be able to fine-tune those characteristics with experience.

"The abilities are off the charts," Rodriguez said then. "He's got the things you can't teach; incredible range, great arm strength. People forget, he's only been playing shortstop for eight years. The more he comes out, the more he gets experience, the better he's going to be."

After being paired with second baseman Stephen Drew up the middle

The first shortstop in Yankees history to hit 20 or more home runs in consecutive seasons, Didi Gregorius's 25 homers in 2017 surpassed Derek Jeter's club record for homers by a shortstop.

for most of the 2015 season, Gregorius received an ideal partner prior to the 2016 season when the Yanks acquired Starlin Castro from the Cubs in exchange for right-hander Adam Warren and a player to be named later (who turned out to be Ryan, the free-spirited backup infielder whom Gregorius had made superfluous). Like Gregorius and outfielder Aaron Hicks, who was acquired in a November 2015 trade with the Twins for light-hitting backup catcher John Ryan Murphy, Cashman was attracted to Castro—then twenty-five years old—because of his youth and flexibility, two qualities that the Yankees sorely needed to showcase more of.

Castro had compiled an impressive 991 hits through his first six seasons in the big leagues, but the Cubs bounced him from his shortstop position to accommodate a younger prospect, Addison Russell, who'd be selected as a National League All-Star in 2016 while helping the Cubs end a 108-year World Series drought. The deal was consummated in early December 2015, but Cashman's pursuit of Castro had started months earlier with several pitches prior to the July 31 trade deadline. Unbeknownst to Chicago, the Yankees' scouts had identified Castro as a player who might benefit from a move to the other side of the bag. When Castro batted .339

with a .903 OPS in 33 games as a second baseman, the shuffle provided a sneak preview that backed the theory.

"Even before the positional switch, we felt by our evaluations that he could be a pretty interesting player over at second," Cashman said. "Then when the Cubs made the switch, we got confirmation of that."

Cubs president of baseball operations Theo Epstein told Cashman that he would be willing to move Castro if he was able to finalize a different transaction during the 2015 Winter Meetings, which turned out to be a four-year, $56 million pact with infielder Ben Zobrist. Moments after that deal was finalized, Epstein told Cashman that he was ready to act, and the Yankees agreed to take on the remaining $38 million that Castro was due through 2019. It was a sizable investment, but one of the more supportive voices in Cashman's ear had been that of Jim Hendry, who'd spent parts of ten seasons as the Cubs' GM beginning in 2002.

"Starlin had this storybook beginning, playing in the All-Star Game at twenty-one and had 200 hits," Hendry said. "The last couple of years [in Chicago] after I left, he had some ups and downs. If anybody would have told us at twenty-two or twenty-three that he wouldn't be hitting around .300 every year with 20 to 25 home runs, it would have been hard to believe."

Born one month apart in the spring of 1990, Castro and Gregorius comprised the youngest Yankees double play combination since Willie Randolph and Bucky Dent in the 1970s, and they instantly hit it off away from the field. Seemingly competing to be the team's flashiest dresser (Castro probably won in a dead heat), the twenty-somethings often peppered each other with snarky remarks in English and Spanish from their adjacent lockers.

The easy rapport between the new teammates prompted the team's in-house "Yankees on Demand" video crew to ask them to participate in a stellar shot-for-shot remake of a scene in the 2008 movie *Stepbrothers*. Gregorius played John C. Reilly's part and Castro delivered a version of Will Ferrell's lines to hilarious results. Had they just become best friends? As Gregorius' character screamed, "Yup!"

"I feel like he is my brother," Castro said. "That's my double play partner, and not only in the field. I think that we've got a really good relationship."

Castro's comfort level shouldn't have come as a surprise. His big league mentor had been former Bombers star Alfonso Soriano, who broke in as a power-hitting second baseman and played parts of five seasons in New York before being traded to the Rangers as part of the A-Rod trade in December 2003.

By 2010, when Castro arrived at Wrigley Field, Soriano had shifted to left field and was playing the role of sage veteran at age thirty-four. The eight-time All-Star took Castro under his wing and taught his fellow Dominican how to dress, how to act, and how to play while tuning out the negativity that often comes with competing in a major market. In appreciation, Castro named Soriano as the godfather to his son, Starlin Jr.

"He took me to his house to live with him, and I appreciated that a lot," Castro said. "I would hang with him every day, work out every day and every morning, just work out with him. He helped me a lot and he taught me how it is in the big leagues."

Though some of the most recognizable names in Yankees history took their positions in the middle of the diamond, Castro and Gregorius accomplished something in their first year playing together that the likes of Jeter, Randolph, Tony Lazzeri, and Phil Rizzuto never could, becoming the first

Few double play combinations around the majors were a tighter fit than the Yankees' Didi Gregorius and Starlin Castro. "I feel like he is my brother," Castro once said.

double play combination in franchise history to each hit twenty or more home runs in a single season.

It would take something significant to dislodge Castro from the Yankees' plans, and that development took place in December of 2017. Despite leading the majors with fifty-nine home runs that past season, reigning National League MVP Giancarlo Stanton was being shopped by Jeter's debt-laden Marlins, who were desperate to free themselves of the $295 million owed to the slugger through the 2028 campaign. Separate deals with the Cardinals and Giants were agreed upon, but fell through when Stanton told the Marlins he would refuse to waive his no-trade clause to all but four playoff-ready contenders: the Astros, Cubs, Dodgers, and Yankees.

Pursuing a power-hitting outfielder had not necessarily been on the Yankees' wish list going into the offseason, but it was difficult to turn down an opportunity to add a player of Stanton's caliber. New York produced the winning offer, obtaining the twenty-eight-year-old Stanton in exchange for Castro, right-handed pitching prospect Jorge Guzman, and infield prospect Jose Devers. The Yankees agreed to take on all but $30 million of the fortune owed to Stanton.

"We still gave up talent," Cashman said. "I appreciate everything Starlin Castro did for us. He was a great pickup for us. A high-character guy. He's tough as nails. He had a great personality. You never saw him have a bad day. He helped us in that win column in many ways."

While Gregorius repeatedly said that he did not consider himself a home run hitter, he was one of several young Yankees who credited veteran Carlos Beltran for helping with his plate discipline during their time together as teammates. Perhaps by virtue of patrolling the same patch of Bronx real estate, Gregorius had also seemed to inherit Jeter's unquenchable thirst for championship hardware.

Despite missing most of April with a right shoulder strain, the 2017 season saw Gregorius set new career highs in runs (73), homers (25), and RBIs (87) while leading the team with 44 multi-hit games and batting fourth in the lineup 42 times. Only the Indians' Francisco Lindor hit more homers (33) among big league shortstops, but despite the gaudy numbers, Gregorius repeatedly said that his performance could have been better.

"A ring. That's my goal," Gregorius said. "That's why you play the game. Winning is our goal. And if one of these guys doesn't have that goal, then you need to sit in my locker and talk about it."

With the help of his lieutenants and some creative thinking, Cashman had stabilized the middle infield by executing a pair of old-fashioned baseball trades. To assemble the rest of the franchise's next dynasty, the Yankees would have to make bold moves in a challenging domestic and international marketplace.

CHAPTER 3

REPAIRING THE PIPELINE

It was the summer of 2005, and Brett Gardner broke a lengthy stare at the fine print resting in front of him. One of the documents featured the midnight blue flowing script of the New York Yankees' logo, along with the iconic mailing address at the corner of East 161st Street and River Avenue in the Bronx.

Gardner did not have any particular loyalty to the Yankees at that time; like many in the South with cable television access to the Turner Broadcasting System superstation, his cheering allegiances had been secured by the Atlanta Braves, who played their home games about four hours from his home in tiny Holly Hill, South Carolina. This piece of paper was making a convincing case for Gardner to rethink those rooting interests.

The Yankees were offering Gardner more money than he had ever seen in his life, $210,000, in exchange for agreeing to join the organization as a third-round draft pick. Though Gardner was aware of the team's reputation of struggling to promote their own young players to the big leagues, the idea of being a member of the farm system sounded a whole lot more appealing than spending his days on an actual farm.

To be clear, the undersized outfielder admired his father John's devotion and commitment in tending to a 2,600-acre patch of the Palmetto State, where the Gardners coaxed corn, cotton, soybeans, and wheat to emerge from the rich soil. Gardner had helped out his mother Faye and older brother Glen on occasion, driving a lawn tractor or a combine, but

Gardner found the early mornings and long afternoons to be something of a bore.

"It's pretty much been his life every day for the last thirty-five or so years," Gardner said. "That's how I grew up. It's definitely not the easiest thing in the world to do, but even though it is hard work, it's something that he enjoys doing and can be rewarding."

When Gardner laced his spikes on the campus of the College of Charleston in 2001, trying out for the baseball team as a non-scholarship freshman, he stood five-foot-eight and weighed a spindly 155 pounds. Gardner remembers having above-average speed at the time and thought that he did fine when the coaches had him run a sixty-yard dash, but the rest of the tryout was admittedly unimpressive.

"There are only a handful of guys that are going to stand out in an environment like that," Gardner said. "You run the sixty, you make some throws to third base from right field, and I didn't have that strong of an arm—still don't, really, but then it wasn't as strong as it is now. You probably get ten, twenty swings in batting practice, and I wasn't going to turn anybody's head hitting singles over the third baseman's head."

After a few days, Gardner had not been invited back by the coaching staff, so he silently dragged his baseball equipment back to Holly Hill. John Gardner had been a minor league outfielder in the Phillies organization in the 1970s, and when he spotted the gear in his home, a note was dashed off to head coach John Pawlowski. Let his son attend practice with the team, the message pleaded. With no promises of playing time in actual games, Pawlowski agreed to let Gardner work out and participate in some of the Cougars' fall scrimmages. Showcasing his fierce determination, Gardner made the coaching staff take notice by leaving the field with the dirtiest uniform nearly every afternoon.

"We're definitely both hard-headed," Gardner said of his father. "I think that work ethic and not taking no for an answer—you try and get the most out of what God gave you. I played with plenty of guys that were way more talented than I am, but guys that maybe didn't want it quite as bad. I feel like that's something that not only has gotten me to where I am, but has helped me stay where I am."

Three years after his first professional at-bats with the Yankees' Class-A Staten Island affiliate, Gardner walked into the original Yankee Stadium during its final season of service in the summer of 2008, joining a club

Brett Gardner is one of five players drafted by the Yankees to tally 1,000 hits with the club. The others are Thurman Munson, Don Mattingly, Derek Jeter, and Jorge Posada.

where Robinson Cano (twenty-five) and Melky Cabrera (twenty-three) stood as the only homegrown position players under age twenty-five. As he watched the Baby Bombers take over the town in 2017, Gardner was impressed by how thoroughly the landscape had changed.

"When I came up, the big-league roster was a roster full of All-Stars and future Hall of Famers," Gardner said. "There wasn't nearly as much opportunity and roster turnover as there's been the last few years. It's all about opportunity."

To illustrate his point, Gardner recalled the case of Shelley Duncan, a big-swinging behemoth of a first baseman who hit 43 homers over parts of seven big league seasons with the Yankees, Indians, and Rays from 2007–2013. In another time and place, Gardner suggested, Duncan's skills should have earned him more of an opportunity with a major league club.

Even the '17 Yankees could have used a player with Duncan's skill set as they tried to recover from an early-season injury to first baseman Greg Bird, instead handing most of those at-bats to strikeout-prone slugger Chris Carter. With the Yanks of the late 2000s, Duncan had been blocked by All-Star talent with massive contracts to match: first Jason Giambi, then Mark Teixeira.

Though the Yankees often seemed to address their on-field issues by waving a checkbook rather than developing the answers in-house, Brian Cashman continually stressed the importance of making the roster younger and more flexible. Cashman said that the talent-rich dynasty of the mid-to-late 1990s had been created partially as a result of walking through fire with losing, frustrating teams in the late 1980s.

"Who knew we were actually sitting on a dynasty waiting to happen? None of us," Cashman said. "All of that talent at the time, it grew into something special. But while that was going on, we were taking hits at the major league level and not making the playoffs on a consistent basis, getting dirt kicked in our face by the 'Bash Brothers' and the Oakland A's dynasty. So I don't forget those times. From adversity and difficult times, you can grow some great things."

The Yankees had not endured a losing season since their 76-win 1992 campaign, and as Cashman considered his roster near the midpoint of the 2016 season, he understood that they couldn't return to the malaise of an era in which pitcher Melido Perez and shortstop Andy Stankiewicz were among the team's most valuable players. Still, Cashman sensed that many in an underwhelmed fan base seemed to be growing open to the idea of embracing a new direction, urging the club to nudge out a stable of aging veterans who were producing diminishing returns.

Due to changes in baseball's Collective Bargaining Agreement that were intended to close the financial gap between large market and small market teams, the art of roster construction had changed markedly since the offseason of 2008-09. That year, the Steinbrenner family opened their wallets to upgrade an 89-win team that missed the playoffs, signing CC Sabathia to a seven year, $161 million deal, handing A.J. Burnett five years and $82.5 million, then inking Teixeira for eight years and $180 million.

That spending spree helped to produce a tickertape parade celebrating the organization's twenty-seventh World Series title, but when the Yankees ripped a page out of that same playbook in the winter of 2013-14, their lavish spending on Carlos Beltran (three years, $45 million), Jacoby Ellsbury (seven years, $153 million), and Brian McCann (five years, $85 million) had not yielded the same results.

They swallowed hard and doubled down by giving pitcher Masahiro Tanaka seven years and $155 million that same winter, and Cashman rationalized it by noting Tanaka's age. Then twenty-five years old, the right-hander was expected to be on the upswing of his career, despite a heavy workload in Japan. Tanaka dominated in his first turns through the league, winning eleven of his first fourteen big-league starts in 2014 before sustaining a partial tear of his right ulnar collateral ligament. Though Tanaka was able to continue pitching without undergoing Tommy John surgery, his health would be a frequently discussed topic for years to come.

Revenue sharing had been a major factor in the strategy shift, as teams found it more cost-effective to turn to homegrown talent in hopes of reaching the World Series, as the Royals did in 2014 and 2015. The Cubs, the Dodgers, and the Red Sox similarly all built rosters around young cores, supplementing with established veterans rather than relying solely upon them. That was the vision that Cashman held for the future, planting the seeds of a sustainable dynasty by maxing out efforts in the domestic and international player pools.

He had an enthusiastic supporter in managing general partner Hal Steinbrenner, who repeatedly stated his belief that clubs should not have to shoulder payrolls in excess of $200 million to have a chance of winning a championship. The 2009 Yankees are the last World Series-winning club to have spent so lavishly for a title; Kansas City won their 2015 championship with a payroll of $112.9 million, which ranked seventeenth among the thirty big league clubs that year.

To build a winner in that fashion, however, New York would need to improve its ability to discover, obtain, and develop elite talent—something they had lagged behind their competition in doing. Cashman said that incremental adjustments were made along the way, a combination of hiring more experienced scouts, improving the team's existing personnel, and tweaking the process that the team used. The Yankees also invested heavily in advanced analytics, which they believed would help those in command make safer bets on players.

"We don't want to walk around with any kind of arrogance that, 'Hey, we're the New York Yankees, the most storied franchise in all of sports,'" Cashman said. "It has meaning, but that's all about the past. It means nothing about the present and the future. We go out of our way to eradicate any arrogance and by doing so, fill that void with a thirst for knowledge and being open-minded to things that potentially exist in the stratosphere."

One of the answers for the Yankees' future was located on the unpaved roads of Santo Domingo in the Dominican Republic, where a young Gary

Sanchez had honed his hand-eye coordination by whacking decapitated doll heads with a broomstick. In his baseball-crazed country, talented young players are quickly snapped up by *buscones,* or street agents, seeking to cash in by representing the next star who warrants a professional contract.

Sanchez's older brother, Miguel, spent six years in the Mariners' minor league chain as a catcher, first baseman, and pitcher, and the Yankees first heard Sanchez's name at age fourteen. He had been working out in front of representatives from big league teams as early as 2005, when he was thirteen years old.

"At that time, I was in a baseball program, and they would take me to the different tryouts," Sanchez said. "Sometimes I did tryouts and all thirty teams were there. On other occasions, I would do one tryout in the morning and then have another late in the afternoon."

Donny Rowland, the Yankees' director of international scouting, was there to take notes. Rowland had been an infielder for the University of Miami's powerhouse teams in the early 1980s before playing professionally in the Tigers organization, making it as far as the Triple-A level. Rowland dabbled in coaching before committing the next three decades of his life to the art of identifying and securing talent.

By age sixteen, Sanchez's body had filled out, with his power and arm drawing attention from big league teams. While Sanchez's catching skills were still clunky and raw, Rowland, longtime pro scout Gordon Blakeley, and Latin American cross-checker Victor Mata each told Cashman that they envisioned Sanchez's future in pinstripes, pushing the GM to commit the necessary funds that would add his talents to the organization.

"He was a high-profile guy. We didn't find him; everybody knew about him," Rowland said. "We saw him a lot, and because we knew it was going to be expensive, we saw him even more. With Gary, back in '09, it was obvious he was potentially a middle of the order hitter. He had extremely advanced plate actions, swagger, confidence. He took up the whole box. It was his batter's box—the plate was his. Supremely confident. It was an absolute no-brainer at the plate."

The Yankees attempted to match Sanchez against the best possible pitching that they could find, scooping up pitchers who had been discarded by other organizations to throw live batting practice. Sanchez raked against all of them. Rowland said that as part of his regular process, he often asks himself what could stop a player from reaching the highest projections, other than injuries. Sometimes it may be susceptibility to a breaking ball, swinging and missing at fastballs, or not generating enough bat speed. None of those registered as a concern with Sanchez.

The only aspect of Sanchez's game that prompted back-and-forth among Yankees personnel concerned Sanchez's large frame and unpolished blocking abilities, making some wonder if he projected as a future first baseman or designated hitter. As the Yankees evaluated their 2009 board of the top Dominican prospects, they also weighed gushing reports on sixteen-year-old slugger Miguel Sano. The Yankees saw the bulky Sano as a corner infielder, outfielder, or designated hitter, and Cashman's lieutenants pushed hard to stress that Sanchez's future was indeed as a catcher. Even if Sanchez had to be moved, Rowland said that they believed Sanchez would have big league value as a right-handed hitting first baseman.

"We thought that he would be, at minimum, an average catcher with a power arm that could shut down the running game," Rowland said. "At that point, the interest level was pretty much a no-brainer. Gary ended up on top of our board because we thought he could stay behind the plate and have the same middle of the order offense as a third baseman. Sano is a supremely talented player and highly valuable, but Gary has that same offensive production behind the plate at a premium position. That's the reason we had him a tick ahead of Sano."

Third on the Yanks' list then was a sixteen-year-old centerfielder named Wagner Mateo, and his saga serves as a prime example of the risk involved with signing international prospects. The Cardinals signed Mateo to a $3.1 million bonus but voided the deal when Mateo failed a physical, having been discovered to have 20/200 vision in his right eye that could not be corrected by laser surgery. Mateo settled for $512,000 a year later with the D-backs and batted .230 over five minor league seasons, two of which were spent trying to latch on as a pitcher before hanging it up at age twenty-one.

"During our training sessions, I tell our scouts, 'When you walk out of that ballpark and you go home to write your report, you have to know that you have nailed the player in an evaluative sense,'" Rowland said. "You've nailed him. Your report is spot on. And then, as soon as you hit submit and send the report in, you know that you've got a ten percent chance of being right.'"

If the Yankees weren't going to sign Sanchez, they were certain that someone else would. Cashman recalls flying to the Dominican to see

Sanchez work out at the Yankees' facility in Boca Chica, then watching Sanchez pack his bags to immediately go across the street to work out in front of the Mets' representatives. Cashman had to fight the urge to physically stop Sanchez, whom he recalls as "a man-child," from leaving the complex.

"I thought I was looking at a college junior physically, rather than a high school sophomore," Cashman said. "The tool package, you could see the hit ability he had. The cannon arm. The physical tool set was undeniable."

A decision was made. Though the Yankees extended contract offers to both Sanchez and Sano, they pushed in most of their chips on Sanchez, who agreed to a $3 million signing bonus—the largest that the Yankees had issued to an amateur international player, or any position player, at that time.

"At the end of it all, the Yankees showed the most interest," Sanchez said. "At the time, I had no money, so it was a great offer by the Yankees."

Sano turned down a lesser amount—Cashman remembers the number as being $1 million—from the Yankees in favor of $3.25 million from the Twins, with whom he would make it to the majors in 2015 and represent as the runner-up to Aaron Judge at the 2017 Home Run Derby.

Sanchez said that he remembers celebrating at home the night that his professional dreams were realized. He may have splurged on a nice dinner, but there was nothing else of extravagance. It wouldn't have been permitted. His parents were separated; Sanchez, his three brothers, and a sister were raised by their mother, Orquidia Herrera, and grandmother, Agustina Pena, in a small community of Santo Domingo called La Victoria. Sanchez said that his father lived nearby and they spoke on a regular basis.

His mother worked as a nurse, taking multiple shifts per day to pay the rent and put food on the table. Sanchez's first major purchase was to upgrade his mother's house in hopes of providing more comfortable living conditions.

"As people, I want to say we stayed the same, but I was able to fix my mom's house and I was able to help out with other things that we needed help with," Sanchez said. "It was definitely an improvement in our quality of life."

Rowland also played a pivotal role in finding a lanky eighteen-year-old Dominican pitcher named Luis Severino, whose athleticism and lightning-quick arm action proved easy to dream on. Raw yet poised, Severino showcased a fastball that sat in the low 90s but had yet to develop the lethal slider that would help him jump to the majors in 2015.

Born and raised in the small town of Sabana de la Mar on the northeast coast of the Dominican Republic, Severino's long march to the big leagues had started around age ten or eleven, when his father taught him how to grip a curveball and make it spin. Around that time, Severino's father also purchased his son's first Yankees cap; it was his most prized possession, and Severino said that he tried to keep it as clean as possible while wearing it daily.

Though Severino seemed to have some pitching chops in his early teens, he lacked the velocity to make a big-league scout pay much mind. In an interview with *The Players' Tribune*, Severino recalled that his first tryout had been with the Braves at age fifteen, when Severino had barely been able to exceed 80 mph with his fastball. Like Sanchez and countless others in the Dominican, Severino hoped that baseball would ease his family's financial strain.

He left home when he was seventeen, traveling about three hours east to pursue better training at an academy in Bávaro, a tourist area of Punta Cana. While there, Severino recalled attending as many as five tryouts in a week, hoping to catch someone's eye. A major advance in his strength and endurance training came when a coach at the academy instructed Severino to begin running for thirty minutes each morning, then to play long toss with softballs instead of baseballs. Two weeks later, Severino's fastball had reached the low 90s.

That was enough to draw interest from the Marlins and Rockies, but when scout Juan Rosario introduced himself with a business card that bore the Yankees' top hat logo, Rosario jumped to the front of the pack. In addition to that well-worn cap with the interlocking NY, Severino had imagined the sandlot down the street from his home to be Yankee Stadium, and he considered Robinson Cano to be his favorite player.

"Sevy blossomed, and Rosario was all over it," Rowland said. "They blew my phone up and I ran down there. He was a great athlete and had an unflappable look to him. The second time I saw him, he was sick as a dog, throwing up between innings, gutting it out. He was 89-93 mph with a flash of a wipeout slider.

"If he were sixteen when we were watching him, he would have gotten $1.5 million or $2 million. I loved the stuff—demeanor, confidence, athleticism. I asked our scouts, 'Who would not sign this guy right now?' Everyone said we had to sign him. So I said, 'Don't let him out of the complex.'"

Rowland personally cut the deal in the dugout that afternoon, settling at $225,000 before Severino was sent to make his professional debut in the Dominican Summer League.

"We negotiated, played the ladder game with each other, and I said: 'Look, he's going to be eighteen in April. Let's get this done. He needs to start pitching,'" Rowland said. "Sure enough, he wanted to be a Yankee."

While Rowland headed the international scouting efforts, director of amateur scouting Damon Oppenheimer and his team of scouts and cross-checkers were responsible for scouring the domestic high schools and colleges for talent. A catcher drafted out of the University of Southern California by the Brewers in 1985, Oppenheimer's playing career had stalled after seventeen hitless at-bats for Class-A Beloit, leading him into a scouting role with the Padres. Oppenheimer was hired by the Yankees in 1994 as a cross-checker, overseeing a group of amateur scouts.

The Yankees first spotted Greg Bird at Grandview High School in Aurora, Colorado, which fell under the territory of scout Steve Kmetko. While Colorado is generally not a mecca for high school position players, Grandview had become a popular destination for teams performing their due diligence on right-handed pitcher Kevin Gausman, who would be selected in the sixth round of the 2010 draft by the Dodgers before opting to attend Louisiana State University. Two years later, the Orioles made Gausman the fourth overall pick in the nation.

In August 2010, Kmetko followed Bird to Blair Field in Long Beach, California, for the Area Code Games, a six day tournament showcase that features approximately 200 of the top players in the country. Bird dressed in the uniform of the Cincinnati Reds, as did every prospect from the states of Colorado, Nevada, and New Mexico. At the time, Bird wasn't even the most touted catcher on his team—those honors went to Blake Swihart, a future first-round pick of the Red Sox. A fair showing during the games didn't do much to distinguish Bird from his competition, but Kmetko urged the Yankees to stay on him.

"Hey, Bird didn't have the greatest [performance], but trust me, this guy has got the right mentality," Kmetko told Oppenheimer. "He can slow things down. He's got a lot of the intangibles we're looking for."

By chance, Grandview High's baseball team made an early 2011 trip to Florida, taking advantage of the Sunshine State's warm weather as snow blanketed their own diamond. The Yankees sent scout Jeff Deardorff to watch Bird, who still was not drawing a great deal of interest from other clubs; Oppenheimer believed that Bird's Colorado mailing address likely had kept him off some radars.

In fact, when the left-handed Bird stepped into the batter's box, Deardorff noticed that he was the only scout who positioned himself for a clear view from the third-base side. He loved what he saw.

"This guy is going to be a monster," Deardorff reported. "He can hit, he's got power. The swing is beautiful."

Later that year, Oppenheimer was on his way to Wyoming for a look at high school outfielder Brandon Nimmo, who would be selected by the Mets in the first round that June. Kmetko urged Oppenheimer to make a detour to Colorado, where Grandview was playing a previously unscheduled game to make up a rainout.

"I get there early on a Saturday morning and he's taking BP, hitting balls out to dead center and really high. Guys don't do that," Oppenheimer said. "Yes, it's Colorado, but high school guys don't do that. Left-handed guys, they're going to pull, hit some line drives. I watch, he's a big-sized guy, he catches, I'm thinking the arm is good enough—and there's only two other scouts there. It was an odd deal."

The Yankees grabbed Bird in the fifth round that June, with a $1.1 million bonus swaying him to bypass a commitment to the University of Arkansas. Oppenheimer said that Bird had done his homework and knew what kind of money he might be able to get three years down the line. At the time, it was believed that Bird would be able to continue catching, but the Yanks also thought his bat was good enough that it would be fine at another position. Bird caught three games in the Gulf Coast League before physical issues prompted a permanent shift to first base.

As it turned out, the Yanks' biggest find—literally—came in the person of Aaron James Judge, though landing the future unanimous American League Rookie of the Year and runner-up for AL MVP had taken a fair amount of luck. They first spotted Judge in tiny Linden, California, population 1,784, a pinprick of a community about 100 miles northeast of San Francisco that does not have a single stoplight. Linden had made its mark as the self-anointed "Cherry Capital of the World" before a barrage of big league homers in 2017 changed that slogan to "The Home of Aaron Judge."

The Athletics had been the first organization to take a swing at Judge, calling his name as a high school player in the thirty-first round of the 2010 draft, but Judge had not been convinced that he was ready for the commitment of playing professionally. Though Judge didn't know it at the time, the Yankees had agreed with that assessment. Kendall Carter, then a national cross-checker for the organization, saw some of Judge's games at Linden High and reported that he'd seen an athletic specimen who still needed to grow into his body and improve his coordination.

Carter recommended that the Yankees keep tabs on Judge, telling Oppenheimer that the prospect might be something special three years down the line. Judge had played first base and pitched in high school, but when he arrived on campus at Fresno State University, that would have to change. Then the nation's leading college home run hitter, Jordan Ribera was manning first base for the Bulldogs, so Judge's choices were the outfield or the bench. Judge had been a three-sport athlete in high school, playing baseball, football, and basketball. Head baseball coach Mike Batesole told Judge that if he could run routes to catch footballs, there was no reason he couldn't do the same with a baseball.

It didn't take long for Batesole to recognize that Fresno State had a special talent in Judge, who was named a Louisville Slugger Freshman All-American and the Western Athletic Conference's Freshman of the Year. Each fall, Batesole organizes a touch football league to help his baseball players maintain their conditioning, with the gridiron running from the right field foul pole across the outfield grass. Then weighing about 230 pounds, Judge dominated from the first snap of his freshman year.

"These are Division I elite athletes, running him down," Batesole told ESPN. "They run a wide receiver screen. There's some Barry Sanders happening here. All five guys on the other team are on the ground, squinting and wrinkling their noses, watching him run for a touchdown. I've never seen anything like it. My first thought was, 'Yes! We've got one!' This isn't a guy that's just going to play in the big leagues for a year or make an appearance. When I saw that, I was like, 'We've got a freak here. This guy is going to play as long as he wants in the big leagues.'"

Fresno State eventually had to keep Judge out of the flag football games, as Batesole feared that one of his players might injure a knee trying to keep up with him. Though he had the physical attributes to patrol the out-field with grace, questions remained about how a player with Judge's build would adjust to professional pitching. Scouts find a safety net in having big league comparisons to call upon, and in Judge's case, there weren't many players his size who had enjoyed sustained success. Yet Oppenheimer also recognized that players who merited legitimate comparisons to Giancarlo Stanton do not come around the block every week.

The Yankees asked Chad Bohling, the team's director of mental con-ditioning, to get a read on Judge. Though other clubs have followed suit in recent years, the Yankees were the first team to interview amateur players instead of issuing written tests, incorporating those assessments into their scouting after hiring Bohling away from the NFL's Jacksonville Jaguars in 2005. The thinking was that by doing so, bad eggs could be weeded out of the system before they ever had a chance to put on the pinstripes. Bohling flew across the country and spent about an hour speaking with Judge at a restaurant near Fresno State's campus, returning with a glowing endorse-ment of the prospect's mindset and background.

"There was still a long way for him to go, but after that combination of what he was tool-wise, the big kicker was the makeup," Oppenheimer said. "The makeup set him apart and made him somebody that we thought could reach those lofty projections."

Judge played left field and right field as a freshman at Fresno State, then center field in his final two seasons, earning a reputation as a solid defender and hard worker whose power still hadn't translated into game action. Though Judge stole twice as many bases (36) as he hit homers (18) over four years in a Bulldogs uniform, there were glimpses of what Judge would become, including during a memorable BP session during a Cape Cod League showcase at Boston's Fenway Park in July 2012.

"Very rarely do we get to see draft kids in a major league setting," Oppenheimer said. "We see them on their high school field or their college field. You put them in that, and all of a sudden, it's a little bit of an eye-opener. It was a different sound and the ball was going into a different spot than the rest of that group."

Matt Hyde, the Yankees scout assigned to the New England region and the Cape Cod League, had filed effusive reports on Judge prior to his junior season at Fresno State. So had Brian Barber, a Yankees national scout, who had seen Judge in the lineup for the Cape Cod League's Brewster Whitecaps on at least four occasions that season.

"You just don't see guys on a baseball field built like this," Barber said. "He played center field that day, and I was like, 'Wow.' Then you notice how hard he hit the ball. It's one of those things in scouting, you happen to be at the right park on the right day, and he hit an absolute mammoth home run the day that I saw him. It was like, 'All right, wow. That's how superstars hit them.'"

Barber had sized up talent like Judge's before, albeit from a distance of sixty feet and six inches. The Cardinals had made Barber the twenty-second overall selection in the 1991 draft, plucking him from an Orlando, Florida, high school and hurrying him to the big leagues four years later at age twenty-two. Injuries ended his career at age twenty-eight, prompting Barber to join the Yankees organization as a scout for the 2002 season.

It turned out to be a good fit. As a starting pitcher, he'd spent many off-days holding a radar gun and charting pitches from the stands, finding that fresh look at the game fascinating. Barber can still recite the report that he filed to headquarters on Judge.

"I remember it exactly," Barber said. "I put him as a definite first-rounder the first time I saw him. He did something at the park every day that made you like him more and more. It wasn't just the power, it was the fact that he was playing center field. You didn't have any inclination to think that he was going to play center field in the big leagues, but he was a quality defender out there…

"The last piece of the puzzle was, this guy is six-foot-seven with really long limbs and he's able to keep his swing halfway short and get the balls on the inner half. I played ten years before scouting and when you saw a guy that big, the first thing you try to do is exploit him inside. You couldn't do that with this guy."

When the Yankees returned to the Fresno campus for a fresh look at Judge, they saw a player who had traveled light years from those formative years at Linden High.

"Damon Oppenheimer asked me to go see him, and it was apparent that there was a 'Wow' factor to him," said Billy Eppler, who was then the Yankees' assistant general manager and is now the GM of the Angels. "To see a human being that big, hitting a baseball that hard. He had the ability to manipulate his swing and put together a quality at-bat, time and time again. And how he moved, at that size, playing center field then? I don't think anybody is surprised with what he's been able to achieve, with the physical talents as well as the character."

Judge compiled a monstrous 1.116 OPS and was named as an All-American during his junior season, when many of those at-bats were witnessed by area scout Troy Afenir.

A former first-round pick who appeared in forty-five big league games for the Astros, Athletics, and Reds in the late 1980s and early 1990s, Afenir would earn a reputation within the Yankees system as a grinder and one of their toughest graders, but 2013 was his first year scouting the Southern California region. He'd inherited a list of players to see from Tim McIntosh, another former big league catcher who'd left to pursue a scouting opportunity with the Angels, and Afenir crossed the names off one by one. Judge's size and athleticism awed Afenir.

"When you get a chance to see him put it into action, it was pretty special," Afenir said. "I remember the coaches always saying that the guys who were the best were the guys who made it look the easiest and Aaron always did that, just from the way he played in the outfield and his natural leadership. Things like that indicated that he had everything that I was looking for."

There was other top talent in the area, keeping Afenir busy. The Astros were preparing to make Stanford right-hander Mark Appel the first player taken in the draft that June, and Stanford outfielder Austin Wilson would go in the second round to the Mariners. With Appel expected to come off the board well before the Yankees would have a chance at him, Afenir recalls weighing Judge against University of Nevada Reno pitcher Braden Shipley, who would go to the D-backs with the fifteenth overall pick. More often than not, Afenir thought Judge would be the better call.

"I remember [Afenir] telling me, 'I don't know exactly what I've got here because I'm new to this, but people aren't going to hit it any harder. They're not going to hit it any farther, and he's a really good *baseball player*,'" Oppenheimer said. "That's the thing that kept coming out, that he was a really good baseball player."

On those recommendations, Oppenheimer made a bleary-eyed trek through security at San Diego International Airport early on the morning of February 24, 2013, boarding a flight north to see Fresno State take the field against Stanford University. Judge didn't do much in batting practice,

In three years at Fresno State, Aaron Judge hit .346 with 41 doubles, 17 homers, and 35 stolen bases. He was a three-time All-Conference first team selection and a 2013 All-America honoree.

but he made plenty of noise in the game, going 5-for-5 with three RBIs, including a long home run to left field leading off the seventh inning.

"It's against Stanford, so it's solid pitching," Oppenheimer said, "and you're just sitting there like, 'Wow. What else do I need to see?'"

Yankees scouts kept tracking Judge, mostly to make sure that he remained healthy and that his performance didn't dip. Some compared Judge's agility to that of NBA superstar Blake Griffin, and as Barber colorfully put it, "This wasn't Herman Munster out there." Afenir said that Judge's placid demeanor impressed him even more than the line drives that seemed to rocket off his bat.

"You didn't know if he had gotten three hits the day before or whether he'd struck out three times," Afenir said. "He was so consistent with his approach to the game."

The MLB draft has existed since 1965, but it does not carry the cache of its NBA and NFL counterparts, in part because college baseball does not garner the television airtime that college basketball and college football do. As such, all but the elite high school and college baseball players remain largely unknown to the public until their names are called, though that has changed somewhat in the Internet era.

The sheer size of MLB's draft also makes it more difficult to track. Big league clubs currently take turns selecting players for forty rounds over three days each June, whereas the NFL draft and NHL entry draft are each seven rounds. The NBA draft lasts for only two rounds. In recent years, baseball has made efforts to entice the same kind of interest that its NBA and NFL counterparts enjoy, televising the first two rounds with live analysis from MLB Network's studios in Secaucus, New Jersey.

Leading into the draft, Oppenheimer ranked Judge as one of the top collegiate hitters on the board, along with Notre Dame infielder Eric Jagielo and Philip Ervin, a right-handed hitting outfielder from Sanford University in Birmingham, Alabama. The Yankees had done plenty of legwork, as they were in the uncommon situation of making three selections in the first round.

While their first selection was slotted twenty-sixth overall, they had also picked up a pair of compensatory draft picks. The thirty-second pick went to New York as compensation for losing outfielder Nick Swisher, who had signed a four-year, $56 million deal with the Indians. The Yankees also scored the thirty-third pick when right-handed reliever Rafael Soriano signed a two-year, $28 million pact with the Washington Nationals.

There was consensus within the organization about Judge's appeal, but Jagielo seemed to be a more conventional selection, a left-handed hitter from Downers Grove, Illinois, with legitimate power who would profile well at either infield corner. It was an opportunity to gamble. If the Yankees selected Jagielo at twenty-six, Oppenheimer believed that Judge would still be there at thirty-two, but the veteran talent evaluator doubted they could land both players by trying the reverse.

Operating from a war room decorated with cluttered dry-erase boards and binders of scouting reports on the third-base side of George M. Steinbrenner Field in Tampa, Florida, the Yankees sent word to their draft representatives in New Jersey that they were to use the twenty-sixth pick on Jagielo. Oppenheimer's heart thumped a few additional beats as the next selections ticked off the board.

The whispered intelligence turned out to be true; the five teams selecting between twenty-six and thirty-two had not been locked in on Judge. Ervin went to the Reds, followed by Rob Kaminsky (Cardinals), Ryne Stanek (Rays), Travis Demeritte (Rangers), and Jason Hursh (Braves).

"I've had a lot of guys since tell me that they really liked him and that there was a split camp with their club," Oppenheimer said. "Some teams had scouts that really liked him and some that weren't on him. For us, we were lucky in that we didn't have a split camp."

Judge was on site at the MLB Network studios, having made his first trip to New York City for the event. His initial read of the Big Apple was that it seemed too busy and hectic for his liking, telling a reporter from the *Fresno Bee* the day before the draft that he was "not sure if I could ever live here."

Good thing that the Yankees hadn't heard that comment. Maybe they ignored it.

"With the thirty-second selection of the 2013 First-Year Player Draft," Commissioner Bud Selig said, his hands cradling the podium as he leaned into a microphone, "the New York Yankees select Aaron Judge, a center fielder from Fresno State University, Fresno, California."

Dressed in a charcoal suit with a gray shirt and purple tie, Judge rose from his seat and embraced his father, then enveloped his mother in a bear hug. Judge said that he had spoken with the Yankees two days before that moment, but did not hear much from them on the actual day of the draft, so it had been "a good surprise" when they called his name.

"We thought we knew there was enough hesitancy within the industry, within baseball, that they were a little bit scared of Aaron Judge," Barber said.

As Judge tried on the pinstripes for the first time, commentator Harold Reynolds said, "I don't think that jersey fits. This kid is *big*." An on-screen graphic then compared Judge to Nolan Reimold, an outfielder who had batted .246 over an eight-year career, mostly spent with the Orioles. It seems in retrospect to be a curious comparison, as Reimold never exceeded 15 homers and 45 RBIs in a single season. In fairness, Judge had connected for only 18 homers in his college career—and six in 388 at-bats over his first two college seasons.

Speaking on a post-draft conference call with members of the New York media, Judge said that he anticipated that the Yankees would move him to a corner outfield spot because it would be easier to cover ground. He also remarked that he was trying to model parts of his game after Giancarlo Stanton—not the first time, nor the last, that comparisons would be drawn between the future teammates.

"He's also a big guy that plays the outfield, so I pay attention to what he does and try to take that into my game," Judge said.

Shortly after Judge accepted a $1.8 million signing bonus, he was invited to suit up for batting practice with the big league squad prior to a June 2013 game against the Athletics at the Oakland Coliseum. Judge remembers being awestruck when he entered the clubhouse, looking around the room at some familiar faces he'd once removed from foil packs of trading cards.

"Mariano Rivera, Robinson Cano, Andy Pettitte, those are guys that I grew up watching," Judge said. "Now they're coming to me saying, 'Hey, my name's Andy. Great to meet you, Aaron.' Andy Pettitte? I know who you are! It's just pretty surreal that those guys are coming up to me and introducing themselves. It shows you what kind of class act guys they were."

Gardner watched Judge take some of his BP swings, offering praise as the young prospect cleared the distant fences with ease. Gardner remembers his initial reaction as being, "Man, this is a big kid. He's a football player."

When Gardner grabbed his glove and jogged to the outfield, Judge followed. The outfielders were preparing to take ground balls in center field from coach Rob Thomson, who was swinging a fungo bat near second base. As Gardner recalls, the very first grounder Judge fielded as a member of the Yankees organization took a bad hop and skipped toward the wall.

"It rolled right under him," Gardner said. "He completely missed it, completely whiffed on it. Thoms has got a great sense of humor; he threw his bat down and maybe even kicked some dirt. He made Aaron think that he was mad at him or upset with him, and I was out there laughing. It was a pretty cool moment to see him that very first day, and to see how far he's come."

At the moment when Judge chased that ball in Oakland, the Yankees' farm system appeared to be stronger than it had been in some time. Sanchez was two months from being promoted to Double-A Trenton, Severino was about to make his stateside debut in the Gulf Coast League, and Bird was mashing in the heart of the lineup for Class-A Charleston. The footsteps were still too far away to be heard in the Bronx, but the Baby Bombers were on their way.

CHAPTER 4

UNLEASH THE KRAKEN

The jewel event of each Major League Baseball offseason is the Winter Meetings, a four day extravaganza that transforms a sprawling hotel and conference center into a bizarre melting pot of team executives, player agents, prospective free agents, current managers, managerial hopefuls, caffeinated reporters, resume-clutching job seekers, and commission-hungry vendors hawking the next great pitching machine or t-shirt cannon.

In another time, they were vital for a team to cross the finish line on transactions. In December 1975, White Sox general manager Roland Hemond found a seat in the lobby of the Diplomat Hotel in Fort Lauderdale, Florida, where he plugged in a rotary telephone and set up a handmade sign that read, "Open for Business." Hemond instructed Buck Peden, the team's publicity director, to ring that line every half hour to make it look as though the team was extremely busy. The ruse worked; the White Sox made four trades that day.

Now that text messaging has replaced landlines, Brian Cashman views the meetings more as a "necessary evil," often secluding himself in the team's suite while appearing sparingly in the lobby, restaurants, or the bar. It is not uncommon for room service to be called upon for each meal of Cashman's day, which generally includes at least one formal session with the media. Reporters are invited upstairs in hopes of tracking down a morsel that hints at the negotiations (or lack thereof) taking place between teams and players.

At times, Cashman opts to skip the briefing altogether. That had been the case in 2008, when he slipped away from the Bellagio Hotel in Las Vegas and showed up on CC Sabathia's doorstep in Vallejo, California, authorized to dangle $161 million of the Steinbrenner family fortune that would make the six-foot-six, 300-pound left-hander the best paid starting pitcher in history. Cashman recognized the palatial estate from an episode of "MTV Cribs," and after a two hour meeting in the hurler's living room, Sabathia agreed to accept the cash. Sabathia's teddy bear personality—and, of course, the 19 wins that tied for the big league lead—would be vital as the Yankees secured their twenty-seventh World Series title that autumn.

Another year, Cashman teased the visitors to his suite by conspicuously leaving a piece of paper on his desk with the names of second baseman Robinson Cano and right-hander Chien-Ming Wang, two of his top prospects at the time. Cashman linked them in a phantom negotiation with the Milwaukee Brewers for right-hander Ben Sheets: "They get Cano & Wang. We get Sheets." One reporter spied the note and surreptitiously placed a notebook over the transaction, hoping to hide it from his competition. Cashman allowed the group interview to run for several minutes before laughing, admitting to the prank out of fear that the reporter would begin to chase down the false rumor. In hindsight, the deal would have been a slam-dunk for Milwaukee.

It was during one of those relaxed interactions that a nickname was born. The 2015 Winter Meetings were held at the Gaylord Opryland

Brian Cashman has served as the Yankees' general manager since February 1998. He joined the organization as an intern in 1986 and is currently the longest-tenured GM in baseball.

Resort and Convention Center in Nashville, Tennessee, a glass-enclosed labyrinth with an indoor river where guests can literally go for days without a breath of outside air. That hermetically sealed structure is where Cashman first uttered his desire to "unleash the Kraken, which is Gary Sanchez, on our roster in 2016 if I can."

"Release the Kraken!" had been a line in the 1981 fantasy adventure movie *The Clash of the Titans*, spoken when Zeus (played originally by Laurence Olivier and later by Liam Neeson in the 2010 remake) orders that a giant sea monster be set free. Cashman said that he actually pulled the reference from the 2006 flick, *Pirates of the Caribbean: Dead Man's Chest,* which features a scene in which Johnny Depp's Jack Sparrow character encounters the colossal octopus.

"It came to me from the movie—'Release the Kraken!'—which was a beast that would unleash fury on its prey," Cashman said. "For some reason, it came to me that Gary Sanchez was a mystical beast, that his bat could unleash fury on his opponents. The one thing that we always talked about when we saw him coming through the system was that the ball off his bat sounds different. The crack of the bat, the Kraken being a mystical beast, it all fit."

The Kraken handle would have staying power; in time, Didi Gregorius would begin using a squid emoji in his postgame tweets to celebrate Sanchez's accomplishments, and Sanchez had an octopus-themed bat crafted for the Home Run Derby in 2017. The Yankee Stadium scoreboard also played the Neeson clip at key points in games, surely generating quizzical stares from fans who hadn't been tracking the offseason of 2015–2016 closely.

Viewed as the front-runner to serve as Brian McCann's backup when the 2016 Yankees began to gather in Tampa, Sanchez arrived early and wowed observers on a back field of the player development complex, unloading a barrage of batting practice homers that forced those peeking through a chain-link outfield fence to take cover.

The potential for a new wave of talent excited the Yankees, who commissioned a fun video in which their clubhouse was transformed into a preschool playroom. Dressed in their pinstripes, Sanchez pushed a toy dump truck across the carpet while Aaron Judge stacked brightly colored blocks and Luis Severino stomped with a plastic dinosaur.

"These guys are taking the 'Baby Bombers' title way too seriously," manager Joe Girardi deadpanned, crossing his arms while bench coach Rob Thomson looked on disapprovingly.

Their acting was passable, but unfortunately, the rest of Sanchez's spring failed to live up to that promise. Pressing to secure the job, Sanchez instead punched his ticket to the minors by producing two hits in twenty-two Grapefruit League at-bats (.091).

"The offensive numbers were not very good," Sanchez said. "I worked really hard every day with my hitting coach…I felt fine playing defense. I felt great. At the same time, I also felt great in my at-bats. It's just that I didn't get the results that I wanted."

He would in time. Summoned to the big leagues for good in August, Sanchez embarked on a remarkable march through the history books with a home run hitting frenzy that captivated much of baseball. For the organization, their patience had been rewarded, dating to the $3 million signing bonus that his natural gifts warranted at age sixteen.

• • •

When a seventeen-year-old Gary Sanchez joined the roster of the Yankees' Class-A Staten Island affiliate for a sixteen-game cameo late in the 2010 season, his defense left much to be desired. Josh Paul, Sanchez's first manager, once told ESPN that Sanchez "couldn't catch a fastball down the middle" in those days. Right-hander Bryan Mitchell wasn't quite so harsh in assessing of Sanchez's receiving skills. A frequent minor league teammate of Sanchez early in their respective careers, Mitchell said that Sanchez's tools had been obvious.

"He always had a great arm," said Mitchell, who was traded to the Padres in December 2017. "His hitting was another level above what you'd see that young. I think you always knew the potential that he had."

Though he would take mandatory English classes after games, Sanchez struggled with loneliness once the stadium lights were turned off and he had retreated to his quiet apartment or hotel room. The place where he seemed to be most comfortable was in the batter's box, where Sanchez had an intrinsic feel for what needed to be done.

Disciplinary episodes peppered Sanchez's progress through the minor league ranks. The most notable incident took place when Sanchez was with Class-A Charleston in 2011, with reports suggesting that he sulked after manager Aaron Ledesma wrote John Ryan Murphy's name into the lineup at catcher for a second consecutive game. Sanchez declined to enter a game as a replacement, and when a coach asked him to warm up a pitcher in the bullpen, he had refused to do so.

The Yankees responded by bouncing Sanchez back to their minor league complex in Tampa for what amounted to a ten-day attitude adjustment. Personally disappointed by his performance to that point, Sanchez returned to the South Atlantic League hungry and belted 13 homers with 31 RBIs over his final 50 games, earning two turns as the league's Player of the Week.

"I remember that I was told that this kid needed a lot of help with his work ethic," said Al Pedrique, who joined the Yankees organization as a minor league manager in 2013. "At times during the games, he didn't run balls out. I remember having a conversation in spring training with Gary that I was there to help him get better, but we'll do things the right way, the professional way. At times, he was stubborn. He wanted to do things his way."

While with Double-A Trenton in 2014, Sanchez was also hit with a five game suspension for what manager Tony Franklin called "a violation of some of our guidelines." Declining to provide specific details of the infraction, Franklin told the *Trentonian* that Sanchez needed to conduct himself "like a professional at all times."

"He grew up, like all of us have to at some point," said Twins hitting coach James Rowson, who served as the Yankees' minor league hitting coordinator from 2014–2016. "Sometimes the spotlight is on you when you're that talented and you're coming up in the New York Yankees organization. You may do something immature here or there, but nothing out of the ordinary. He was just a kid who was being a kid."

Rob Refsnyder said that he first saw Sanchez play in 2013, when the two were teammates with Class-A Tampa. Refsnyder recalls Sanchez "oozing" talent, instantly showcasing the best arm and raw power that the infielder had ever seen. While some wondered if Sanchez was destined to become another Jesus Montero, a promising catcher whose career fizzled soon after being traded to the Mariners following the 2011 season, Refsnyder saw few signs of the moodiness that Sanchez was reputed to exhibit.

"People are blown away by this, but Gary is one of my favorite human beings on the entire Earth," Refsnyder said. "No exaggeration. I love Gary.

He's an awesome guy, he's an awesome husband and father. I consider him one of my closest friends in baseball still. I know Gary got a lot of flak about work ethic and stuff like that, but to this day, I'll swear by it—Gary is one of the best teammates I've ever had.

"I saw that guy go like 0-for-20, terrible at-bats, at-bats that a player would be sulking or consumed by. He was on the top step, giving high fives. I learned a lot from Gary. If you go 0-for-4, it's a shrug of the shoulders, kind of an 'I'll get them tomorrow, I'll figure it out.'"

Sanchez said that he was in the process of becoming a more mature player even before he followed a hallway of fluorescent lights into a Trenton, New Jersey hospital room during the 2015 season, where Sanchez's wife, Sahaira, gave birth to a daughter that the couple named Sarah. As Sanchez snipped the umbilical cord, he admired the girl's cherubic face and made a silent promise to be the best father he possibly could.

"Imagine, just like that, you're a dad," Sanchez said. "The responsibility that comes with that, being a dad, it's a big responsibility. It's something that you have to take very seriously. There's a kid now that you want to provide for and make sure that she's comfortable and has a good life."

Gary Sanchez received a $3 million signing bonus in July 2009. Pictured here with the Tampa Yankees, Sanchez was consistently rated among the organization's most exciting prospects.

Then twenty-two, Sanchez remembers being "very surprised" when he found out that Sahaira was expecting, but "at the same time, very happy." He recalls being afraid to hold Sarah, fearing that he would somehow harm the delicate newborn. Sanchez eased into fatherhood, and Sarah grew into an adorable toddler with curly black hair who loves to babble and play with her daddy.

"Once she was born, it was kind of like a switch went off," Sanchez said. "I saw the opportunity in front of me. I just decided, whatever I need to do and whatever it takes to get to the big leagues, let's get it done now. When you have a daughter, it's kind of like a source of energy and motivation. It pushes you to do more, to be better."

When Sanchez rejoined his Trenton teammates, coaches noticed Sanchez taking a more purposeful approach in batting practice, which he'd sometimes treated like a home run hitting competition. Sanchez also spent more time in the weight room and seemed to pay closer attention during games, returning to the dugout and tipping teammates off to patterns that opposing pitchers had fallen into.

"You could tell he was a different guy," said Pedrique, the manager of that Trenton squad. "He was more serious about his approach during batting practice, what he was trying to accomplish. During the game, he would communicate more with his teammates. He started being more aggressive handling the pitching staff and understanding the game plan for each guy. You could tell that he was growing up."

Posting a robust .274/.330/.485 split line between Double-A Trenton and Triple-A, Sanchez polished his defensive skills with lessons picked up from Josh Paul, instructor Julio Mosquera, and bench coach Tony Pena, prompting his first call-up at the end of 2015. Sanchez pinch-hit twice, going hitless, and was on the roster as a third catcher for the Wild Card game against the Astros. Pena said that the big-league coaches had been pleased by Sanchez's progress.

"Before, you had to force him to do things," Pena said. "Now he understands that he needs to keep improving. He's doing it. Sometimes it's the nature of human beings. Some people grow up faster than others. I think there are a lot of Latin American players that it takes a long time to grow. I love to see the way he handles himself."

Sent to play against top competition in the Arizona Fall League, Sanchez sparkled, slugging seven homers while throwing out sixty-two percent of runners attempting to steal. Word filtered to Cashman that something had clicked; Sanchez knew he was probably going to be a good big-league player, but now he was determined to be great.

"If you have a tool package that's exceptional, which he does, then the sky is the limit," Cashman said. "It's a very difficult game, and one you can't play unless you have talent. He has exceptional power, he's a big man, he's got a good arm. If you can refine your ability to sharpen the lens of your craft, you can tap into that physicality and that's clearly what has happened."

When the Yankees gathered for their organizational meetings that autumn, John Ryan Murphy was listed as their backup catcher. A baby-faced twenty-four-year-old from Bradenton, Florida, the easygoing Murphy was generally regarded as a sharp defender with some offensive potential, having batted .277 with three homers and 14 RBIs in 155 at-bats during the 2015 season. Murphy seemed to be a nice player to have, but Cashman was so convinced of Sanchez's readiness that the Yankees dealt Murphy to the Twins for outfielder Aaron Hicks that November.

But when Sanchez flopped in the spring of 2016, the Yankees decided instead to carry Austin Romine as their backup catcher, optioning Sanchez to Triple-A.

"Probably a guy trying to do too much and trying too hard in spring training," manager Joe Girardi said. "That happens. It happens all the time. The key is that he learned from that."

While Sanchez moved his gear across the street to the minor league complex, Romine savored having finally caught a break. Then twenty-seven years old, Romine carried strong baseball bloodlines. His father, Kevin, had enjoyed seven years as a Red Sox outfielder from 1985–1991, and his older brother Andrew has played in the majors with the Angels and Tigers.

Once a touted prospect who was considered a possible heir apparent to Jorge Posada, Romine had been designated for assignment prior to the 2015 season, a procedural move that exposed him to waivers and freed any other club to make a claim. They all passed, and Romine returned to Scranton/Wilkes-Barre, where he resurrected his career by earning selection to the International League's All-Star Game.

Upon his return from those festivities in Omaha, Romine's heart sank, learning that Sanchez had been promoted from Double-A and would take Romine's job as the RailRiders' everyday catcher. Romine respected

Sanchez's talent and understood why the organization wanted to accelerate his development, but he also had hoped that his play was being noticed by the decision-makers in the front office.

"It put a chip on my shoulder—a positive chip," Romine said. "Sometimes, you can put a negative one up there and it can go against you in certain ways. I just put a positive one up there. I know what I can do when I stay within myself."

Though the Yankees weren't ready to use Sanchez at the major league level, some of their competition was willing to. The untouchables in the system at that time were listed as Greg Bird, Aaron Judge, Jorge Mateo, and Luis Severino, but Cashman would listen if one of his GM counterparts mentioned Sanchez's name. Cashman said that he received "some very strong proposals" to trade for Sanchez, but the Yankees ultimately rejected all of them.

"You walk through the process, dissect it, and walk away from it," Cashman said. "We were never close to doing anything, never brought anything to ownership, but a lot of different clubs tried to push a lot of different concepts that made us go through the process and go through offers. When Gary started turning the corner in Double-A, he entered the category that he was going to be a success or a failure here in New York."

Following his spring stall-out in 2016, Sanchez played in seventy-one games at Triple-A. The opportunity to play every day had served as a blessing in disguise for the twenty-three-year-old, who posted a .807 OPS with Scranton/Wilkes-Barre, accumulating valuable reps that would not have been available if he were backing up McCann in New York. Having Sanchez lose the spring battle to Romine also created an inadvertent long-term benefit for the team, as it delayed Sanchez's free agency until after the 2022 season.

The Yankees called up Sanchez for a one game cameo on May 13, plugging his right-handed bat into the DH spot against nasty White Sox left-hander Chris Sale. Sanchez went hitless in four at-bats that night, then was summoned for good prior to an August 3 Subway Series game at Citi Field, in which Sanchez notched his first big league hit—a seventh inning single off Mets reliever Hansel Robles.

Finally, Sanchez had a chance to begin showing why the organization had been so excited about his progress. Over the final eight weeks of the regular season, Sanchez equaled a dusty record that had been set by out-

Bursting onto the big league scene late in 2016, Gary Sanchez was the fastest player in baseball history to reach 11, 18, and 19 home runs in terms of games played.

fielder Wally Berger of the 1930 Boston Braves, hitting an incredible 20 home runs in his first 51 big league games.

When Alex Rodriguez played his final game on August 12, the veteran slugger remarked that Sanchez's loud bat had helped to nudge him out the door. Sanchez had gone 4-for-5 in a win at Fenway Park two nights earlier, a performance that included Sanchez's first big league homer, an eighth inning solo shot off Red Sox reliever Junichi Tazawa.

"The game is tough. I saw Gary Sanchez have a series in Boston and I looked at him and said, 'I can't do that anymore,'" Rodriguez said. "And I was happy about it. I'm at peace."

Sanchez's homer off Tazawa was the first installment of a barrage that would see him take seventeen different pitchers deep, with Cody Martin, David Price, and Marco Estrada each serving up a pair. Sanchez hit a sizzling .389 with 11 homers in August, earning selection as both the AL's Player of the Month and Rookie of the Month. Sanchez was the first Yankees catcher to win either award.

"Gary's been doing this from Double-A, Triple-A, and now he's up here to do it on the big show," Aaron Judge said. "It didn't matter who was throwing, what the count was, what the situation was. He was going to go with his plan and he was executing it. That's tough to do at the major league level, and he did it for a month and a half there."

Quickly elevated to the number three spot in the lineup, Sanchez also set a record for the fewest games played by any player to hit 20 homers in a season (previously Giancarlo Stanton, who hit 27 in 74 games in 2015). The only other Yankees to ever hit 20 home runs between August 10 and the end of any season were Babe Ruth (1927) and Roger Maris (1961), so Sanchez was in fantastic company.

"I think everybody on the team calls 'home run' when he steps up there," said fellow rookie Tyler Austin, who made some history of his own by belting back-to-back homers with Judge on August 13 of that 2016 season. "When you get on a roll like he's on and the way he's swinging the bat, I feel like every time he steps in the box, it could be a home run."

In 229 plate appearances, Sanchez produced an impressive .299/.376/.657 slash line, with 32 of his 60 hits going for extra bases. T-shirts bearing Sanchez's uniform No. 24 became a hot seller while the Yankees gained steam in the postseason chase, and those who witnessed the early installments of Sanchez's rise were not surprised by what they were seeing.

"There's no better teacher than experience," Rowson said. "He continues to make adjustments at every level. You have to change your swing at times as you progress. You tend to make your swing a little bit shorter. You're not swinging as hard as you can for the long ball all the time."

The Yankees were equally pleased with Sanchez's demeanor behind the plate, as he'd frequently pop-up mid at-bat to wrap an arm around a hurler and go over their next pitch sequence. Starlin Castro compared Sanchez's throwing arm to that of the elite Cardinals backstop Yadier Molina, and in a telling take of Sanchez's focus, CC Sabathia said that he was able to navigate through his starts without shaking off a single one of Sanchez's signs.

"He has good suggestions, which is rare for a young catcher," Sabathia said. "That makes you feel good and confident that he knows what he wants to call."

With Major League Baseball continuing to operate on an unbalanced schedule, the Yankees play against their American League East rivals (nineteen games against the Blue Jays, Orioles, Rays, and Red Sox each) more than the teams in other divisions. Having to see Sanchez so frequently was an unsettling thought to Rays manager Kevin Cash, who said that he spent a half of an inning on the bench discussing the catcher's breakout with first baseman Logan Morrison during a September 2016 series.

"We were trying to figure out if we've ever seen anybody come up and do something like this," Cash said. "What a talented player—offensively, defensively. We saw as strong an arm as I've ever seen from a catcher. And then, offensively, he just has a very, very good approach at the plate and a ton of power."

Gary Denbo, who was then the Yankees' vice president of player development, said that he believed the organization's coaches deserve applause for helping Sanchez realize his potential. Denbo specifically mentioned catching instructors Jason Brown, Michel Hernandez, Julio Mosquera, and Josh Paul as being crucial, as well as Al Pedrique and hitting coaches Marcus Thames, P.J. Pilittere, and Tommy Wilson.

"They spent hours and hours with this guy," Denbo said. "He's matured mentally and physically and he's become one of the best young players in the game. We're very proud of that."

Sanchez finished second to Tigers pitcher Michael Fulmer for the American League's Rookie of the Year Award, receiving four first place votes, twenty-three second place votes, and two third place votes (full disclosure: one of Sanchez's second place votes was cast by the author of this book). Upon returning to the Dominican Republic in the winter, Sanchez focused on strength work, saying that he needed to prepare his body to catch more than 100 games in 2017.

Though Sanchez remained a man of few words, exhibiting an introverted demeanor when surrounded by microphones and notepads, his success quickly made him recognizable on the streets of New York. During a staged January 2017 visit, Sanchez stunned the lunchtime crowd at a Bronx bodega when he donned a chef's hat and stepped behind the counter to slap together ham and cheese sandwiches, part of a promotion that the Yankees launched in part to sell the city on their next generation of stars.

"I don't feel any pressure to be 'the guy' off the field," Sanchez said. "On the field, you're trying to win games and that's the focus. I don't feel any pressure at all. I've got to keep doing the same things I've been doing. Just to play baseball is what I know how to do."

Seemingly at ease behind that bodega counter, Sanchez was about to get settled behind home plate at Yankee Stadium. The Yankees had made their intentions clear at the tail end of the '16 season, when Cashman said that the starting catcher job had become Sanchez's to lose. By trading Brian McCann to the Astros for a pair of young pitching prospects, the Yankees announced they were ready to send Sanchez into 2017 as the unchallenged starter.

"We can count on him being one of the top five hitting catchers in the AL at very least, with a great arm and defense," Cashman said. "He's extremely bright, and one of the better intellectual young hitters that our staff has come across. It took a little longer than we wanted, but he was projected to be a middle of the lineup type hitter and a very exciting defender. Boy, what he did was amazing."

CHAPTER 5

BIRD IS THE WORD

The home run that helped clinch the fifty-third postseason appearance in Yankees history was launched from Greg Bird's bat on the afternoon of September 24, 2017, a three-run shot to right-center field off the Blue Jays' Joe Biagini. While Didi Gregorius and Ronald Torreyes raised their arms and clapped in the first-base dugout at Toronto's Rogers Centre, Bird cracked the slightest sliver of a smile, satisfied in having reminded his team why they were correct to not have given up on him.

Bird had always seemed to exude patience, but the past two years had tested that admirable character trait. After surging onto the big-league scene with 11 homers at the tail end of 2015, Bird lost all of 2016 to injury and was slammed with more bad fortune early in 2017, when the impact of a seemingly innocuous foul ball wound up erasing the twenty-four-year-old from the lineup for more than two-thirds of the season.

So, while his teammates gleefully sprayed each other with Bottega Prosecco and created a miniature Lake Ontario in the center of the clubhouse carpet, Bird made sure to savor the moment for a few extra beats—articulating his excitement while staying true to his tranquil demeanor.

"Whatever your job is, you've got to do your job," Bird shouted over the celebration, while cans of Budweiser exploded around his head. "At points this year, my job was to get better and try and come back. Just to be back now is huge for me."

After sitting out all of 2016 while recovering from right labrum shoulder surgery, the disabled list was the last place that Bird expected to be in

2017. Mark Teixeira had marched into retirement on a high note, hitting a September grand slam off Red Sox hurler Joe Kelly for his 409th and final big-league homer, opening the door for Bird to take over as the next in a succession of terrific Yankees first basemen. Bird's eight spring training homers raised optimism that he could be a worthy successor to the likes of Don Mattingly, Jason Giambi, and Teixeira.

Then came a March 30 exhibition against the Phillies in Clearwater, Florida, the Yankees' final game in the Sunshine State before their bags were packed to head north. Batting in the third inning against veteran right-hander Joaquin Benoit, Bird hacked at a pitch and sensed a lightning bolt of pain rush through his right ankle. He winced and hobbled around the batter's box but remained in the game, working a walk before yielding to a pinch runner.

In the clubhouse, Bird had the ankle wrapped in ice and thought little of it, believing it was another in the long line of bumps and bruises that come with playing every day. A precautionary set of X-rays were taken, which came back clean, and Bird had no reason to assume he had sustained anything other than a particularly nasty contusion.

His concern grew when the ankle throbbed throughout April, a month in which Bird managed six hits in sixty at-bats (.100). Bird was placed on the disabled list in early May, beginning a quest for answers that would necessitate office visits with no fewer than seven noted orthopedists.

After Bird's discomfort aborted a twelve-game rehab stint in early June, there was at least one moment of frustration in which an unnamed Yankees insider questioned Bird's desire to return, telling the *New York Daily News*, "You really have to wonder what's with this guy. You'd think with Judge and Sanchez, the guys he came up through the system with, doing so well up here, he'd want to be a part of this. Apparently not."

Bird wisely refrained from returning fire, though he was clearly irked.

"I want to play. I've always wanted to play since I can remember," Bird said. "I love baseball. For me, I'm doing everything I can to get back. That's pretty much all I know. I would hope people see that."

Cashman dabbled with first base alternatives, giving 184 at-bats to the strikeout-prone Chris Carter before trading with the Brewers for minor leaguer Garrett Cooper and offering a chance to fourth-stringer Ji-Man Choi. Cashman maintained that Bird was still the team's best choice for the present and the future.

Cashman said that Bird reminded him of former big-league outfielder Bobby Abreu, in that he could seemingly roll out of bed and be an exceptional hitter. That remained possible, but first someone would need to figure out what was keeping Bird off the field. The root of Bird's inflammation issues was finally identified in a mid-July consultation with Dr. Martin O'Malley at New York's Hospital for Special Surgery.

O'Malley explained that Bird was dealing with an excess growth in the os trigonum of his right ankle, describing it to the player as an accessory bone that had been present at birth and served no real purpose. O'Malley's suggestion was to remove the bone altogether, with the hope of getting Bird on the field within six weeks. Though manager Joe Girardi said that they couldn't necessarily count on that timetable after so many false starts, Bird vowed that his season was not over.

"Being able to go out and play with these guys again and be part of the team, that's what I'm looking forward to the most," Bird said. "I'll have a scar. It's a bone I won't need. One less bone."

Touching base with Mets general manager Sandy Alderson in advance of the July 31 trade deadline, Cashman revealed that he had spoken about Jay Bruce, Lucas Duda, and Neil Walker, all of whom would soon be traded when the disappointing Mets turned the page toward their 2018 season. They were all capable of playing first base, with Duda the most experienced of the trio. Cashman told Alderson that he was interested but only as a rental, since Bird was supposed to be activated in August.

"I do remember him saying, when he wasn't getting what he needed from me in one of the conversations, 'Are you really going to rely on Greg Bird, who hasn't played all year?'" Cashman said. "I said to him, 'I know this guy and I know what he's capable of. He's going to be healthy. He's coming back and he will hit because that's what he's always done. He's not going to need much time.'"

• • •

Before Aaron Judge and Gary Sanchez were the celebrated young muscle in the big-league lineup, Greg Bird was being talked about as the next big thing in New York. That ripple began in the spring of 2015, when Alex Rodriguez watched a group of prospects including Bird and Judge put on a batting display at George M. Steinbrenner Field. Rodriguez returned to his locker and—unsolicited—remarked that the Yankees had something special brewing.

Say what you will about Rodriguez's tumultuous career, but he seemed to read the game at a different level between the white lines, picking up on trends and storylines quicker than his coaches, teammates, and the media. That was the case then, when Rodriguez lauded Bird and Judge as "two of the finest young hitters I've seen in a long time."

When Rodriguez made that proclamation, Bird was a few months removed from having been named the Most Valuable Player of the Arizona Fall League, coming off a campaign in which he batted .271 with 14 home runs and 43 RBIs in 102 games for Class-A Tampa and Double-A Trenton.

"You don't see those type of young hitters come around very often," Rodriguez said. "We're lucky to have two of them."

Born in Memphis, Tennessee, to parents Jim and Lee, Bird lived with his family in nearby Cordova, Tennessee, until age ten, when his father pursued an opportunity as a Colorado property realtor. Though he initially lamented the loss of his schoolyard friends, Bird soon discovered that life in the Rocky Mountain state suited him fine.

"The winters were different, more snow, but it was great," Bird said. "You'd play basketball in the street, go to the movies, normal stuff—just suburban cities. In Colorado, there's more to do in the outdoors; go to the mountains, skiing, fishing, camping. We did that more."

Introduced to baseball by the 1993 movie *The Sandlot*, Bird swiftly moved on from Smalls, Ham, and Squints to study the Rockies' games on television, often mimicking the left-handed swing of power-hitting first baseman Todd Helton. He remembers being enthralled by the 1998 home run chase between the Cardinals' Mark McGwire and the Cubs' Sammy Sosa, and later counted shortstop Troy Tulowitzki as one of his favorite players to observe.

"My mom always tells me that I was good at watching and doing it," Bird said. "When I started to understand how baseball worked, I just liked to watch the good hitters hit."

Dabbling in basketball, football, and hockey as a youth, Bird's brooding over a poorly-timed game of hoops during his freshman year at Grandview High helped outline his future priorities. He remembers sitting in one of his classes, deciding not only that he should play baseball, but that he was going to get drafted by a big-league team out of high school.

"I was upset. I missed baseball tryouts because I was playing basketball," Bird said. "It wouldn't have made a difference, but I stopped. I didn't like that. I always liked baseball. It wasn't a matter of trying to focus on it, I enjoyed it the most, so why not do that one?"

A stellar student who juggled his sports commitments while bringing home report cards filled with As and Bs, Bird played two seasons as a catcher (2009–2010) on the varsity squad, where he enjoyed calling the games and being involved in every pitch.

"The big thing for me was just the attitude that he had, the type of person that he was," Dean Adams, Bird's baseball coach at Grandview, told the YES Network. "What he brought to the table besides being able to play. It was the attitude and the work ethic and the personality. He is an extremely mature young man."

Future Orioles pitcher Kevin Gausman was one of Bird's teammates and recalls marveling after Bird stepped into the batting cage on his first day of winter baseball workouts.

"I was like, 'This guy is the best guy on our team, right now,'" Gausman said. "It wasn't close."

Named as Colorado's Gatorade Player of the Year during his senior season, there are still tales told at Grandview about Bird's bombs. Aided by an aluminum bat and Colorado's thin air, Gausman said he was awed when Bird cleared the centerfield fence 400 feet from home plate, reaching the netting of a tennis court that sat about fifty feet behind the ballfield.

"It was dead quiet," Gausman said. "Nobody could say anything, just looking around."

Those sorts of displays intrigued the Yankees, who selected him in the fifth round of the 2011 draft after he had hit a Colorado-best 27 homers with a .574 average during his final two years of high school. Bird wrestled with his decision as he weighed the allure of a pro contract against a scholarship offer from the University of Arkansas. He loved the small-town appeal of the Fayetteville campus and the idea of playing in the Southeastern Conference, but also couldn't resist picturing himself in pinstripes. Bird's parents told him that they would be supportive of whichever path he chose.

"They were never the type that said, 'Hey, you've got to do this, play this sport,'" Bird said. "They just always told me, do what you want to do, we'll support you. Have fun, enjoy it, give your all, and that's kind of how it was. After a bad game, it was, 'Go get 'em tomorrow.'"

Greg Bird during his 2013 season with the Charleston RiverDogs, when he batted .288 with 20 home runs and 84 RBIs in 130 games.

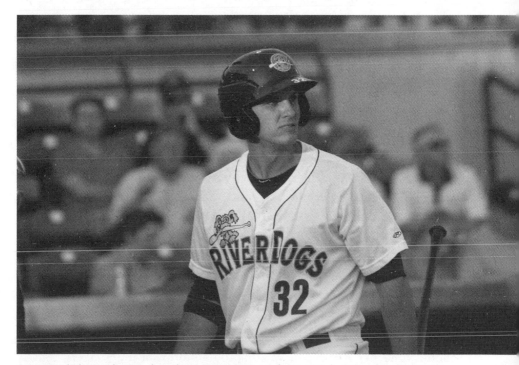

Greg Bird drew the Yankees' interest at Grandview High School in Colorado, where he batted .553 with 12 homers and 38 RBIs as a senior and was named the 2011 Gatorade High School Player of the Year.

"My dad never played baseball, so he never really coached me, if you will, but he was always there for me if I needed it. Eventually, I kind of grew out of what he could do, and then I always kind of joked that my mom was my best hitting coach. She'd tell me, 'See the ball, hit the ball. You always have, so do that.'"

Accepting a $1.1 million signing bonus, Bird's signature dried in time to participate in four Gulf Coast League games at the end of 2011, beginning his long climb toward New York.

"It's something growing up that you always want to do," Bird said. "I think there was a little period where I signed, you're a little bit overwhelmed by everything that's going on. Once that slowed down, I think deep down I always kind of knew. Baseball is tough and you have to take it day by day, and that's part of the process. I think hearing that from other guys, coaches, staff, definitely helped keep that confidence."

Once Bird was in the pipeline, concerns over the health of his back prompted a conversion into a first baseman. Bird embraced the challenge, spending many hours drilling on the minutia of the position with Carlos Mendoza, then one of the team's roving instructors and now a coach on the big league squad. As his confidence increased, Bird started to envision himself playing the position at Yankee Stadium, where a five-time Gold Glove Award winner and three-time Silver Slugger was winding down an outstanding career.

• • •

For years, first base in the Bronx had belonged to Mark Teixeira, who signed an eight-year, $180 million contract with the Yankees prior to the 2009 season and played a key role in helping the franchise win their most recent championship title. That season, Teixeira was a monster, tying the Rays' Carlos Pena for the American League lead with 39 home runs while pacing the Junior Circuit with 122 RBIs, 85 extra-base hits, and 344 total bases.

During slumps, Teixeira often invited questioners to look at "the back of my baseball card," a not-so-subtle way of pointing out the ongoing string of seasons in which he had slugged 30 or more homers while driving in 100 or more runs. From 2004 through 2011, Teixeira averaged 36 homers and 117 RBIs while wearing the uniforms of the Rangers, Braves,

Angels, and Yankees. Indeed, the flip sides of his Topps-issued collectibles were impressive.

That consistency began to slip in 2012, when a nagging cough, wrist inflammation, and a calf strain forced Teixeira to miss thirty-nine games. A routine workout in preparation for the World Baseball Classic spoiled Teixeira's 2013 season; taking a practice swing at a ball on a tee, Teixeira experienced a painful grab in his right wrist. The diagnosis was a partially-torn tendon sheath that eventually required surgery. Teixeira batted .209 over the next two seasons before rebounding with a resurgent 2015, earning his final All-Star Game selection.

Arguably the Yankees' MVP to 2015's midway point, having hit a team-leading 31 homers, Teixeira sustained a small fracture when he fouled a ball off his right shin in an August game against the Twins. In a parallel to Bird's 2017 ankle issues that did not go unnoticed, the severity of Teixeira's season-ending injury wasn't properly diagnosed for another four weeks.

That opened a door for Bird, who had been named the organization's minor league Player of the Year in 2013 after hitting .288 with 20 home runs, 84 RBIs, and a minor league-leading 107 walks for Class-A Charleston of the South Atlantic League. Al Pedrique, who managed Bird that season, compared his plate approach to big league veteran Lyle Overbay.

"He had great plate discipline," Pedrique said. "Very smart, hit the ball the other way with authority. When he needed to pull the ball, he would pull the ball. I had Overbay in Arizona in Double-A, and he was basically the same type of hitter. Line drive, gap-to-gap power, very good plate discipline with runners in scoring position."

Though the start of Bird's 2014 season was delayed by a lower back injury, scouts raved not only about his power upside, but also a level swing that promised to allow him to hit for average. To the organization's delight, Bird cut down on his strikeouts, reducing that number from 132 in 2013 to 97 the following year. Opposing clubs took notice, and Bird became one of the most commonly requested players in Cashman's dealings with other GMs.

In July 2015, Cashman volleyed proposals to upgrade his starting pitching but made it known that Bird was one of his untouchable prospects, along with Aaron Judge, Jorge Mateo, and Gary Sanchez. Rebuffed in their attempts to pry one of those players loose, the Phillies instead dealt left-hander Cole Hamels to the Rangers (for a package that included five quality prospects and veteran pitcher Matt Harrison). The Tigers shipped left-hander David Price to the Blue Jays, where he helped Toronto lock up the AL East by going 9-1 with a 2.30 ERA in eleven starts. Price netted three pitchers for Detroit: Matt Boyd, Jairo Labourt, and Daniel Norris.

At that time, the Yankees had also considered pursuing relievers Aroldis Chapman and Craig Kimbrel, but ultimately opted to stand pat. Chapman would eventually land in New York, but only after his value was lowered by an October 2015 incident that prompted a thirty-game suspension under MLB's domestic violence policy. Bird remembers being excited because the Yankees seemed to have the fortitude to keep their group of rising prospects intact.

"We dreamed of playing together here and figuring it out along the way," Bird said. "We enjoy each other and enjoy playing with each other, and we always have. You build a good clubhouse with talented guys, you've got something."

Though they declined to make a splashy trade, Cashman found an alternate route to bolster the roster by promoting Bird and Severino from Triple-A Scranton/Wilkes-Barre. Bird made his debut on August 13, 2015 against the Indians in Cleveland, which he called "the best 0-for-5 ever." Six days later, Bird hit his first two big league homers off the Twins' Ervin Santana in a 4–3 victory at Yankee Stadium. Girardi raved that the Yankees seemed to have a "professional hitter" on their hands in Bird.

"He's got a slow heartbeat and you can see it," Girardi said. "He doesn't go out of the zone, he knows what he wants to do and has a plan. I think it's in his DNA, especially at that age."

Yankees radio broadcaster Suzyn Waldman, who has covered the team in some form or fashion since the late 1980s, recalls exchanging pleasantries with Bird's parents during his first few weeks in the majors. During that interaction, she paid the young man a compliment of the highest order.

"These players have all grown up where winning is the only important thing," Waldman said. "You hear it come out of Greg Bird all the time. The things that they say, it's more than they're having fun. They've got an idea of what it takes to be a Yankee and succeed here. I remember meeting Bird's parents and I said, 'Your son is a born Yankee.' He's just like that. He's Mattingly. I don't know how good he's going to be; you don't know. But I said that to his parents."

Proving he had the chops to take over a key position in the midst of a pennant race, Bird came through in the clutch again on September 22, mashing a three-run homer in the 10th inning off the Blue Jays' Mark Lowe that lifted New York to a 6–4 win at Rogers Centre. After watching Bird snare a ball out of the first few rows of the seats in another game at Yankee Stadium, Cashman compared Bird's demeanor to that of John Olerud, who hit .295 over a seventeen-year career in the big leagues, including a cameo with the Yankees in 2004.

"It wasn't an easy play. A lot of people would have come out with the crowd roaring, with the fist or smirk or pride, showing what a great play they'd made," Cashman said. "Bird was the same demeanor, as if he just received the throw from shortstop for the final out of the inning. Just jogged, trotting in to the dugout. He's got a real special way about him that I think will serve him well in his career, especially in a big market. He's not excitable."

Eight days later, at Yankee Stadium, Bird squinted through the first champagne celebration of his life as the Yankees secured the American League Wild Card with a 4–1 victory over the Red Sox that also happened to be the 10,000th win in franchise history. He was four years removed

Greg Bird's 11 homers in 2015 tied the Mets' Mike Jacobs (2005) for the most by any player in his first big league season after debuting in August or later.

from his first professional at-bat, and the journey seemed to have transpired in an instant.

"It's like, all these years you put in and then all of a sudden you're just there," Bird said, snapping his fingers for emphasis. "All of a sudden, you wake up and you're in the playoffs."

The fun was short-lived. Astros left-hander Dallas Keuchel limited the Yankees to three hits in the Wild Card game, one of which was a single by Bird. The Yankees went silently against a trio of relievers before trudging toward the clubhouse with a 3–0 loss, having no interest in watching the Houston players turn the Yankee Stadium diamond into a beer-soaked playground.

Bird could not have imagined it at the time, but that would mark his final time on a big-league diamond until 2017. Bird had missed a month of the 2015 season while with Double-A Trenton, complaining of discomfort in his right shoulder, but a regimen of rest and rehab calmed the issue. After the Wild Card game, Bird's agent Jim Murray informed the Yankees that Bird's shoulder was bothering him again.

"It was not structurally right," Bird said. "Early on in the year, I was getting frustrated with the feeling that I had. Hitting is a big feel for me. I couldn't feel what I normally wanted to feel, so I figured out how to work through that and get by."

Rest and rehab were again recommended, but as Bird began ramping up his workouts for spring training, he continued to experience issues. Evaluated by two doctors, the diagnosis this time was a right labrum tear. Bird had a season-ending procedure, then attended spring training, often sitting forlornly in a corner locker while his teammates hurried to the fields for drills.

There was one positive from that time on the sidelines, as Bird fell in love—with a cat. A family friend from Colorado, Kelly Westover, persuaded Bird to adopt the hairless feline, who is named Mr. Delicious and is a fourth-generation descendant from Mr. Bigglesworth, the wrinkled companion to Mike Myers' Dr. Evil in the 1997 comedy *Austin Powers: International Man of Mystery*.

Bird was skeptical, but he invited Westover to bring the cat to Tampa, where she showed him the paperwork that confirmed his Hollywood lineage. That was a fun talking point, but more importantly to Bird, he discovered that the cat's personality meshed perfectly with his own.

"She had 'Lish' for a long time and always wanted me to take him, and I just never had the time," Bird said. "Couldn't do it. Finally, I took him. I've never been a cat person, but he's great. He's more like a dog. Everyone is a little bit standoffish at first with him, but once they meet him and get around him, he's super social. He's great."

Not all of Bird's friends saw the appeal—at least, not right away. It can take some time to adjust to the idea of petting a living creature that feels like a warm peach. Gausman, the Orioles pitcher, has noticed that Bird has a tendency to talk about Mr. Delicious like a proud parent.

"He's like, 'You've got to meet him. He's got a great personality,'" Gausman said. "It's like, 'Dude, it's a cat.' He told me he had a cat, and I said, 'Cool.' Then he showed me a picture of it and I was like, 'Oh man, what's wrong with your cat? Is your cat dying?'"

When the Yankees packed up their gear to head north and begin the 2017 season, Bird pointed Mr. Delicious toward Colorado, not certain how to balance the demands of playing in the big leagues and caring for a feline during the summer months. They were reunited in the Big Apple that September, in time for Bird to turn another season of pain into a postseason of pleasure.

"I bet on myself," Bird said. "I knew I could come back and be a part of this."

CHAPTER 6

DEADLINE DEALING

From his first days carrying a Yankees credential in the summer of 1986, Brian Cashman had heard the organizational mantra drummed into his head. George M. Steinbrenner once famously said that "winning is second only to breathing," and it was more than a pithy catch-phrase for The Boss. Steinbrenner was clear on this topic: the Yankees were supposed to win the World Series each and every year, and anything short of that was a failure.

General manager of the New York Yankees may be one of the most impressive titles in professional sports, but it had never been Cashman's dream job. After spending his early childhood in Washingtonville, New York, Cashman moved to Lexington, Kentucky, before high school, where his father John—a horse racing enthusiast—managed the Castleton Farm, helping to raise Standardbreds for harness racing.

A scrappy second baseman, leadoff hitter, and history major during his time at Catholic University in Washington, D.C., Cashman had a summer job driving a truck for the United Parcel Service, and briefly entertained thoughts of becoming a full-time employee. He was able to upgrade those plans to an internship with the Yankees; Cashman's father had served a stint at Florida's Pompano Park, a track that Steinbrenner had been known to frequent in the days when the Yankees called Fort Lauderdale their spring home.

Cashman worked in the minor league scouting department during the daytime, then assisted with Yankee Stadium security at night, an assignment that sometimes included breaking up scuffles between rowdy fans.

More than a few times, the five-foot-seven, 160-pound Cashman returned home with fresh scrapes for his efforts.

"I was bigger than I am today," Cashman said. "If you look at my college baseball pictures, people say, 'Wow, you've got a neck!' I'm the same height, but my physical side was a lot different than it is now. It's easy when you have a lot of gigantic security people grabbing one person. Four or five on one, it's pretty easy to deal with. They'd leave me an ankle to grab."

Upon his college graduation, Cashman was offered a full-time position as a baseball operations assistant, when Woody Woodward was the Yankees' GM. During that 1987 season, Cashman roamed the hallways at Yankee Stadium and watched Woodward struggle with his role on a daily basis.

Once a light-hitting infielder with the Braves and Reds, Woodward had played nine seasons in the majors. Now he was being referred to as "The Pharmacist," an in-house reference to the desk drawer stash of aspirin and blood pressure medication that Woodward needed to deal with Steinbrenner's frequent tongue lashings.

In June of that season, Steinbrenner pushed Woodward to deal knuckleballer Joe Niekro to the Twins for backup catcher Mark Salas. When Niekro returned to Yankee Stadium a month later, firing six scoreless innings against his former team, Steinbrenner ordered Woodward to face the media and take full responsibility for the trade. (Woodward was granted a one-night reprieve when the Yankees rallied for twelve runs against Minnesota's bullpen.)

"It was a war zone," Cashman said. "It was a very difficult place to work. Tensions were high. The turnover was extreme and the pressure was off the charts. It's still the same type of pressure, but it's not the same type of atmosphere. It was a pretty intimidating place back then."

Promoted to assistant GM late in 1992, Cashman became the second-youngest general manager in baseball history in February 1998, taking the reins of the Yankees following Bob Watson's resignation. Then thirty years old, Cashman was the sixteenth GM to hold the office under Steinbrenner, and never dreamed he'd be the last. Uncertain if he wanted the position long-term, Cashman told Steinbrenner that he would operate through his first year on a handshake agreement.

"My attitude at the time was, I don't want the Yankees tied into something if they don't know if it is going to work or not," Cashman said. "I was smart enough to realize this is too great of an opportunity to turn down, but I understood this job is so much more important than yourself."

When Joe Torre's team started the season with four losses in its first five games, Steinbrenner panicked and placed a call to Gene Michael, who'd served as the Yankees' GM from 1990–1995 and was settling into a role as the team's director of major league scouting. Steinbrenner told Michael that a mistake had been made and that he should return to his old office, taking over for Cashman.

Michael stalled for time, assuring Steinbrenner that Cashman would be capable of handling the job if given a chance. The 1998 Yankees proved to be a powerhouse team, going on to set an American League record with 114 wins (later surpassed by the 2001 Mariners, who won 116 games) and sweeping the Padres in the World Series. Cashman received a legitimate contract following that season, eventually becoming the longest-serving Yankees GM since Ed Barrow led the team from October 1920 through February 1945.

"This would be nothing I ever would have thought was possible, in any shape or form," Cashman said. "The general manager I happen to be today is radically different than the one that started this job. Experience has served me well, but it doesn't hold me back in recognizing that I don't have all the answers. I don't ever have this job figured out."

Given his damn-the-torpedoes education in the Yankees family, Cashman could have been tempted to overlook the red flags popping up as his team approached the midway point of the 2016 season. Six years after The Boss' passing, "rebuilding" remained a dirty word in the offices, and few would have faulted Cashman if he wanted to pitch the idea that the aging roster could capture some magic and sneak into the playoffs.

It would have been a message that played well upstairs at Yankee Stadium and on the fourth floor of the Tampa facility that now bore Steinbrenner's name, where Hal Steinbrenner—a self-described "finance geek"—spent many of his hours poring over forward-looking spreadsheets. Perhaps they could add to the roster; Cashman had enjoyed a fair amount of success when approaching ownership with requests to add salary, despite his current boss' oft-repeated statement that a chance to win a title should not require more than $200 million.

Yet as Cashman surveyed the roster that bore his fingerprints, he could not convince himself that it was a team capable of great things. For example, their offense had been built around the expectation that Alex Rodriguez and Mark Teixeira would combine for 60 homers and 200 RBIs; the tandem would manage 24 homers and 75 RBIs that season. In what Cashman would later characterize as a series of the most difficult conversations that he had ever presented to ownership, the GM was forced to explain to Steinbrenner why his team wasn't good enough to win the 2016 World Series.

That was the bad news. The good was delivered as Cashman detailed to Steinbrenner how he envisioned re-establishing the Yankees as a "super team," with this seeming to be a prime opportunity to accelerate that process. Cashman's recommendation was to flip some of the Yankees' better-known assets in order to replenish the farm system for 2017 and beyond. If executed properly, that tactic would accentuate the youth movement that had already delivered Luis Severino and Greg Bird (when healthy) to New York. It was the only viable route; Steinbrenner would never authorize an outright rebuild like the Astros and Cubs had recently endured.

"The easy thing is to see that cliff and recommend, 'Let's just drive off the cliff,'" Cashman said. "Then, all of a sudden, you're in that tanking mode and you're not straddling that halfway mark where you're rebuilding and trying to compete at the same time. That could bring you to the middle of the pack."

The Yankees were in Houston when the first domino fell, with Cashman agreeing to ship left-handed closer Aroldis Chapman to the Cubs in exchange for a four player package that included nineteen-year-old Venezuelan infielder Gleyber Torres, who was rated as Chicago's top prospect. Cashman referred to Torres as "the equivalent of a firstborn," and the move would have been recognizable to any Wall Street insider as a classic turnaround flip.

Chapman had been what Cashman called "an asset in distress" when the Yankees acquired him on the cheap from the Reds prior to the season, facing what would be a thirty-game suspension under Major League Baseball's domestic violence policy. A trade that would have sent Chapman to the Dodgers during the 2015 Winter Meetings was called off when reports surfaced that he and his girlfriend had been involved in an October disturbance during which Chapman allegedly fired eight gunshots toward a garage wall.

When the Yankees acquired Gleyber Torres from the Cubs in July 2016, general manager Brian Cashman referred to the standout infielder as "the equivalent of a firstborn."

Police were dispatched to the pitcher's home in Davie, Florida, and though Chapman was not arrested and no criminal charges were filed, the optics of the incident were enough to scare the Dodgers off. Cashman and Steinbrenner spoke at length about the delicate situation. Chapman was the hardest thrower in history, regularly exceeding 100 mph with his fastball, and had been an All-Star during his final season in Cincinnati. The Yankees fully expected that the league would discipline Chapman for his actions, but they also believed it wouldn't be a season-long suspension and that he would pitch *somewhere* in 2016. It might as well be for them.

The Reds told Cashman that they were now willing to make a deal without obtaining any of the Yanks' untouchables, and so three days after Christmas, a trade was consummated in which Chapman went to New York for four mid-level prospects: right-hander Caleb Cotham, right-hander Rookie Davis, third baseman Eric Jagielo (who'd been selected twenty-sixth overall in 2013, ahead of Aaron Judge at thirty-two), and second baseman Tony Renda. In his remarks following the trade, Cashman said he recognized that because of the ongoing circumstances, "The price point on acquisition has been modified."

That deal had created a three-headed bullpen monster of Dellin Betances, Andrew Miller, and Chapman, and now Cashman saw a chance to cash in on Chapman's restored value, two months before Chapman would be eligible for free agency. Smartly tagged "No Runs DMC," the trio had been as good as advertised: the Yanks were 19-2 when Betances, Chapman, and Miller all pitched, combining for a 1.36 ERA and 13.70 strikeouts per nine innings in those games.

Cashman said that the thought of flipping Chapman for prospects had been part of those initial conversations with Steinbrenner prior to the trade with the Reds.

"If it played out well enough with all aspects of the club, then we'd see where it would take us," Cashman said. "If it did not, we knew we would be in a situation where, as long as he stayed healthy and performed to his norms, there would be potential upside on someone that was going to be a free agent in almost two months. We decided to maximize that value."

In addition to Torres, the Yankees re-acquired right-hander Adam Warren, who had been traded to the Cubs in the Starlin Castro deal, plus minor league outfielders Billy McKinney and Rashad Crawford. Cashman said that it had been "an easy call, and the right call" to move Chapman because the Yankees were able to trade from an area of strength to complete the transaction.

Theo Epstein, the Cubs' president of baseball operations, said that the Yankees' insistence on receiving big league-ready starting pitching forced the teams to work on a more creative package. Warren's inclusion helped to convince Steinbrenner to offer his stamp of approval, as his impact on the big-league roster would be immediate, not years down the line.

"This isn't a white flag," Cashman said. "This is a rearrangement."

Cashman said that the Yankees had maintained strong interest in Torres since 2013, when they viewed the Caracas, Venezuela, native as the top international free agent available. Born less than two months after third baseman Charlie Hayes squeezed the final out of the 1996 World Series, Torres instead signed with the Cubs, from whom he scored a $1.7 million signing bonus and quickly established himself as one of the brightest prospects in the sport.

McKinney was a toolsy left-handed hitter from Plano, Texas, who had emerged from high school to become the twenty-fourth overall pick in the 2013 draft, hearing his name called by the Athletics. Cashman said that the Yankees had intended to select McKinney if he fell to them at twenty-six, and they watched closely when McKinney landed with the Cubs a year later as part of Chicago's return for a trade involving pitchers Jeff Samardzija and Jason Hammel. Cashman referred to Crawford, a raw lefty-swinging outfielder from Atlanta, as "a lottery ticket."

"The total package was something that we targeted and strived to get, and if we got it, we would move toward a recommendation," Cashman said. "I made the recommendation to ownership that they thought on, and they gave the sign of the cross to it."

Steinbrenner instructed Cashman to continue assessing market values, both coming and going. Cashman reported to Steinbrenner, team president Randy Levine, and chief operating officer Lonn Trost that it seemed to be a "very volatile time" throughout the baseball landscape. The addition of a second Wild Card was partially responsible for that, making it more difficult for teams to honestly assess if they should consider themselves contenders or pretenders.

• • •

The clock at Tropicana Field read 8:57 p.m. ET on the evening of July 30, when Rays closer Alex Colome zipped a 94.8-mph fastball past Starlin Castro for the final out of a 6–3 Yankees loss, their third straight. The Yankees were now a game over .500 at 52-51, in fourth place, and 6½ games behind the division-leading Blue Jays. Having been among the 25,883 in attendance at the dimly-lit Trop, Steinbrenner crossed the Howard Frankland Bridge toward Tampa and decided that he had seen enough.

Shortly before midnight, Steinbrenner told Cashman that he was free to trigger more trades. Cashman was reminded that it was not in ownership's DNA to permit a strategic tank job, recalling his marching orders to walk the fine line between rebuilding and contending, "but not to fall off." Cashman and his lieutenants worked their sources in the overnight hours, eschewing sleep in favor of encouraging opposing clubs to ask about everyone and anyone on the roster.

"Any business entity or corporation needs to be honest with itself," Cashman said. "If you're going to change course, you can double down or triple down like a guy who's losing his shirt at the poker table and try to win it all back, or you have an honest assessment and say it's time to change course. If it's a poker player, it means folding up your tent and walking away because I don't want to lose anymore, or it's we need to plot a new course and do it fast because things can get much worse if you don't."

The Yankees had not acted as midseason sellers since their dismal 1989 season, when they traded future Hall of Famer Rickey Henderson to the Athletics for pitchers Greg Cadaret and Eric Plunk, plus outfielder Luis Polonia. Suffice it to say that these opportunities did not come around very often in the Bronx, and so Cashman was intent upon securing both quality and quantity.

"The Yankees have acted a certain way for a long time, and trying to change course from that was difficult," Cashman said. "But at the same time, it's continuing to remind everybody that the chess board that we're playing is way different than the one their dad was playing. They have limitations on the international amateur space, they have limitations in the domestic amateur space, they have penalties on winning, and a significant portion now is the luxury tax and revenue sharing. There are a lot of different things dragging you under that are preventing us from being all we can possibly be."

On the morning of July 31, Andrew Miller reached for his buzzing cell phone, expecting to see an alarm going off. Instead, Cashman's name popped up on the caller ID, and Miller realized that his final pitch as a Yankee had been thrown. Miller was informed that he had been traded to Cleveland for a four player haul of outfielder Clint Frazier, left-handed starter Justus Sheffield, and right-handed relievers J.P. Feyereisen and Ben Heller.

Indians president Chris Antonetti described the talks for Miller as having been "excruciating," but the Yankees knew there was great value baked into the player, given that his team-friendly contract offered Cleveland control for two more seasons after 2016.

"I think most trade talks are excruciating. Most don't go anywhere," Cashman said. "The more interesting dynamic in the Miller discussions were negotiations with ownership, simultaneously with opposing clubs. Even if I got satisfied from an opposing team standpoint like we did with Cleveland, there was no guarantee that ownership would relinquish the short-term for a longer view. It was a lot of heavy lifting I was going through, from all ends."

A tall, personable southpaw with one of the game's most lethal sliders, Miller had bypassed asking for a no-trade clause in his four-year, $36 million Yankees contract. That occurred in part because the Tampa resident loved having spring training near his home, which allowed him an extra two months of the year in his own bed. Unfortunately for Miller, the Indians hold their spring camp in Goodyear, Arizona.

"I was focused on being a Yankee," Miller said. "The important thing was being part of a winning team. I made a lot of good friends; I miss those guys in New York. They were great teammates, it was a great team to play for, it was a great city to live in. But I've got a chance to be a part of a team that's going to the World Series, and you couldn't ask for anything better."

In surveying the Indians' assets, the Yankees had refused to be moved off of Frazier, an energetic twenty-two-year-old outfielder nicknamed "Red Thunder" whom Cashman said "shows up for the National Anthem in a dirty uniform." During that same conversation, Cashman lauded Frazier's bat speed as being "already legendary," and that skill promised to carry the right-handed swinger all the way to the majors from his modest upbringing in Loganville, Georgia.

Having moved from third base to the outfield prior to his junior year, Frazier was the first high school position player taken in the 2013 draft, going fifth overall to Cleveland. Frazier received a $3.5 million signing bonus to bypass his commitment to the University of Georgia, which was the largest bonus that the Indians had doled out at the time.

The cash influx was desperately needed. Frazier's father, Mark, was a building supplies salesman who had been laid off twice and was struggling to keep up with the mortgage of their home. With a few dashes of a pen, those problems were erased; Frazier insisted upon using his bonus for that purpose, a gesture that prompted tears of joy from his mother, Kim. For good measure, Frazier gifted his father a new Dodge pickup the next Christmas.

Ten days after the draft, the reigning Gatorade National Baseball Player of the Year was invited to take batting practice at Progressive Field. The Indians' big-league roster celebrated the occasion by wearing bright red wigs, a nod to the distinctive red curls that flowed out of the back of Frazier's batting helmet as he slugged a school record of 63 homers at Loganville High.

Frazier thought the goof had been "awesome," as were the long conversations he enjoyed that day with Indians manager Terry Francona and veteran Jason Giambi, with whom he played video games before exchanging cell phone numbers. Soon, Frazier was boarding a jet to take his first professional at-bats with the Indians' rookie-level club in Arizona, fulfilling a dream that he had identified while most of his classmates were busy finger painting and learning the alphabet.

"It's what I always wanted to do," Frazier said. "My mom still has a picture that I drew in kindergarten that she saved and put away in a scrapbook. We had to draw what we wanted to be when we grew up, and I drew a baseball player."

Cashman personally reached Frazier on the day of his trade, welcoming him to the organization and informing Frazier that he should report to the Yankees' Triple-A affiliate.

"I remember having the conversation with Brian Cashman," Frazier said. "One of the first questions I asked him was, 'Do I have to cut my hair?' And I did."

Left unsaid during that call was that the Yankees believed Frazier had been aggressively promoted to Triple-A by the Indians; at twenty-one, he was more than five years younger than the average player at that level. Cashman thought that Frazier probably should have spent the entire 2016 season in Double-A, but ultimately the GM decided that adding a demotion to the trade would over-complicate the situation.

Cashman had more work to do as the minutes ticked off to 4:00 p.m. ET on August 1, with the trade deadline pushed a day from its usual July 31 place on the calendar. Though trades could still be completed after that date, all involved players must pass through waivers, providing opponents with an opportunity to block the moves.

It was a risky game within the game. In August 2000, the Yankees placed a claim on the Devil Rays' Jose Canseco, intending to keep the aging slugger from impacting the division race. To Cashman's surprise, Tampa Bay gave Canseco's contract to the Yankees, gratis. A spare part that Joe Torre never seemed sure how to use, Canseco appeared in thirty-eight games for Yankees, including a pinch-hit appearance in Game 4 of the World Series. He struck out looking.

Chapman and Miller were now gone, and as the Yankees shopped the rest of their wares, Cashman bluntly labeled his team as a "playoff pretender." Carlos Beltran and Ivan Nova soon became former Yankees, on their way to join the Rangers and Pirates, respectively. A well-respected switch-hitter from Puerto Rico with a promising Cooperstown case, Beltran netted a three player package of pitchers Nick Green, Dillon Tate, and Erik Swanson, with the Yankees kicking in approximately $3.7 million to offset the thirty-nine-year-old's remaining salary.

"This organization has never been [like] this," Beltran said. "But it's the new baseball, man. It's the new generation. Organizations no longer are making dumb decisions."

The only member of the Yankees' starting rotation at that time who had been developed through the team's farm system, Nova said that he was running on a treadmill at 3:55 p.m. that afternoon at Yankee Stadium when he looked at the clock, thinking to himself, "OK, I'm not going to get traded. I'm going to stay here." A minute or two later, the sweat session was interrupted by bullpen catcher Roman Rodriguez, who relayed the news that Nova been dealt to Pittsburgh in exchange for outfielder Tito Polo and left-handed pitcher Stephen Tarpley.

The moves were met with sour reactions in the clubhouse; third baseman Chase Headley had observed after the Miller trade that "we're probably not as good a team as we were ten days ago, seven days ago." No matter. Cashman had a bigger picture in mind. In exchange for four veterans, the Yankees had acquired ten prospects, three of them highly rated. Frazier and Torres merited the largest headlines, but Tate had also received a $4.2 million signing bonus when the Rangers made him the top pitcher selected in the 2015 draft.

"I was like, 'It's time,'" Cashman said. "We need to do certain things that we've never really done. I'm glad ownership signed off on it, and I think that the future is brighter because of it."

As they had done by adding Adam Warren in the Cubs trade, the Yankees attempted to cushion the blow to their big-league squad, adding right-hander Tyler Clippard in a trade with Arizona. Cashman said that the Yankees could have decided to "take a nose dive," but tanking would not have served the team's fan base—particularly their loyal season-ticket holders, most of whom seemed to understand and embrace the shift to a new generation of players. Patching the ship with free agents in the post-Derek

Jeter and Mariano Rivera era had not yielded the desired results; they had played nine postseason innings since 2012.

"Brian and his staff and the organization are trying to put this team in a good position to have a long run of not just playing well, but winning championships," Joe Girardi said. "It's not about being a second Wild Card team and winning one game, or losing one game. We want to win championships. That's what we've always been about. And I think what we're trying to do is position ourselves to do that."

Now without two of his big three bullpen arms, Girardi installed Dellin Betances as the closer for the rest of the 2016 season. The six-foot-eight Betances, a proud Dominican whose 265-pound build and high 90s fastball juxtapose against his gentle bilingual monotone, seemed to be stunned by the Miller trade. Though Betances said that he was "trying to get over the fact that we traded the best of the best," the Yankees believed that Betances was capable of handling the ninth inning.

Betances was excellent in twelve August appearances, pitching to a 0.68 ERA, but his statistics took a hit as September dawned. In eleven outings after August 31, Betances allowed 13 runs (10 earned) in 9⅓ innings for an obscene 9.64 ERA, tagged with two losses and a blown save. Those numbers resurfaced the next spring in a conference room of the Vinoy Renaissance hotel in St. Petersburg, Florida, where Betances and the Yankees clashed in a four-hour salary arbitration debate over $2 million.

Shortly after a three person panel of arbitrators determined that Betances's 2017 salary would be $3 million and not the $5 million sought by the player, the team's beat reporters were ushered into a tiny office at the rear of the George M. Steinbrenner Field press box. They exchanged quizzical glances while Yankees president Randy Levine took the verbal equivalent of a victory lap over a speakerphone, stating that Betances had been "a victim" of agent Jim Murray's "attempt to change the marketplace in baseball" by requesting closer money for a setup man.

"It's like me saying, 'I'm not the president of the Yankees, I'm an astronaut,'" Levine said. "Well, I'm not an astronaut, and Dellin Betances is not a closer, at least based on statistics."

Betances had the deepest connection to New York of any current Yankee, having been born in Manhattan's Washington Heights neighborhood and raised in the Lillian Wald Houses on the Lower East Side. His father, Jaime, has navigated the city streets for more than two decades as a livery taxi driver, and a ten-year-old Betances was in the Yankee Stadium bleachers for David Wells' 1998 perfect game against the Twins—he still has the $7.00 general admission ticket stub. Betances played high school ball at Brooklyn's Grand Street Campus before the Yankees called his name in the eighth round of the 2006 draft.

It had been a dream story, but this arbitration process served as an official introduction to the business side of the sport. Incensed by Levine's comments, Betances held a media gathering of his own as soon as the Yankees were off the field, saying that the team seemed to value him only as a setup man. Betances suggested that he might become more "selfish" as a result. Though Betances remained under team control until 2020, he acknowledged that the experience made the idea of free agency somewhat more palatable.

"They take me in a room and they trash me for about an hour and a half," Betances said. "I thought that wasn't fair. I felt like I've done a lot for this organization, especially over the last three years. I've taken the ball, time after time. Whenever they needed me, I was there for them. I never said no."

While Betances' feelings clearly needed to be massaged, the moves worked out exceptionally for both the Cubs and Indians, who rode Chapman and Miller to a historic World Series showdown between the two clubs with the longest championship droughts in the sport.

It seemed fair to wonder how the eliminated playoff clubs might have fared had they pursued either reliever more aggressively; the Dodgers, for one, balked at the Yankees' asking prices for both Chapman and Miller before being bounced by the Cubs in a six-game National League Championship Series.

"I'm happy for both of those players and I'm happy for both of those teams, because they paid a steep price for instant impact," Cashman said. "We drove the hard bargain for impact down the line. Hopefully everybody gets what they wanted out of this thing."

When the Indians celebrated their American League Championship Series victory over the Blue Jays, owner Paul Dolan acknowledged that there had been a high price paid, but they had viewed Miller as the reason that they were celebrating their first pennant since 1997.

"Yeah, years from now I suspect we'll look at some of these guys that we traded and say, 'Why did we trade them?'" Dolan said, expressing hope that Cleveland would be able to point to a few championship trophies as the payoff.

The ripple effect of those 2016 moves were evident. Frazier and Torres were widely regarded as the Yankees' top prospects, and neither had been in the organization before July. In Game 7 of the Fall Classic, Chapman served up a game-tying homer to Rajai Davis, then was credited with the win as the Cubs celebrated their first title since Theodore Roosevelt was in office.

A 108-year drought was unfathomable, but Cashman believed that his actions had moved the Yankees closer to their next celebration. His own pinstriped championship dry spell had now reached the age of a first grader, all of seven years old.

"Clearly Cleveland and Chicago are getting what they bargained for," Cashman said, "and we expect over time with all the cast of characters— not just the ones we got in these deals—that we'll be having a much better, [more] impactful future than we would have had."

Cashman viewed the team's outlook as being brighter than at any time since his days serving as the farm director underneath Gene Michael, who was widely credited as the architect of the 1996–2000 dynasty. That occurred in large part because Michael was able to fortify the farm system over the two plus years while George Steinbrenner had been banned from day-to-day management of the club for consorting with a known gambler.

"When I started with the Yankees back in the day, that was some of the best young talent we had," Cashman said. "And I think our system now that is currently in play is starting to hopefully mirror what that system started to produce, which propelled us into the '90s. We're trying to get back to a situation where we can build an uber team, a sustainable one. I think the fans should be excited by that."

Tim Naehring was. Having been recently promoted from a professional scout to the Yankees' vice president of baseball operations, Naehring now enjoyed access to the team's secure database of player evaluations, both inside the farm system and across the industry. Previously, he'd only been able to peruse his own reports, but now Naehring was free to dig into what everyone in player development and scouting was feeding to the mother ship.

"As I started to read what we had, I was very excited," Naehring said. "It was the first year in a number of years that I actually went out and scouted all these guys with my own eyes. I told Brian Cashman, probably a month into the season, I was very impressed with the level of talent that we had throughout the system—Triple-A all the way down.

"The culture in our minor leagues, as far as how they went about their business, day-to-day individual work and how these guys were developed as individuals; it was very refreshing to see how well-oiled a machine it was. The environment that Gary Denbo and his staff had put in place and continues today, it's a good working atmosphere for these guys to develop as young men and start their baseball careers."

• • •

The Yankees had swallowed hard to make the pivot from a veteran-laden roster, creating a collection of young talent that promised more tomorrows than yesterdays, but there was still one expensive loose end to tie up. Alex Rodriguez had more than a year remaining on the ten-year, $275 million contract that he had signed following his 2007 American League Most Valuable Player campaign, a deal negotiated after news of his opt-out from his original Yankees contract leaked during Game 4 of that year's World Series between the Red Sox and the Rockies.

At the time, even with some viewing Rodriguez as a "clean" successor to Barry Bonds' career record of 762 home runs, there were those within the Yankees brain-trust who believed the organization would be ill-advised to continue the relationship. Cashman was one of those voices, but he had ultimately been overruled by ownership. Less than two years later, on a February morning in Tampa, Cashman listened as Rodriguez held a press conference in which he admitted to having used performance-enhancing drugs during his three seasons in Texas. Cashman reacted as though someone had spiked his coffee with lemon juice.

"This is Humpty Dumpty," Cashman said then. "We've got to put him back together again and get him back up on the wall."

They had, to some extent. On one occasion, Cashman acknowledged that the Yankees would not have won the 2009 World Series were it not for Rodriguez, removing his glittering championship ring and resting it on a table in front of him for emphasis. But the Yankees were now carrying a diminished version of that player on their 2016 roster.

Despite having improbably repaired a litigious relationship with Major

League Baseball and the Yankees to enjoy a resurgent 33-homer campaign in 2015, the forty-one-year-old's playing time had dwindled. He'd once seemed to be a lock as the fourth player to hit 700 homers, joining Bonds (762), Henry Aaron (755), and Babe Ruth (714), but A-Rod's chase stalled at 696.

On the evening of August 12, a crowd of 46,459 witnessed the end of Rodriguez's eventful career, concluding a bizarre week in which he and the organization had jointly announced that the fourteen-time All-Star would be released from his contract following that game. As part of the agreement, Rodriguez would stay on to serve as a special advisor and instructor for the Yankees through the final day of 2017.

Threatening skies had cleared for Jeter's farewell on the captain's final day at the Stadium in 2014, but they did the opposite for Rodriguez. Loud thunder-cracks and a torrential downpour seemingly appeared out of nowhere to interrupt an on-field ceremony, forcing all involved to scurry into the dugout for cover. Rodriguez quipped that it had been a "biblical" storm, but it passed quickly. In what was the 2,784th game of Rodriguez's

Alex Rodriguez hit 351 of his 696 regular season home runs in a Yankees uniform, playing 12 seasons in New York after being acquired from the Rangers in February 2004.

career and his 1,509th as a Yankee, he laced a run-scoring double off Chris Archer in the first of four at-bats before giddily returning to his locker, retrieving a glove to play third base for one batter in the ninth inning.

As the right-handed hitting Mikie Mahtook stepped in, Rodriguez not-so-quietly rooted for Betances to record a strikeout. Why? Rodriguez later revealed that his last time in the field—May 19, 2015—had also been his last time strapping on a protective cup. Betances took care of his concerned teammate, freezing Mahtook looking at a curveball.

"I was very stressed and I got really low," Rodriguez said. "I screamed to Betances the same thing that, ironically, Cal Ripken screamed to Roger Clemens in the All-Star Game in 2000 when we switched [positions]. He said, 'Strike him out, Roger.' I said exactly the same thing."

Rodriguez's departure, followed by Teixeira's upcoming retirement, would leave two players in uniform from the last group of Yankees to claim so much as a single postseason victory. Though Brett Gardner and CC Sabathia were the only men remaining from that 2012 roster, the next generation of winners was about to enter the building.

CHAPTER 7

PASSING THE TORCH

The championship rings grew more ornate as the Yankees morphed into what would be referred to as "the team of the decade," but for those lucky enough to score more than one of those treasures, the 1996 version with a half-carat diamond at its center and twenty-three diamonds ringing the outside stands apart as one of the most special in franchise history.

"It was the first. You never forget your first," Derek Jeter said. "Everything was new: going to cities on the road for the first time, playing in different stadiums, playing against guys you watched on television at a young age. That was the beginning. The Yankees hadn't won in a long time.

"You remember the excitement in the stadium, you remember the excitement in the city. You're walking the streets and people are recognizing us for the first time; it's kind of awkward. This was a special group because The Boss said if he won, he'd keep us together, and we continued to win. You never forget that first time."

Jeter was on the left side of the Yankee Stadium infield during the afternoon of August 13, 2016, mere hours after his longtime frenemy Alex Rodriguez had hunched over near that very spot, filling the back pockets of his uniform pants with souvenir dirt. No matter what transpired in the game against the Rays, it had already promised to be a memorable day. With temperatures inching into the mid-nineties and some puffy cumulus clouds looking on, preparations were underway for the Yankees to celebrate their history as few organizations can.

Twenty years prior, the roots of a dynasty had taken hold when the

Yankees defeated the Atlanta Braves in a six-game Fall Classic, memorably ending when third baseman Charlie Hayes settled underneath a Mark Lemke pop-up in foul territory at the original Yankee Stadium. The title was the Yankees' first since 1978, and elation was in the crisp October air. Wade Boggs made an impromptu decision to join a mounted NYPD officer for a victory gallop around the stadium's warning track, the future Hall of Famer momentarily forgetting that he happened to be deathly afraid of horses.

There was no cavalry protecting the outfield on this day, only thirty-two members of the team that enjoyed a ticker-tape parade through Manhattan's Canyon of Heroes, donning untucked pinstriped jerseys emblazoned with their old uniform numbers and a commemorative "96" patch on the left sleeve. Assembled behind the loading dock gate in left-center field before being called one by one across the grass, they smiled and laughed, dusting off their inside jokes as though they'd wandered into a time warp.

If the players had glanced up to read the current Yankees' starting lineup, they would have seen that their old teammate Joe Girardi was sending out a batting order that slotted first baseman Tyler Austin seventh and right fielder Aaron Judge eighth. Both were about to make their major league debuts, and that realization inspired something approaching the intersection of awe and jealousy in some of the old-timers.

"I definitely believe these youngsters have a great opportunity to shine," Jorge Posada said. "The moves that the Yankees have made, it will create a lot of opportunity for the youngsters to play the game and show that they are capable to play in the big leagues. They will definitely need some older players that can lead them, but at the same time, they're rebuilding and doing what is right for the team."

The "Core Four" of Jeter, Posada, Andy Pettitte, and Mariano Rivera drew some of the loudest ovations that afternoon, as did Boggs, David Cone, Dwight Gooden, Paul O'Neill, Darryl Strawberry, Bernie Williams, and manager Joe Torre. Coming off a heartbreaking loss to the Mariners in the 1995 American League Division Series, those '96 Yanks had found their identity in a blend of proven veterans and promising rookies. They adopted a rallying cry from infielder Mariano Duncan, whose enthusiastic nature and heavy Dominican accent helped modify a phrase that would appear on T-shirts that season: "We play today, we win today, das it!"

And they did plenty of that, posting ninety-two victories before powering past the Orioles and Rangers in a pair of memorable playoff series. Aiming to end an eighteen-year title drought, George Steinbrenner had entrusted the lineup card to Torre, who hadn't yet compiled anything resembling what would be a Hall of Fame managerial resume. Torre inherited a club that went against the grain of the game's mid-1990s power surge; these Yankees would get the job done with pitching, clutch hitting, and intangibles.

As that 1996 team broke the seal on the newly-constructed Legends Field facility in Tampa, Florida, Williams recalled that Torre told his players, "'You've got two rules with me. You play hard, and you be on time. If you do that, I'll go through a wall for you.' He did, and he gave us that confidence to know that if we did those things, we were going to be fine."

There were in-season maneuvers that bolstered the squad, adding Strawberry, Graeme Lloyd, Luis Sojo, and Hayes, but perhaps the most crucial moves were the ones not made. Panicked by Jeter's inconsistent fielding in the spring, Steinbrenner suggested trading Rivera for light-hitting infielder Felix Fermin. The dynasty could have ended before it began—Rivera would have been in Seattle and Jeter banished to Triple-A. Instead, Rivera was setting up for World Series Most Valuable Player John Wetteland while Jeter earned honors as the AL's Rookie of the Year.

"That was a gutsy call from The Boss," Rivera said. "To have four youngsters on the team, that was a gutsy call. We were anxious and we wanted to do something, because we knew that we belonged in the big leagues."

It was the first title for many, including Cashman, who was then the Yankees' assistant general manager under Bob Watson. Cashman recalls cheering from Watson's private box on the suite level of the old Stadium when Lemke fouled out to Hayes, then tagging along with many other staffers to continue the celebration at a watering hole on the Upper East Side. On their way, they discovered that the championship had turned the city upside down in euphoria.

"People were on top of cars," Cashman said. "It was just a complete block party of entire Manhattan. It was just truly amazing."

Yet if the Yankees thought a title gave them license to rest, Steinbrenner quickly corrected that. Cashman was among the groggy group nursing coffee a few mornings later while they boarded buses from Yankee Stadium, preparing for a celebratory ride along Broadway. It was the city's first baseball title since the Mets defeated the Red Sox in 1986, and Cashman smiled when he saw that Mets owner Fred Wilpon took out a full-page advertisement in the *New York Daily News*, congratulating Steinbrenner on bringing a title back to the city.

"I said to myself, 'Oh, George must be in all his glory, the Wilpons are taking a knee and we're king of New York again,'" Cashman said. "Then I got off the bus when we arrived down the Canyon of Heroes and literally first step off the bus, there was The Boss. This was our first rodeo, but not his. He had choreographed out exactly how the parade would be and where people would be. I remember him screaming at our players, Boggs, Leyritz, and Wetteland: 'Get your wives off the float!'"

Steinbrenner's plan, as he loudly informed Yankees vice president of marketing Debbie Tymon, had been to have the players riding atop floats while their wives were assigned to the lower level of the double-decker buses that were also rolling along the parade route.

"He was ballistic," Cashman said. "I said to myself, 'He's a world champion, but he's a perfectionist. If he can't be happy now, I don't know if we'll ever make him happy.' It was 8:00 a.m. and he was just crushing our guys. Guys were looking at The Boss yelling at them, and then they were looking at their 'boss,' and they had to pick between which boss, the wives or the Boss. The wives stayed, but he was not happy."

Fortunately, there would be more parades to orchestrate.

Flash forward twenty years to the nostalgic atmosphere that awaited to celebrate that special club, the air thick with tales of "remember when," and you have a sense of the atmosphere that enveloped Aaron Judge as he walked into the Yankees' clubhouse for the first time as a big-league player. His day would be fueled by adrenaline; Judge had been dining with his parents at a Dinosaur Bar-B-Que restaurant in Rochester, New York, prior to midnight, ready to dig into a postgame bite when RailRiders manager Al Pedrique wandered over to their table.

"He came up to me and said, 'Hey, you'd better hurry up with this meal. You've got to be up in New York tomorrow,'" Judge said. "So, pretty special. At first, it was kind of a shock, but he meant it and it was pretty cool."

Judge's parents, Patty and Wayne, had been looking for an opportunity to meet up with the RailRiders for weeks, seeing a few games at PNC Field in Moosic, Pennsylvania, before accompanying the team on a road trip. They had perfect timing. The Judges paid their bill, piled into a rental car, and drove through the night to cover the 336 miles between the barbecue joint and Yankee Stadium, arriving in New York after 6:00 a.m.

Now-retired teachers from California's San Joaquin County, where they instructed students in physical education and leadership, Patty and Wayne Judge adopted Aaron the day after he was born in April 1992. Judge's older brother, John, was also adopted and is currently an English teacher in Korea. Wayne Judge once told the *New York Post* that during pediatric check-ups, Aaron was always at the top of his age group, and that doctors had taken note of his large hands and feet.

"We kind of joked that he looked like the Michelin Tire baby," he said. "It wasn't long before the four ounces of formula was just the appetizer and it had to be the formula with the oatmeal to pacify him."

The major summer event in Judge's bucolic hometown of Linden, California is the annual cherry festival, and Judge recalls the 7½ square mile area of shady walnut groves, peach orchards, and vineyards as being "a perfect environment to grow up in." He quickly earned a reputation as a special athlete; Judge's tee-ball opponents scattered when he came to the plate, unwilling to risk bodily harm by fielding his hard grounders and line drives.

"It was just a small community," Judge said. "I had a mom in every single house down the street. I had people always looking out for me and people in the community looking out for me. Growing up in something like that was something special. I always had a place to go and there was a friend on every corner you looked."

Judge said he has never had any contact with his biological parents and has not spoken publicly about his ethnicity. He said that he was about ten or eleven years old when he came home with a question that Patty and Wayne—both of whom are Caucasian—had anticipated would one day be asked.

"I think it was like, 'I don't look like you, Mom. I don't look like you, Dad. Like, what's going on here?'" Judge said. "They just kind of told me I was adopted. I was like, 'OK, that's fine with me.' You're still my mom, the only mom I know. You're still my dad, the only dad I know. Nothing really changed. I never really asked any questions after that. There's no need to."

Judge said he hardly remembers the conversation because it was not that important to him. When his parents asked if he had any questions, his response had been, "OK, can I go outside and play?"

Already standing six-foot-three as a sophomore, he'd shot up another four inches prior to that senior season, and opponents often simply refused to pitch to him. More than a few times, scouts asked coach Joe Pimbio Sr. to set up the batting cage following one of Linden's games because Judge hadn't been given anything to hit that afternoon.

Judge would then good-naturedly hit for another hour, with a dozen or so scouts roaming the outfield to shag fly balls. Though Judge loved watching Giants slugger Barry Bonds, he'd also been a hurler, showcasing a low 90s fastball and a sharp curveball to go 9-3 with a 0.88 ERA in his senior year. With 65 strikeouts and 25 walks, there was a legitimate debate over whether Judge's future path should be at the plate or on the mound.

When Oakland area scout Jermaine Clark filed a breathless report on the Linden High first baseman and pitcher, calling him an "untapped monster," the A's invited Judge to work out at the Coliseum. As Oakland called Judge's name in the thirty-first round of the 2010 draft, Judge's parents told him that the decision was his to make, but that he should consider the value of continuing his studies.

"They wanted me to always make sure I put education first and make sure I prioritized everything," Judge said. "If I was going to make plans, stick to them. Make sure I'm on a tight schedule and make sure I don't miss anything. I think having that background in education really helped them give me some of the qualities as a teacher.

"It was tough at times growing up. I wanted to go outside and play with my friends or play some video games, but they were tough on me. They'd say, 'Hey, you've got homework to do. You've got to finish your math homework and science homework, then if you have time left over before dinner you can go play,' something like that. I didn't like it as a kid, but looking back on it, I really appreciate what they did for me."

Judge's performance in other sports forced him to make difficult choices. During the 2009–2010 school year, Judge averaged 18.2 points and 12.8 rebounds per game as Linden's center. He would later say that his favorite memory of high school basketball was the bonding experience Judge and his teammates had on the streets of Linden, picking up garbage as part of a community service program. On the football field, Judge reeled in 54 catches, setting single-season school records in receiving yards (969) and touchdowns (17).

One of Linden's most effective plays, as coach Mike Huber remembers it, was to send Judge down the field with what they called the "Jump Pass."

If Linden was within the red zone, Huber would signal for the play by raising both hands in the air, as though he were signaling a touchdown. The quarterback would lob the ball above the defense, and it usually didn't matter if the opponents knew it was coming; they couldn't defend it.

Judge's high school senior yearbook took note of his athletic endeavors, including an action shot of him dunking a basketball, while his classmates tagged him with the superlative of "Most Flirty." Seemingly every day, the Judges received another invitation on collegiate letterhead. Stanford, Michigan State, Notre Dame, and UCLA were among the programs expressing interest in the wide receiver/defensive end; a coach at UCLA told Judge that they would probably ask him to put thirty to forty pounds on and convert him into a tight end.

Many believed that Judge could have had an NFL career, had he wanted one. Late in 2017, when an autumnal crisp began to fill the Bronx air, he'd occasionally run pass routes across the Yankee Stadium outfield with Matt Holliday, who took the opportunity to revisit his own days of high school quarterback stardom. But baseball had been Judge's strongest passion since those early days terrorizing T-ball opponents, and so he was off to Fresno State, where he declared kinesiology as his major.

Aaron Judge was selected by the Athletics in the 30th round of the 2010 draft but opted to attend Fresno State, where he was named the Western Athletic Conference's Freshman of the Year after hitting .358.

"It was the first time being away," Judge said. "You're kind of on your own, learning the things that your parents did for you. Now you're on your own and nobody is there for you. You've got to grow up and adapt and learn, otherwise you're going to sink and have a miserable time in college."

Though he had been drafted by the Yanks in June 2013, a quadriceps injury sustained during a base running drill kept Judge from beginning his climb to the majors until 2014, when he made his professional debut with Class-A Charleston. Infielder Tyler Wade, then entering his first full pro season, recalls meeting Judge on their first day together as members of the RiverDogs.

"He was a gentle giant," Wade said. "I was eighteen years old and didn't really know what to expect. He came through the clubhouse and he was like the first guy to introduce himself to me. I was like, 'This is a really nice guy.' I think we went out to lunch and ever since, we've been friends."

Judge hit .333 with nine homers and 45 RBIs in 65 games to earn selection as a South Atlantic League Midseason All-Star. Wade said that Judge quickly established himself as "a man amongst boys," remarking that he had never seen anyone hit the ball farther or harder.

"It was like the first month. We were in Charleston and I was at second base, and he hit a ball probably ankle-high at me," Wade recalled. "I was at second base, getting my secondary [lead]. I didn't know what to do, so I laid down and the ball skipped right over me. He hit it so hard, I didn't know what to do."

Judge was promoted to Class-A Tampa in June of that season, where he batted .283 with eight homers and 33 RBIs in 66 games while getting a taste of the pitcher-friendly Florida State League. Judge made a positive impression quickly on Tampa manager Al Pedrique, who recalled Judge as being humble, respectful, and easy to coach.

"I was very impressed with his makeup," Pedrique said. "The one thing I realized on a daily basis was his work ethic was great. I had to really help him a little bit in having a routine in all the areas, but for the most part when I had him the second half of that year, you could tell the kid knew what he wanted to do to get better."

James Rowson, then the Yankees' minor league hitting coordinator, also said that Judge's determination stood out at that early stage. Rowson observed that once Judge figured something out, he had the ability to maintain and hold on to it.

"He always wanted to know 'Why?', which I think is the most important question that a young hitter can ask," Rowson said. "Any time you're making adjustments or you're talking about the game, it was like, 'Hey, tell me why you want me to do that?' When guys ask that question, you really know that they're going to make it their own. If they understand it, they're going to make it their own and they're going to repeat it and do it more consistently. His ability to not just do things, but to understand why he was doing things, was pretty special."

With Judge's 78 RBIs leading all Yankees minor leaguers, he was selected to participate in the Arizona Fall League, where he hit .278 with four homers and 14 RBIs in 24 games for the Scottsdale Scorpions. The Scottsdale roster was comprised of some of the top talent in the Yankees, Mets, Phillies, Pirates, and Giants farm systems, many of whom were getting their first opportunity to see Judge on a daily basis.

The Mets' Brandon Nimmo, one of Judge's teammates that fall, said that the Scorpions "were in awe of him" and immediately started making comparisons to Giancarlo Stanton, who had led the National League in homers for the first time in 2014 while finishing second in the MVP race to Dodgers ace Clayton Kershaw. The Scorpions had their own version of that talent to watch, gawking when Judge would connect on hard liners that improbably carried over the outfield walls or uncorked an impressive throw with his strong right arm.

"We all knew that he could break us if he wanted to," Nimmo said. "That's the thing about him; he never imposes that. He's a very gentle soul, and I appreciate him very much for that because he can throw his weight around very easily...A great friend, a great leader, and then he has that huge presence about him. I just loved being around Aaron and being his teammate, and then secondly getting to see that he's quite a talent on the baseball field."

In the AFL, teams wear the home and road uniforms of their big-league organizations, with only a customized cap to identify them as being on the same team. Scottsdale's caps were black with a red embroidered arachnid on the front, and the mish-mash of temporary teammates bonded during their six weeks together.

Since the first pitches of games were normally scheduled for noon, the players had some post-game free time to explore what Scottsdale—once described by *The New York Times* as "a desert version of Miami's South Beach"—had to offer. Nimmo recalls a few lengthy meals at Mastro's City Hall, a high-end steak and seafood lounge where he broke bread with Judge, Greg Bird, and P.J. Pilittere, a former minor league catcher who had transitioned into one of the Yankees' most respected hitting instructors.

"They had this tomahawk ribeye that was like thirty-six ounces and we ordered three or four of those. It was awesome," Nimmo said. "We were all grabbing the bones at the end and gnawing on them. We had a lot of fun together out there, talking about what the major leagues would be like if we were so lucky to get there. A lot of dreaming."

The nutrient-rich red meat, as well as the development time in the desert, proved beneficial. Judge split his 2015 campaign between Double-A Trenton and Triple-A Scranton/Wilkes-Barre, batting a combined .255 with 20 homers and 72 RBIs. He led all Yankees minor leaguers in homers and RBIs, enjoying a fourteen-game hitting streak while wowing his teammates with a series of awesome BP displays at Arm & Hammer Park in Trenton.

"Some of the same mutual friends that I have that were in the lower levels were saying, 'This guy is awesome. You're going to love playing with him,'" said Rob Refsnyder, who counts Judge among his closest friends in baseball. "We had a similar family background, being adopted. He's pretty down to earth, straightforward, honest. We clicked right away."

One of the better-regarded hitting prospects in New York's system, Refsnyder batted .241 over 91 games with the Yankees before moving on to the Blue Jays organization in 2017. Born in Seoul, South Korea, Refsnyder was adopted at five months old by Jane and Clint Refsnyder, who raised him near the Pacific Ocean in picturesque Laguna Hills, California. The adopted-son link came up only briefly; Judge told Refsnyder that he maintained no curiosity about his biological parents, saying that his adoption had been meant to be.

"What impressed me the most about Aaron was he was an awesome teammate," Refsnyder said. "He could be struggling, but he was still the same every day at the ballpark. I think that's what New York should be most excited about. He's very self-driven. He sets goals and every day he works at it. I think that's indicative of his parents. His parents are awesome, awesome people."

Promoted to Triple-A in late June, Judge participated in the All-Star

Futures Game at Cincinnati's Great American Ball Park, then returned to Scranton/Wilkes-Barre to open 2016, where he batted .270 with 19 homers and 65 RBIs in 93 games. His place in the Yankees organization could be directly traced through Nick Swisher's departure as a free agent following the 2012 season, as Swisher netted New York a compensation draft choice when he signed a four-year, $56 million deal with the Indians. The Yankees had used that pick to select Judge.

Though the fun-loving Swisher was an Ohio State University alum who unofficially renamed a section of Cleveland's Progressive Field as "Brohio," the excitement over his homecoming faded when injuries limited Swisher to a .208 batting average in his first season with the Tribe. When the Braves released Swisher in spring 2016, eating the remaining $15 million on his contract, the thirty-five-year-old gave his career one last chance by returning to the Yankees organization on a minor league contract.

As one of the oldest players in the RailRiders clubhouse, Swisher submitted his surgically repaired knees to 220 Triple-A at-bats and became a regular at the tiny Waffle House restaurant on Davis Street in Scranton, Pennsylvania. He'd order his hash browns "smothered, covered, and chunked"—onions, cheese, and ham, for the uninitiated—while inviting all of his teammates to enjoy breakfast on his tab. Judge, Gary Sanchez, Ben Gamel, and Luis Cessa were among those who took Swisher up on the offer regularly.

"It's definitely not the best food to be putting in your body," Swisher said, punctuating his observation with a loud cackle. "We ate at Waffle House, I don't know how many times. I think it was almost like a competition, who could eat the most waffles. I feel like that was the hot spot in Scranton. By the way, that was like the cheapest meal I've ever bought in my life. I'm like, 'Bro, you guys can come here all the time, no problem!'"

With the clatter of dishes and the hum of traffic on the two-lane roadway serving as their background ambiance, Swisher and Judge spoke often about baseball and life in general. Over twelve years in the majors, Swisher said that he saw plenty of players struggle after enjoying immediate success, but those meals reinforced that there would be no such concerns about Judge.

"I think Aaron has got that right idea," Swisher said. "He knows the man that he is, he knows what he stands for and he's continuing to do that. I think that's his parents. They built such a good man. As a role model, now that I have kids myself, that's the kind of guy that I want my children to look up to. I think he's doing it the right way. That smile is infectious."

At the time of his major league call-up, Judge was ranked second in the International League in RBIs and home run/at-bat ratio (18.53), and fourth in runs (62), homers (19), and slugging percentage (.489). With Beltran on his way to join the Rangers, right field had become wide open, and Cashman said that Judge was guaranteed to play every day.

When the transaction hit the wire, Yankees director of amateur scouting Damon Oppenheimer sent out a celebratory e-mail blast to the scouts who had been involved in delivering Judge and Tyler Austin to the organization. Watching Austin and Judge make their major league debuts on the same day would be, Oppenheimer said, like watching two sons walk to collect their college diplomas.

"There are so many times where in scouting you feel like an independent contractor," Oppenheimer said. "You don't have that daily connection with the organization. You don't go into an office, you're not with the team. You have hours and hours and days and days in a car or hotel rooms, losing your mind because you're by yourself. When that kind of stuff happens, it's huge to the guys. It's a camaraderie builder. There's a real feeling of euphoria for the whole group: look what they accomplished and what we were part of."

Dating to that spring of 2016, Girardi had been impressed by the cohesive nature of the minor leaguers, noticing that they tended to congregate in groups of eight, nine, or ten like a jovial college team. He hoped that Austin and Judge saw something of themselves in the collection of graying ex-ballplayers who ribbed each other that day.

"I think it's good for them to be here today to see that these guys were young, these guys performed at a high level, and they had a long run," Girardi said. "Let's go do the same thing."

As it had been in spring training, Judge's size 52 jersey was embroidered with the uniform No. 99, which his teammates saw as a perfect numerical representation of his supersized appearance. Judge had not originally requested the number. With No. 44 retired for Reggie Jackson, Judge had favored No. 35, which had been his father's favorite number. That was also already assigned, to pitcher Michael Pineda.

No. 99 grew on Judge, and equipment manager Rob Cucuzza made him the third Yankee ever to wear it in a big-league game, joining outfielder Charlie Keller in 1952 and pitcher Brian Bruney in 2009. It hadn't brought Judge much luck in the spring of '16, when he went 1-for-19 in Grapefruit League play, but spending the spring in big league camp added value because Judge's locker had neighbored Carlos Beltran's.

"There was actually a moment when we were doing relay throws on the back fields, and I asked him, 'How's it been for you, with the ups and downs each year?'" Judge said. "He said, 'You've got to realize, you could be hot for the first couple months, or you could be bad the first couple months, but that's baseball. It's all going to even out. If you can stay as even-keeled as possible, don't try to ride the ups and downs, try to stay positive with everything, your results and the team's results will even out at the end of the year.' So, to hear that from a veteran presence in that situation was pretty cool to hear."

The locker setup was an arrangement that Beltran had personally requested, hoping to impart some wisdom on his heir apparent. Beltran remembers hearing coaches talk about how inconsistent Judge was with his swing at that time and what they would do to fix him, but Beltran thought that Judge showed more polish than he was being given credit for.

"Watching him in spring training, when I saw him hit and I saw him coming to the ballpark every day, the guy is mature," Beltran said. "He just needed the opportunity. Sometimes when you get called up, maybe for a time he wanted to try too hard, he wanted to do more than he's capable of doing. He didn't need to try to do anything different. He just needed to put the barrel on the ball and the ball will fly. The guy is a huge human being."

Judge had been nervous on that first day huddling up with Beltran, and he sensed similar anxiety here in the Bronx. So did the twenty-four-year-old Austin, who had a wide-eyed look as he surveyed the scene. Austin had been at the team hotel in Rochester, New York, the previous afternoon, preparing to take the second bus to Frontier Field—home of the Rochester Red Wings—the Twins' top farm affiliate—when Pedrique's number lit up Austin's cell phone, ordering him to get to the clubhouse as soon as possible. It could only mean one thing.

"I was excited," Austin said. "I called my mom. It was an emotional phone call; same with my girlfriend. This is something that I worked for my entire life. To finally get an opportunity to come up here and play, it was a special moment."

Once a high-ranking prospect whose stock had dipped due to a nag-

Tyler Austin was the fourth Yankees player ever to homer in his first at-bat, joining John Miller, Andy Phillips, and Marcus Thames. 114 seconds later, Aaron Judge became the fifth.

ging wrist injury, Austin was hitting .323 with 13 home runs and a 1.051 OPS in Triple-A at the time of his promotion. The Yankees booked Austin's travel to New York, but when that flight was canceled, he audibled by taking two car services—one from Rochester to Scranton, and then another from Scranton to New York.

For Austin, a 350-mile highway trek was nothing worth complaining about. He overcame testicular cancer at age seventeen, having been diagnosed with a fast-growing teratoma that required surgery. Fortunately, Austin mentioned the pain and his cancer was discovered early, blocking it from spreading. He vowed not to let the diagnosis change his life. A few days after having his stitches removed, Austin was strapping on his catcher's gear in San Diego, playing in a major high school showcase game.

Austin's tenacity impressed a Yankees area scout, Darryl Monroe, who pushed the organization to select him in the thirteenth round of the 2010 draft. Austin signed for $130,000, with the club envisioning him as a corner infielder or corner outfielder. After an impressive start to his pro career, the wrist injury popped up at Double-A Trenton in 2013, forcing him to repeat the level the next season.

When the Yankees designated Austin for assignment late in 2014, he passed through waivers unclaimed and attended big league camp as a non-roster invitee the next spring. Austin could handle that challenge; as a senior at Heritage High School in Conyers, Georgia, he'd experienced far more daunting situations while making summer money assisting his father, Chris, in his duties for a local eviction company.

"It was pretty scary," Austin said. "The cops are there every time you're there, so nothing really gets out of hand, but you've got to deal with the people. There was one in particular that sticks out. My dad goes up and knocks on the door with the cops and it's just this woman and her kid, a young infant. It sucks to do it, but when the bank says you've got to do it, you've got to do it. They didn't have anywhere to go, I don't think. It's sad, but what can you do?"

• • •

Yankees broadcasters Michael Kay and John Sterling had completed their emceeing duties in front of the first-base dugout, and an employee wheeled a mahogany podium bearing the team's interlocking NY logo to its usual place in the press conference room. As the grounds crew made their final preparations to the diamond, pounding the dirt on the pitcher's mound and touching up the chalk baselines, the '96ers had already started to enjoy cocktails and snacks in a luxury suite upstairs.

Other than a possible hit on the Yankees' TV and radio network, their work was done for the afternoon, and now it was time for the kids to take over. Andy Pettitte watched with interest as Rays right-hander Matt Andriese turned the Yankees aside in the first inning, pitching around a single and a stolen base. Pettitte recalled that he anticipated the post July-trade Yankees were headed for a rocky patch, one that never materialized.

"I thought it would be a little bit of a lull and these guys would have to develop," Pettitte said. "They developed real quick. You just didn't think that was going to happen, but they've done it. Now what you have is, you start feeling like, 'OK, we've got a chance to have something real special here with these guys' ages. I think everybody thought that this team was a few years away from being where they're at right now."

Austin waited on deck, then prepared to walk to home plate after Gary Sanchez grounded out for the second out of the second inning. Gripping a bat at the dugout steps, Judge leaned over and told his teammate, "Do your thing, T."

With those words of encouragement, Austin stepped into the right-handed batter's box for his first at-bat in The Show. His upper cheeks streaked with heavy black smears, Austin worked the count to 2-2 before Andriese tried to put away the rookie with a 92-mph fastball. Austin swung hard and caught up with the heater, barreling it toward right field.

Austin tracked the ball's flight as it pelted the first row of seats beyond the 314-foot marker down the line for a home run. Austin quickly pumped his right fist, then charged quickly around the bases. Yankees 1, Rays 0.

"There's no other feeling," Austin said. "You know the people that have worn this uniform throughout history with the NY on their chest. It was just an overwhelming, special day, and I wouldn't change it for anything."

The last Yankee to have homered in his first big league at-bat was Marcus Thames, who happened to be in the first-base dugout on that afternoon, serving as the club's assistant hitting coach. Thames hit the first of his 115 big league homers on June 10, 2002, a shot to left-center field off future Hall of Famer Randy Johnson at the original Yankee Stadium.

It was a moment that diehard Yankees fans still recalled fondly, and the 41,682 sweaty witnesses on hand for Austin's homer only had to wait 114 seconds to see the feat equaled. Judge said that he had been "ecstatic" for Austin while waiting on deck, thinking to himself, "Oh man, I've just got to make contact now."

Andriese got ahead of Judge with two strikes before missing outside the zone, then tried to float an 87-mph changeup by him. Judge unloaded on the pitch, clubbing a drive to center field that struck a small ledge atop the restaurant before plopping onto the netting that covers Monument Park. Yankees 2, Rays 0. The blast was calculated at 446 feet by MLB's Statcast system, and as researchers would quickly discover, Austin and Judge had become the first teammates to hit home runs in their first big league at-bats in the same game.

"I couldn't believe that it happened to me, let alone when he did it back-to-back," Austin said. "That was unbelievable. It was special. It had never been done before. I was just super excited for him because I know the path that he has taken, the work that he has put in to get up here."

Some 3,000 miles from Yankee Stadium, the scout who'd been credited with selecting Judge from Fresno State three years prior beamed.

After homering in his first big league at-bat, Aaron Judge promised that there were more memorable moments on the way. "We have a lot of guys coming up. It's exciting. It's a great time to be a Yankee," he said.

"It was awesome. It was the first guy that I'd ever had drafted, period, in my whole career," Troy Afenir said. "You knew that it was in there. I'm fifty-four, so I had seen guys like Dave Winfield, which was a good example of a guy that's close in size and hit the ball with the same ferocity and consistency. He had the same kind of power—had that unbelievable rising line drive type of power. You dream. You hope, and you think, 'Maybe someday.'"

Someday was today. Judge was the third player to hit the ball off or over the glass panels above Monument Park, joining the Mariners' Russell Branyan in 2009 and the Astros' Carlos Correa earlier in 2016. Judge was about to make the rarely-seen feat a regular occurrence, especially in batting practice, when teammates and opponents would make it a point to be on the field when Judge's group was scheduled to hit.

"It's must-watch TV," Dellin Betances said. "We take turns in what time we shag [fly balls] for bullpen guys. Some guys go out for the first half, some guys go out for the second half. I try to make sure I'm always out there for Judge because I'm just trying to see where that ball is going to land."

Meredith Marakovits, the YES Network's clubhouse reporter, was assigned to speak with the parents of both Austin and Judge during the game. She also interviewed the tandem on the field after the Yankees' 8–4 victory.

"What made it even more unbelievable was that they were honoring the '96 team that day," Marakovits said. "It almost seemed like they were passing the torch a little bit and you were seeing the new young guys who were supposed to be the core. The fact that they were there, seeing these young kids we'd heard a lot about, it was a big day for the organization and for the fans to get that first peek."

Judge's first 27 big-league games produced mixed results—both of which would hint at performances to come. The first player in Yankees history to record an extra-base hit in each of his first three games, Judge also struck out 42 times in his first 84 big league at-bats. Cashman and Girardi shrugged the 50 percent strikeout rate off as growing pains, believing that Judge was in the early stages of adjusting to the best pitching in the world.

"He always will have strikeouts as a part of his game," Girardi said late in 2016. "He won't always have strikeouts like this."

Though the Yankees ultimately fell short of qualifying for postseason play in 2016, finishing with a negative run differential of 680-702 that identified them as a poor hitting club, Hal Steinbrenner's hopes had been buoyed by the late-season surge. A 9-17 start forced them to battle until June 10 to get over the .500 mark, and they had been 53-53 on the morning of August 3, when Gary Sanchez was summoned from Triple-A.

Though the Yankees finished fourth in the American League East, missing the playoffs for the third time in four years, they posted a 48-33 (.593) mark at home and were 32-26 (.551) from August 1 through the end of the season. Didi Gregorius saw evidence that this refreshed group could play at that level over the course of a full season, which would make them capable of accomplishing some special things.

"Everybody gave up on us, that's the first thing," Gregorius said. "And then we knew that we were not giving up. We all talked to each other. They made all the trades but you've got to stay positive and push each other, help each other out any way we can. I think we scared everybody, to be honest, because nobody expected us to be all the way here."

No wonder they were able to laugh as the rookies dressed in Yankees onesies, complete with bonnets and pacifiers, to embrace the Baby Bombers theme for their flight home following a September 22 game at Tropicana Field. Unfortunately, Judge missed out on that fun, having landed on the disabled list with a season-ending right oblique strain after taking a mighty cut eight days earlier against the Dodgers.

The injury saved Girardi from having to make a tough call; he'd penciled Judge's name in the lineup regularly down the stretch, but indicated that might not have been the case if Aaron Hicks had not been mending a hamstring injury at the time. The strikeouts didn't bother Judge as much as his overall lack of success. In his first 84 big league at-bats, Judge had managed 15 hits, a .179 batting average.

It echoed the adjustment process that Judge had gone through after being promoted to Triple-A for the first time, when he'd hit .224 with 74 strikeouts in 61 games. The addition of a leg kick had helped Judge identify pitches better then, and now he needed to make another alteration. Aiming for more consistent contact, Judge spent time working with Rowson during the offseason, and also traveled to New York to drill with Cockrell and Thames, the Yanks' hitting coaches.

"I've been making adjustments my whole life," Judge said. "I've been a work in progress for twenty-five years now. Every offseason, I've got something I try to work on."

During that time, the number .179 was scalded into Judge's consciousness. He programmed a note into his iPhone that displayed the unattractive batting average, making it one of the first things that he saw every morning.

"In some of the tougher times, you start to see players really doubt themselves," Rowson said. "He's one of those guys who never doubted himself. He stuck with it, he learned a lot from it, and instead of getting down about it, he figured out how to fix it. That's what good players do."

As spring training neared, Judge vowed that 2017 would be different. .179? Never again.

"It's motivation to tell you, 'Don't take anything for granted,'" Judge said. "The game will humble you in a heartbeat."

CHAPTER 8

SPRING FORWARD

George M. Steinbrenner Field serves as the Yankees' home during the sun-splashed months of February and March, when spring training is in full swing. Once the team goes north, the field is entrusted to a group of athletes in their early twenties who comprise the roster of the Yankees' Florida State League affiliate, while the upper levels of the stadium serve as the base of operations for a multi-billion-dollar corporation and the most recognizable brand in professional sports.

Every decision of significance either comes directly from or is vetted through Tampa, where Hal Steinbrenner can often be found in his fourth-floor office, perched high above the diamond. Though he'd served as the day-to-day control person of the organization since 2008, running the Yankees as a family business alongside his siblings Hank, Jennifer, and Jessica, the youngest of the Steinbrenners retained many interests outside of baseball.

He'd been passionate about the family's hotel and horse racing ventures, held an affinity for aviation, and had earned a reputation around Major League Baseball as something of a meteorological savant, frequently using radar data to scan the skies from afar to determine if his team should prepare for a rain delay. Steinbrenner's input saved one game of the 2009 ALCS against the Angels from being postponed, as he told the league that his data showed the storm would dissipate. It did, saving a considerable amount of money and headaches with television and ticketing.

Originally named Legends Field, the Steinbrenner Field facility sits adjacent to Raymond James Stadium—home of the NFL's Tampa Bay Buccaneers—and was constructed to replicate the exact dimensions of Yankee Stadium, circa 1996. The windows lining Steinbrenner's office provide a view of palm trees that sway with the traffic whizzing by on Dale Mabry Highway, a major commercial thoroughfare that connects Interstate 275 with fast food restaurants, big box retailers, auto dealerships, and more than a handful of adult entertainment venues.

It was here, shortly after the conclusion of the 2016 season, that Steinbrenner peered into a glowing computer screen and monitored the social media conversation surrounding his club. Most of Steinbrenner's clicks summoned phrases of positivity, and the Yankees managing general partner smiled.

"This feels different," Steinbrenner said. "I mean, we've got a great crop of good young players, and a good crop of veterans as well. It's a great mix and I think the veterans are going to be great dealing with the kids, mentoring them. We've seen that in the past. But they've got to prove themselves, a number of these guys. This is their big chance and they're going to get it this year."

Steinbrenner had sensed the uptick in excitement in 2015, when the Yankees gave Greg Bird and Luis Severino late-season reps on the big-league stage, and that sentiment was reinforced in the weeks that followed the decision to retool the roster in July of 2016. With every "like" and retweet, Steinbrenner believed that the fan base was lending its approval to the new course.

Steinbrenner repeatedly mentioned Gary Sanchez and Tyler Austin as promising reasons to watch the Yankees in 2017, while also noting that he looked forward to tracking the progress of Clint Frazier, Ben Heller, Justus Sheffield, and Gleyber Torres, among others.

Chance Adams, Dustin Fowler, Jorge Mateo, James Kaprielian, and Tyler Wade also received hype, but no one had more placed upon his broad shoulders than Aaron Judge. Shrugging off Judge's high strikeout rate during his first taste of the majors, Steinbrenner had boldly stated that he expected Judge to establish himself as the Yankees' starting right fielder.

"He's got some work to do. He knows that," Steinbrenner said. "We're going to figure out exactly what we think is wrong. My expectations are, he's going to be my starting right fielder this year. That's a big deal and a big opportunity. I know he's going to make the most of it."

The Yankees organized a "Winter Warm-up" event in January 2017 that introduced several of their youngest and untested players to the icy New York City streets. Adams, Frazier, Kaprielian, Sheffield, and Torres served lunch and danced with seniors at a Manhattan church, wandered the corridors of the Intrepid Sea, Air and Space Museum, sampled Italian delicacies along storied Arthur Avenue in the Bronx, and attended a Knicks game at Madison Square Garden.

For Frazier, the highlight of the trip was a private tour of the museum at Yankee Stadium, during which they were invited to hold one of Babe Ruth's game-used bats, a jersey that belonged to Lou Gehrig, and a glove worn by Mickey Mantle. As he wandered the expansive Great Hall, a long corridor along the first-base side of the Stadium, Frazier couldn't resist peeking out at the stadium grass and envisioning the opportunity to patrol those grounds.

"I don't know when I'll be there, but I'm happy to be here," Frazier said. "I'm proud to say I'm a part of the Yankees organization. It's the goal to make it up there this year."

Joined by big league second baseman Starlin Castro, most of the prospects took part in a one hour "Town Hall" Q&A at the Hard Rock Cafe in Times Square, speaking to approximately 300 invited fans in an event that was live-streamed on the Internet. Cashman said that the event gave those players a chance to "sword fight a little bit" with the press, which could prove to be valuable experience down the line. The GM returned to his stadium office enthused about what was coming through the pipeline.

"We have a lot of quality, young, hungry, talented players, and we still have some veterans mixed in here," Cashman said. "I think if we stay healthy and perform up to our capabilities, I think we can start writing a new chapter in Yankee-land."

Prognosticators generally held mixed views of the 2017 roster, with the Yankees expected to be in the early stages of a rebuild. Their big winter move had been to re-sign Aroldis Chapman to a five-year, $86 million deal, and Chapman created a stir during a conference call with reporters when he said that he believed Cubs manager Joe Maddon had "abused me a bit." Chapman threw ninety-seven pitches in the final three World Series games, seeing a drop in velocity while blowing the save in Game 7 against the Indians.

"I believe there were a couple of times where maybe I shouldn't be put in the game and he put me in, so I think personally I don't agree with the way he used me," Chapman said. "But he is the manager and he has the strategy."

The Yankees' other notable signing was to add thirty-seven-year-old Matt Holliday on a one-year, $13 million deal, intending to use the veteran as their designated hitter. The Yankees kept a small piece of their budget available and considered signing a pitcher to bolster their shaky rotation, but instead spent it on first baseman Chris Carter when his market crumbled. Despite leading the National League with 41 homers for the Brewers in 2016, Carter merited a one-year, $3.5 million contract—an indication of how teams' views of big-swinging, strikeout-prone sluggers with low on-base percentages had changed.

At least on paper, adding Chapman, Holliday, and Carter—while trading Brian McCann to the Astros for a pair of teenaged pitching prospects—hadn't drastically moved the needle from where the Yankees were at the end of 2016. Not one of eight *Sports Illustrated* writers picked the Yankees to win the American League East or a Wild Card in the publication's preseason issue, while the stats-friendly website *Fangraphs* forecast them to finish last in the five-team American League East, with eighty-three losses.

"Somebody brought to my attention early in spring training, I think it was one of the writers, that we were predicted to be an 80-82 or an 81-81 team," Brett Gardner said. "I thought we had a chance to be way better than that."

Cashman also shrugged off the slights, believing that with health, the Yankees would be good enough to at least make a run at one of the AL's two Wild Card slots.

"What sank us in 2016 was offense. It wasn't pitching," Cashman said. "A-Rod, Beltran, and Teixeira, that's the middle of our lineup. They did not produce and our offense was one of the worst in the American League last year, which was unexpected. I thought, if you take those three guys at Triple-A—Bird, Judge, and Sanchez—and pop them three, four, five [in the lineup] for 162 games next year, it'll significantly out-produce what we got from Beltran, Tex, and A-Rod."

Many of the recent World Series winners fielded young players with veterans mixed in, and manager Joe Girardi said that it was a formula that had served the Yankees well during a lengthy run of consecutive winning seasons that started in 1993—twenty-four years and counting as of the spring of '17, second only to the Yankees' own thirty-nine-year winning streak from 1926–1964. He saw the Yankees as having adjusted to a landscape where players do not become free agents as soon as they once did, with many opting for the security of a long-term contract early in their careers.

"I think our young players are very talented, but talent is one thing, production is another," Girardi said. "We believe that they are going to be able to produce. We will help them get through the tough periods, but we think that they can produce at a high level."

Pitchers and catchers were scheduled to report to George M. Steinbrenner Field on Valentine's Day 2017, with position players due a week later, but many of the Yankees' brightest prospects were invited to Tampa early for what the organization called its "Captain's Camp." A four-week crash course devised by player development head Gary Denbo, Captain's Camp evolved into something of a seminar on leadership in which some of the team's greatest players were called upon to help shape the next generation of stars.

In 2017, Derek Jeter, Andy Pettitte, Jorge Posada, CC Sabathia, and Alfonso Soriano were among the recognizable names to address the Baby Bombers in a classroom setting at the club's player development complex— all of them unpaid for their appearances. Pettitte said that he had been honored to be tapped as a resource, seeing the program as a natural extension of the Yankees' star-studded roster of guest instructors.

During his own playing days, Pettitte recalled sharing the clubhouse with the likes of Yogi Berra, Whitey Ford, and Ron Guidry, readily-accessible icons of Yankees teams gone by. Speaking to the next generation of Bombers, Pettitte said that he tried to relay how he had dealt with adversity, the importance of preparation, and shared tips on how to handle the mental aspects of the game.

"I hope it helps somebody," Pettitte said. "For me, it was the coolest to have Yogi and to see Whitey and to see Gator around, the guys that you knew were just kind of the Yankees legends when I was a young man coming up."

Having spent so much of his career at the Himes Avenue facility, where Jeter was perennially among the team's earliest arriving players, the Tampa resident opted instead to treat about twenty players and front office personnel to an off-campus dinner. No discussion topic was out of bounds, and much of Jeter's advice centered on how to properly represent the Yankees and coping with the pressures of playing in the majors. Judge tried to absorb as much as he could.

"He was big into 'stay even-keeled,'" Judge said. "You're going to have those times where you're going to go 0-for-20, 0-for-25, 0-for-30. You've got those months where you can't get out and the ball looks like a watermelon, but just try to stay even-keeled and stick to the process. It's a long process. If you have a bad April or a bad May, you might bounce back in June or July. Just keep the pace and focus on whatever you can do to help the team."

Denbo said the concept for the Captain's Camp was hatched in the wake of Jeter's retirement, when officials had gathered in a Tampa conference room to brainstorm about which names might step up as the next prominent figures in the organization. A few times each week, the prospects' routines of preseason conditioning and on-field workouts would be interrupted by a visit from a new voice. Former GMs, scouts, and media members were among those invited to offer perspectives otherwise unavailable to the prospects.

"We get to talk to a lot of old veterans and older scouts and a lot of our staff members about how they handle themselves on and off the field, how they respected the game, how they played the game," Judge said. "That's great. A lot of guys don't get that opportunity to hear from a lot of great players like we have."

It could be viewed as a positive sign that the most significant controversy of the spring revolved around Clint Frazier's long locks. Frazier had several inches trimmed off the day before the Super Bowl, but the twenty-two-year-old still took the field for the team's first full-squad workout with a healthy amount of red peeking out from under his ball cap. Frazier loved those curls; he'd been heartbroken when his parents made him chop them down as a seventh grader, and had vowed never to do anything so drastic again.

The media took notice, and Girardi initially laughed off the comments, joking that there were probably more than a few people in the clubhouse who would have gladly traded hairlines. But when the conversation trickled upstairs to ownership, Frazier relented and told Girardi that he would trim the mop more. The Yankees tried to put a positive spin on the moment, tweeting a photo of Frazier in mid-shear on the morning of March 10.

"Just after thinking to myself and talking to a few people, I finally

One of Clint Frazier's first questions after being traded to the Yankees in July 2016 was, "Do I have to cut my hair?" The highly-touted outfield prospect was told that he did.

Clint Frazier's first four big league hits were a double, homer, triple, and single, making him just the second Yankee to hit for the cycle with his first four hits. The other player was pitcher Johnny Allen in 1932.

came to agreement that it's time to look like everybody else around here," Frazier said. "It had started to become a distraction. I just want to play. That's what I want to do. I like my hair, but I love playing for this organization more."

In camp that day as one of the team's guest instructors, Reggie Jackson recalled a terrific quote from Mariano Rivera, who once said that, "the pinstripes are heavy in New York." Jackson said that he believed Frazier was beginning to feel that weight.

"When you first come here, I think it takes time for some of the younger people to understand the Yankee way," Jackson said. "The whole organization has a feeling about continuing—and I can say this with respect—the way the old guard wanted it. The way the sheriff wanted it is how we want to continue to do things."

The Yankees' hair policy had been in place since 1973, shortly after a group led by Steinbrenner had purchased the franchise from CBS for the remarkable price of $10 million. Accounting for inflation, Steinbrenner's purchase price was the equivalent of $57.9 million in 2017 dollars, twenty times less than what Jeter and controlling owner Bruce Sherman paid for the Marlins.

When the team stood along the baseline prior to the '73 season opener, Steinbrenner pulled out a scrap of paper and jotted down the uniform numbers of players who needed an immediate trim. Those were handed to manager Ralph Houk, who reluctantly relayed the owner's orders to Thurman Munson, Bobby Murcer, Sparky Lyle, and Roy White, among others.

Steinbrenner's demands morphed into a written rule, stating that no player, coach, or executive may display facial hair other than a mustache and that scalp hair may not be grown below the collar. Hall of Fame closer Goose Gossage's distinctive look came as a direct result of those rules, as he shaved off a beard but left an exaggerated, bushy mustache. Though Girardi acknowledged that Frazier's hair did not specifically violate Steinbrenner's code, the manager said that he believed the 1973 edict still had value.

"It's a tradition by a man that meant so much to this organization, and if it's important to him and it's important to his family, then it needs to be respected by all of us," Girardi said.

Jackson's input helped Frazier, and it was not the first time that Mr.

October had come through for him. Following the trade from Cleveland, Frazier posted an underwhelming .674 OPS in 25 games with the RailRiders and was sent to continue his season in the Instructional League. A three week program that runs from late September into October, the circuit's sparsely-attended games are played within the confines of chain-link fences on the back fields of Florida complexes.

Sensing that Frazier was struggling to find motivation within those serene surroundings, Jackson approached the prospect after a game and invited Frazier out for frozen yogurt. Frazier loaded into Jackson's rental car, still wearing his full uniform as though it were a throwback to his Little League days. Frazier said that he didn't recall discussing baseball with Jackson that day, but they both believed that they had connected on a personal level.

"I don't know if I can remember back how I thought when I was twenty-two, but I sure as hell was a wild antelope in the woods, that's for sure," Jackson said.

Frazier had a more contemporary role model in Brett Gardner, whom he shadowed through drills early in camp, studying the veteran in hopes of applying something to his own game. Gardner said that it was only natural for a young prospect to attempt to better his play in such a fashion; he'd done so himself not that long ago with Johnny Damon, whom Gardner still credits for helping him learn how to be a major leaguer.

"He's one of the guys that really helped kind of take me under his wing and feel comfortable, and at the end of the day I was trying to take Johnny's job from him as a young guy," Gardner said. "Clint's trying to do the same to me. I've got to respect his work ethic and the way that he goes about his business, and I'm sure that he does the same to me. It's my job to be as good as I can be and try to keep him from taking my job. That's how it works, man."

Cashman made it clear that he was not counting on Frazier to be in the mix for a starting role as soon as 2017, believing that Frazier would benefit from additional development time at the Triple-A level. Remember, if Frazier had been a Yankee for all of 2016, he likely would have spent the entire year in Double-A. Yet Cashman had seen players with outstanding tool packages force the Yankees' hand before; Robinson Cano had been one such case.

"We anticipated [Cano] coming out of Double-A and being ready in two years; he moved that up a full year, came to spring training after a good winter ball and crushed it," Cashman said. "All of a sudden, everybody was like, 'We have to get this guy on the team.' [Alfonso] Soriano was the same way when he was coming through our system, the shortstop we moved to second and left. It was, 'How do we get this guy on the roster?' When you have that type of tool package, once it all comes together—Gary Sanchez is the more recent example—it's like a flood."

There was similar buzz around Gleyber Torres, who had been named the youngest Most Valuable Player in the Arizona Fall League prior to his twentieth birthday, leading the circuit with a .403 batting average and a .513 on-base percentage. Getting a chance to see Torres on a daily basis that spring, the Yankees raved about the infielder's maturity and ability to use the entire field with his lively bat. When shortstop Didi Gregorius injured his right shoulder in late March, some members of the coaching staff pushed for Torres to make the leap from A-ball into the majors.

"We had the injury to Didi, and all of a sudden, our major league staff wanted him now," Cashman said. "They wanted him to break camp and play him at shortstop. I can understand why, but you take careful steps when you have that type of ceiling. At that age, he had never played in cold weather in his career. I didn't want him drinking out of a fire hose in April."

The Yankees stuck to their plan, telling Torres that there was nothing he could do to force his way to New York that spring. Understanding that, Torres said he set his goals upon continuing to mature and gaining experience in what he called "a very unique opportunity."

"I worked really hard so that I wouldn't feel out of place," Torres said. "You want to keep working hard. That's a key."

• • •

Once a jewel of the Florida State League, Steinbrenner Field had started to show its age in recent seasons, especially with newer, flashier structures starting to pop up along the coastlines. A $40 million renovation project was underway to add a new main entrance, a two-story gift shop, lounges, cabanas, and a walkway that offered a 360 degree route around the field. As the Yankees took their first batting practice hacks of 2017, they did so amid a cacophony of jackhammers and clanging steel. No one made more noise than Judge, who blasted a memorable drive over the large left-field scoreboard and dented the structure often.

"We actually worry about the construction workers a little bit," Girardi said. "I just think the ball is really going off the bat from a lot of our players, younger players, and that's kind of exciting to see. I know it's BP, but the potential is there to have huge run production from some of these guys. And that kind of excites me."

The Yankees entered the spring with two vacancies in the pitching rotation, having guaranteed spots to Masahiro Tanaka, CC Sabathia, and Michael Pineda. A crowded mix followed for the final slots, with Cashman often rattling off the names of Luis Cessa, Chad Green, Bryan Mitchell, and Luis Severino as his prime candidates. Despite going 14-5 with a 2.13 ERA at Double-A Trenton and Triple-A Scranton/Wilkes-Barre in 2016, Jordan Montgomery's name had been scarcely mentioned as a serious contender.

Wearing uniform No. 90, the twenty-four-year-old lefty's most memorable appearance of the spring came on March 23 against the Rays in Port Charlotte, Florida, a contest that was nationally televised on ESPN. Montgomery struck out eight, including fanning three-time All-Star Evan Longoria twice. Seated in the dugout, Girardi and pitching coach Larry Rothschild exchanged impressed glances throughout the performance.

By this point, most of Montgomery's peers had been dispatched across the street to minor league camp, leaving the soft-spoken South Carolinian to dress in a row of empty lockers. When a bulletin was posted on the clubhouse wall, urging players to bring their vehicles to Steinbrenner Field so they could be loaded onto a carrier for New York, Montgomery tried to keep his head down in case the club brass had forgotten he was still there.

"He'd been on my radar, but we had him as more depth than taking a legit shot at the fifth spot," Cashman said. "He came to camp and took it. That's why it's great to have spring training, because guys can change the narrative. He was entering spring training as starting pitching depth that we could turn to if we had injuries and maybe be an up-down guy for us, but he said, 'Nope, my time is now.'"

A finesse pitcher who features a fastball, slider, curveball, and changeup, Montgomery made a career out of proving people wrong. He once recalled how he had initially been tabbed to be a specialist at the University of South Carolina, trusted to enter only in relief against left-handed batters. Growing up in Sumter, South Carolina, where his father Jim was a government farm service agent and his mother Raury was a substitute teacher, Montgomery had gone undrafted out of high school.

Sumter was perhaps best known as the home of former Yankees second baseman Bobby Richardson, whom Montgomery correctly identifies as the only player from a losing team ever to be named World Series MVP (1960). The Yankees dropped that Fall Classic on a series-ending Game 7 homer by the Pirates' Bill Mazeroski off pitcher Ralph Terry, despite Richardson's .367 average and 12 RBIs.

"You'd see him around Sumter all the time," Montgomery said. "He would talk to us a lot with our high school and American Legion teams. He would tell us that we had to work hard and put our faith first."

Montgomery carried the nickname "Gumby," which he said was given to him by a fifth-year senior at South Carolina because of a doughy, gawky frame that Montgomery had yet to grow into. Montgomery initially hated the moniker but learned to embrace it, eventually using it as part of his Twitter handle: @gumbynation34.

"I was so uncoordinated," Montgomery said. "I hadn't matured into my body yet. Really, I don't think I started maturing until my junior year of college, which is really when I grew into my body. I had a bunch of baby fat and I kept growing, and my body wasn't catching up to it."

The Yankees watched Montgomery often as a member of the Gamecocks, relying on both old-school scouting and advanced analytics to home in on his performance. The Bombers have a staff of fifteen analytics staffers who pore over that sort of collegiate and professional data on a daily basis, including Scott Benecke, who holds a PhD in applied statistics.

While scout Adam Czajkowski filed reports on Montgomery's swing-and-miss stuff, the Yanks' software also distilled Trackman radar data that highlighted Montgomery as a pitcher of interest. In April 2014, Yankees national scout Brian Barber brought his radar gun to the stands at Baum Stadium in Fayetteville, Arkansas. Barber filed a positive report after watching Montgomery dominate the Razorbacks' lineup, striking out nine over seven innings.

"It's probably the best game he threw the whole spring," Barber said. "It's just the luck that you have to be at the right park on the right day. I was able to see the Jordan Montgomery that you guys are seeing now. He had a good fastball that day, he was up to 93 mph. He had a really good changeup that day. You saw the size, the pitchability that he had, with the stuff. Other people saw bits and pieces of that, but I saw the total package."

Barber's review was so enthusiastic that Damon Oppenheimer booked a trip to Nashville to watch Montgomery start against Vanderbilt University. Montgomery struck out eight over seven sharp innings that evening, impressing with a changeup that Oppenheimer viewed as being an above-average big-league pitch at that time.

"Because he didn't light the radar gun up at 93, 94, 95, in today's world, he slides," Oppenheimer said. "But the rest of the stuff—the location on the fastball, the slider, the changeup, you saw the secondary stuff, you saw the composure he had in a big Friday game at Vandy."

Oppenheimer said that a consistent piece of draft strategy echoed by old-time scouts and farm directors is that a team should try to pick a legitimate left-handed pitcher within the first seven rounds. In Montgomery, the Yankees saw one with pitchability, size, and a funky overhand delivery. The Yankees called Montgomery's name in the fourth round that June, making him the 122nd selection in the nation.

Jordan Montgomery shows his form during the 2015 season with the Tampa Yankees, when he went 6-5 with a 3.08 ERA in 16 games (15 starts).

Girardi believed that Montgomery's poise stemmed from his experience in the 2012 College World Series, when Montgomery had a trial by fire as a freshman, pitching in front of large, enthusiastic crowds. Montgomery pitched well in an elimination game against Arkansas to help South Carolina advance to the finals, and had they made it past Arizona, Montgomery would have started the championship game.

During the spring of 2017, Girardi observed that Montgomery's overhand delivery reminded him somewhat of a young Andy Pettitte, another baby-faced left-hander who also opted to shave on his bullpen days so he could take the mound with a slight amount of scruff. Pettitte quickly took an interest in Montgomery's career path, exchanging contact information so they could swap text messages throughout the season.

"Jordan's a little different mechanically, he's straighter over the top, but he's left-handed so I can relate with a lefty," Pettitte said. "Me and Jordan stay in touch with each other and we'll continue to talk. I know he wants to talk to me about the cutter and stuff like that. He's a great kid. He's got a great makeup. I love everything about him and I think he's got a great future if he stays healthy."

● ● ●

There is an old saying that reminds baseball people not to believe what they see in March or September, since the influx of minor league players participating in the major league starting lineups dilutes the talent pool. Still, in the spring of 2017, the Yankees had a difficult time finding reasons not to buy into Greg Bird's performance.

Looking like the best hitter on the planet for an extended stretch of the spring, Bird batted .451 (23-for-51) with eight homers in Grapefruit League play, convincingly answering any questions about his return from the right shoulder injury that cost him all of 2016. As he stepped into the batter's box during a March 30 exhibition against the Phillies in Clearwater, Florida, Bird only was trying to get to Opening Day healthy.

The foul ball that Bird whacked off his right ankle that afternoon would change the course of his season, but the Yankees didn't know that as they traveled to Atlanta, helping to open the Braves' sparkling new SunTrust Park in an exhibition game (Bird hit the stadium's first homer, off the ageless Bartolo Colon) before returning to the Tampa-St. Petersburg area for the season opener at the Rays' Tropicana Field.

The experts were still lukewarm on the Yankees' chances. *Fangraphs* softened their prediction to say that the Yankees would finish a few games above .500, in fourth place. *USA Today* had the Yankees finishing 80-82, also in fourth place, and the *New York Post*'s front page for April 1 touted a fan poll declaring that "the Mets are the kings of New York." As the hours ticked off until Opening Day, Cashman said that he thought the 2017 Yankees were capable of more than they were being given credit for.

"We contended all the way to the end last year. That was proof in the pudding," Cashman said. "Listen, if our current roster stays healthy and performs up to their maximum capability or close to their maximum capability, we're without a doubt a Wild Card contending team at the very least. We'll see. You've got to play it out."

CHAPTER 9

ALL RISE

The concept of "The Judge's Chambers" was first floated in the spring of 2017, during a time in which team officials were brainstorming avenues to make Yankee Stadium more appealing to a younger generation of fans. Work had already begun in the Bronx to add children's play areas, terraces, and party decks to the facility, which was readying for its ninth year of service. Noting the popular response that Aaron Judge had received during the exhibition games in Florida, the Yanks' decision-makers deemed a dedicated cheering section to be a logical next step.

Similar concepts had been successful in other ballparks, such as the Astros' "Keuchel's Korner" for ace Dallas Keuchel and the Mariners' "King Felix's Court" for standout pitcher Felix Hernandez. It may not have been groundbreaking, but it seemed that way for the Yankees, a team that had to fight the temptation of simply leaning upon their storied history to sell tickets. Though some would argue that there had never been a special section devoted to Derek Jeter or Mariano Rivera, the willingness to innovate represented a refreshing change of pace.

Judge told the Yankees that he thought the idea was "cool," but first, he had to actually make the team. It may seem difficult to believe in hindsight, given how sensational Judge's rookie season turned out to be, but there was serious consideration given to having Judge begin 2017 in the minors. Since Judge still had minor league options remaining and Aaron Hicks did not, the Yankees decided to carry Judge on the roster only if he

Though Aaron Hicks came up short in his battle to win the right field job from Aaron Judge in the spring of 2017, the switch hitter still was able to set single-season career highs in runs, doubles, homers, RBIs, and walks.

won the starting right field job, believing that a backup role would stunt his development.

"He never had a full year in the big leagues," Cashman said. "He had competition that was legitimate with Aaron Hicks. Aaron Hicks had performed just as well for a period of time, if not better, for the first half of the spring. It was a tight competition. I'd say halfway through camp, Hicks was winning by a hair."

Driven to convince management that he was ready for the opportunity, Judge said that he locked his focus upon having quality at-bats for thirty days straight. The organization held daily meetings in the final weeks of camp, with Cashman, Tim Naehring, and numerous other assistants disappearing into Girardi's office. Judge ignored their lengthy chats, saying that he couldn't afford to waste time worrying about whether he would begin the season as a RailRider or a Yankee.

"I wasn't getting paid enough to make that decision," Judge said. "I had one goal in my mind, to go out there and compete and do whatever I can to fight for a job. Every day I was just taking that mindset, I've got to go out there and work my butt off to get this job."

Seven minutes after 10:00 on the morning of March 30, the heavy steel door to the manager's office swung open, indicating that a decision had been made. Someone joked that it reminded them of the clouds of smoke that rise over the Sistine Chapel to announce the selection of a new Pope. Girardi summoned the team's beat reporters and lauded both Hicks and Judge for making it a very tough call, but announced that Judge's late-spring surge had tipped the scales in his favor.

Hicks needed a couple of days to stew over the decision, and though he was disappointed with the outcome, he acknowledged that the team had given him a fair shot. The job had been given to the man who had played the best.

"The last two or three weeks of camp, Hicks didn't necessarily lose it as much as Judge took it," Cashman said. "Those weren't false conversations. It was more like, you've got to win that everyday job or you're going to Triple-A, and Judge knew that. Aaron Hicks is an above-average right fielder in this game, but Judge has turned out to be an MVP candidate. It was real. I guess we made the right decision."

Judge, meanwhile, was elated. He responded by saying that "now the real work starts," adding that the challenge would be to ward off the competition from Hicks and the team's stable of talented minor leaguers. Girardi said that the Yankees were now locked in and would give Judge plenty of leeway if he got off to a slow start. With the Yankees about to open the regular season, Judge called his folks in California, urging them to hop on the next flight to Florida.

"They were worrying about it, just like any parent would," Judge said. "They just wanted to know what was going on, so I just called them and let them know, 'Hey, I'll be in Tampa on Opening Day.'"

Judge was one of five players on the Yankees' active roster who participated in their first big league Opening Day, joined by Gary Sanchez, Greg Bird, Jonathan Holder, and Bryan Mitchell. Judge hit eighth in the season opener and, upon returning to New York, opted to settle into an art deco hotel in the heart of Times Square, living out of two suitcases between road trips. It was the same hotel where the Yankees had sent him after his first big league call-up the previous August.

"I didn't know where else to live," Judge said. "This is my first go-round, so I just kind of thought, 'I'll live in New York.' It was just busy. There were a lot of things going on. That was probably the first thing I noticed when I came here, especially from a small town in California. Then you come here, and usually on the sidewalks back home there's nobody on the streets. Here, you're shoulder to shoulder with people."

Judge's plate appearances quickly became the ones that no one wanted to miss, easing traffic at the concession stands and the stadium lavatories. Judge tied a major league record by hitting 10 home runs in April, and the top spot in the books would have been his alone if not for an April 16 drive against the Cardinals that was inexplicably ruled to be a fan-interference triple after video review.

"Last year was kind of like a practice test," Judge said. "I saw the league a little bit, got a chance to face some pitchers. Now I'm seeing some familiar faces and just getting used to the league, going out there and trying to compete and just keep continuing to have quality at-bats."

Hitting them high, far, and often, Judge quickly won a fan in Matt Holliday. After Judge homered twice in a 14–11 slugfest victory over the Orioles, the fourteen-year veteran gushed that he thought Judge was "probably the most gifted baseball player I think I've ever been around." That was no small compliment, considering Holliday had shared a clubhouse with Albert Pujols for four seasons in St. Louis.

"You just look at the guy in batting practice and he hits the ball 550 feet," Holliday said of Judge. "He can run and he can throw at six-foot-seven, 280 pounds. You just don't see it. I haven't seen anything like it. It's fun to watch. He's fun to watch. I think the whole stadium stops when he comes up to bat. That doesn't happen all the time."

When Nick Swisher stopped by Yankee Stadium in a new role as an analyst for FOX Sports, Judge's former minor league teammate and Waffle House dining companion marveled at how far the slugger had come in such a short period of time.

"He's a whole different player now than he was at Triple-A," Swisher said. "He's got a new stance, he's got a new swing. Everything has changed. He went home in the offseason and I think what really got him was when he missed those last few weeks of being up here in the big leagues. When he left here, I know that man went home and busted his tail to get ready for this year. He knew that once this season came around, this was his shot."

Exit velocity was the new buzzword for hitters around Major League Baseball, and the Yankees had started displaying those miles per hour readings in the top right corner of the center-field scoreboard, as they would for a pitcher's velocity. It did not take long for Swisher and any other observer with eyes and ears to realize that Judge's thirty-five-inch, thirty-three-ounce Chandler bat was impacting the ball with more thunder than any other in the league.

"I've never seen anybody hit a baseball like that," Swisher said. "He's the red circle in the lineup now. Guys don't want him to beat them, but this man hits pop-ups for home runs."

Judge's mighty strokes were incredible to watch from a safe distance, while unnerving for those who had the misfortune of standing sixty feet and six inches away. Pitching for the Rays, reliever Jumbo Diaz surrendered a game-tying single on April 12 that rocketed off Judge's bat at 116.5 mph, whistling past the hurler's right ear into center field.

"It was very close. I felt the wind go by my head," Diaz said. "When I got back, I received a message from my wife. She was a little scared, a little jolted by it. She was just grateful I was OK."

Judge celebrated his twenty-fifth birthday on April 26 at Fenway Park, where he had captured the Yankees' attention a few years earlier with that memorable batting practice session in a Cape Cod League showcase. The party started quickly, as Judge mashed the first pitch he saw from Rick Porcello over the wall in right-center field for his seventh homer of the season.

He then showed off his fearless defense an inning later, approaching the stands before flipping over a short wall and into an empty red seat to snare an Xander Bogaerts pop fly in the webbing of his glove. Watching from the mound, Luis Severino doffed his cap. Judge found a way to thank a teammate for his daring catch; after the game, Judge mentioned that former Red Sox outfielder Jacoby Ellsbury had walked him through some of Fenway's intricacies.

"He won two World Series here and knows this outfield pretty well," Judge said. "He helped me with positioning a little bit, where to start, where to move over on certain guys. Having that advice and giving me a couple of extra steps to the foul line really helped me out."

The disregard for self-preservation reminded Brett Gardner of Jeter's bloody tumble into the third-base seats, an oft-replayed highlight from a July 1, 2004 game against Boston at the old Yankee Stadium. Gardner chuckled when he imagined what the fans sitting in Fenway's front row must have thought, seeing Judge rumbling toward them at full speed.

"That's a big boy to be piled up on the nachos and peanuts in the front row," Gardner said.

Girardi's first inclination was to hold his breath, recalling a similar 2014 play at Tropicana Field that sent Carlos Beltran into an MRI tube. There were no such tests for Judge that night, but later in the season, Judge was frequently seen wearing a heavy ice pack on his left shoulder during his postgame interviews. He'd travel to Los Angeles to have arthroscopic surgery a month after the season, removing loose bodies and cleaning up cartilage, and it was speculated that the discomfort could have started with that tumble into the Fenway box seats.

"I can't really pinpoint what it is," Judge said in late August. "There have been quite a few falls that I've had. It's just part of the season. Everybody goes through this."

Through the season's first month, the Yankees spent a fair deal of time being fascinated by the contrast between the six-foot-eight Judge and five-foot-seven Ronald Torreyes, an unlikely sparkplug from Venezuela who had won a place on the roster in the spring of 2016 by consistently barreling baseballs. Torreyes' versatility was a valuable asset, permitting Girardi to plug him in at second base, shortstop, and third base, as well as the out-field. Had the Yankees required an emergency third catcher, those tasks would also have been delegated to Torreyes.

At this time, the Yankees needed his services at shortstop, where Torreyes opened the season as the starter after Gregorius injured his right shoulder while playing in a World Baseball Classic exhibition. Torreyes' solid play helped patch over the absence of a key star, while also providing some valuable levity. In a celebratory act that never failed to crack up the bench, Judge would raise his hand as high as possible, forcing Torreyes to take a running start in order to high-five his towering teammate. On one occasion, Gregorius literally picked Torreyes up as though he were a child, and Judge needed only a tiny bunny hop to slap Torreyes' hand.

"I feel super happy about that, just having the guys give me so much support," Torreyes said through an interpreter. "It's really nice, you know? But the feeling is mutual. I really like my teammates as well. I come in here and try to do my work. That's what I like to do."

As a teenager in Venezuela, Torreyes' father Alcides urged him to hit more, run more, and outhustle the more physically blessed competition at many of the academies run by pro organizations in the country. Scouts

Ronald Torreyes was an extremely popular figure among the Yankees' players for his diminutive size, his defensive versatility, and a surprising ability to barrel baseballs consistently.

found it difficult to envision Torreyes' slight frame on a pro diamond, but the Reds took a flyer in 2010, signing him as a non-drafted free agent.

Stints in the Cubs, Astros, Blue Jays, Dodgers, and Angels organizations followed until Torreyes finally seemed to find a home with the Yanks at age twenty-four. Gregorius played with Torreyes in Cincinnati's system and delighted in telling anyone who would listen that Torreyes would be a good big-league player—and didn't let them forget it when Torreyes did something to back up that boast. Most of the Yankees, including Judge, considered Torreyes to be among their favorite teammates.

"He's doing an amazing job," Judge said. "That's the great thing about 'Toe,' you can put him anywhere and he's going to produce."

Judge's production carried the Yankees early, as he became the youngest player in major league history to hit at least 13 homers through his team's first 26 games of the season. The only other right-handed-hitting outfielder of any age to accomplish that feat had been Hall of Famer Willie Mays, who did it for the Giants in 1964.

It was during this time that Judge received a call from Mike Batesole, his baseball coach at Fresno State. Having once been a high school teammate of Lenny Dykstra and a scout league teammate of Darryl Strawberry,

Batesole told ESPN that he wanted to make sure that the temptations of New York City weren't having a negative impact on Judge.

"On his first day off this year, I said, 'Look, dude. Bars across America are full of guys who had one good month,'" Batesole said. "'You haven't done anything except piss the rest of the league's pitchers off and now they all want you extra bad. You're better off shutting your phone off. Get some alone time, call Mom, give thanks. I don't want to hear that you had dinner with Jay-Z and Beyoncé on your first day off. Make sure you're keeping your feet on the ground and taking care of business.' His response, as it always is, was, 'Yes, coach.'"

The national media enthusiastically embraced the storyline of a hulking Yankees superhero with an aw-shucks demeanor. A May 15–22, 2017, double issue of *Sports Illustrated* featured Judge on the cover, depicting his pinstriped cut behind the words, "All Rise! The Yankees' Youth Movement Is in Session. The Powerful Aaron Judge Presiding." Stephanie Apstein's accompanying article traced Judge's roots, painting him as a shy rookie from a small California town whose career happened to be off to the most prolific start ever.

The next week, NBC's *The Tonight Show* aired a hilarious segment in which Judge tested his acting chops with a Clark Kent impression, donning a blazer and glasses behind a desk in New York's Bryant Park to quiz Yankees fans about…Aaron Judge.

After asking one fan how much he thought the rookie might be able to bench press, Judge nonchalantly replied, "400? You're right." One fan referred to the prospect as "Adam Judge," and another passerby wearing a Yankees jersey figured out the gag when Judge held up his *SI* cover, offering a double take before taking note of Judge's toothy smile.

"It was the gap," he said. "There's only two gaps in New York, you and [Michael] Strahan, man."

The Yankees were visiting Kansas City the day after that segment aired, and Judge said that his phone had been overwhelmed with text messages and voice mails. Judge had tipped off his parents to the upcoming bit, asking them to set their DVRs, but the late-night appearance had come as a surprise to most of Judge's friends and family.

"I'm not really a comedian at all, but I think it turned out great," Judge said. "I was nervous the whole time. When I was going through it, I didn't

All Rise! "The Judge's Chambers" became one of the most coveted seating locations at Yankee Stadium during the 2017 season.

think I was doing well at all. They did a lot of editing and it really turned into something great."

When several groups of fans began attending games in black robes and white powder wigs, waving signs that included variations of "All Rise," the Yankees responded by unveiling the project that they had discussed during the spring. When the Yankees took the field for batting practice on May 22, The Judge's Chambers appeared at the rear of Section 104 in right field, eighteen seats boxed in by wood to create the appearance of a courtroom jury box.

New York versus Kansas City was first on the docket. It would only be Judge's sixty-sixth major league game, but Jason Zillo, the Yankees' director of media relations, said that the Judge's Chambers had simply continued the momentum that the fans established on their own.

"It's all part of a shift toward making the experience more interactive," Zillo said. "It's a different era. It's a different group of fans. Fans are looking for things in their trip to a stadium that fans weren't looking for ten years ago, twenty years ago, thirty years ago."

The seats became a wildly popular attraction, with fans lining up early for the opportunity to snap selfies in the area. The team's ticket office was flooded with inquiries about the section and were told that they could not buy their way into the Judge's Chambers; instead, Yankees employees roamed the concourses prior to first pitch, looking for guests who were wearing Judge paraphernalia and offering them the opportunity to upgrade their seat location.

Upon entry, the lucky seat-holders were issued black robes with the Yankees logo on the front and Judge's No. 99 on the back, as well as foam gavels. The gavels (also sold in stadium gift shops) were theirs to keep, but the robes were washed and re-issued for the next home game. On one occasion, Associate Justice of the Supreme Court Sonia Sotomayor spent a few innings in the Chambers, cheering along with her fellow Yankees fans.

"It's pretty unreal," Judge said. "I never would have thought [this could happen] so soon. But the fans like it, so I'm glad they're having fun."

Named the American League's Rookie of the Month in both April and May, Judge was the first Yankee to ever win the award twice in a season and the first Yankee since Don Mattingly in 1985 to win *any* monthly award in consecutive months. Holliday had made an exceptionally comfortable living by pounding pitching for more than a decade, and even he had to admire what Judge was doing at the game's highest level.

"I think we've all come to realize that he hits the ball harder than anybody else," Holliday said. "I think all the stats prove it. It feels like he's hitting a ball every day where I'm like, 'Whoa.' He's not swinging at many bad pitches, and when he gets his pitch, he doesn't miss it."

Taking a lesson from his days at Fresno State, where players had to place a dollar in a shoebox every time they used the words "me," "mine," or "myself" in a boastful manner, Judge struck a humble note. He had never been fined for self-centered talk in three college seasons, and so that wasn't going to happen at Yankee Stadium. Offering a knowing smirk, Judge would pause for a few extra beats before answering a question that invited him to thump his chest, then credit his teammates for getting on base so pitchers were forced to throw him hittable pitches.

"It's been a fun first half so far," Judge said on July 8, having hit his thirtieth homer to shatter Joe DiMaggio's record for the most blasts by a Yankees rookie, a mark that had stood since 1936. "I'm blessed to be in this position with my teammates around me, always putting me in the right spot and helping me do my best and helping me succeed."

Judge's polish with the media came as no surprise to Zillo, who organizes a seminar with the Yankees' younger players each spring, attempting to prepare them to represent a franchise that arguably receives as much media coverage as any in the country. In one exercise, players assume the role of reporters and attempt to bait their teammates into losing their temper or saying something controversial. Zillo listed politics, gun laws, religion, and gay teammates as topics that were covered at one point or another; Judge aced them all, as Zillo had been pleased to tell Brian Cashman.

"Clearly, he has a wonderful upbringing, starting with his family and his parents. It takes a village," Zillo said. "Cash and I have a lot of dialogue. He wants to know what I'm picking up on the young guys that I'm interacting with every day and we're putting them through the media training program at a young age. I told him, 'Aaron Judge, on my end, is locked and loaded.' I think he understood at a very young age what it meant to be a professional baseball player and what it could mean to be a New York Yankee."

Whenever the stadium lights blinked off and Judge hailed his nightly Uber to Times Square, he enjoyed the convenience of that junior hotel suite overlooking the Crossroads of the World, savoring the ability to satisfy a sweet tooth craving at any hour. After games, he'd walk outside in search of frozen yogurt or ice cream, thrilled that such pleasures were readily available. But Judge had also been living out of the same tired pair of suitcases for two months, and so with Gardner's family out of town for the week, Gardner urged Judge to crash in his guest room and see what life was like in suburban Armonk, New York.

"He was tired of living in the hotel, so he stayed with me for a week or so," Gardner said. "I remembered that Dave Robertson stayed with Johnny Damon for a while when we were rookies; same kind of deal. He was really good. He has proper etiquette: puts his dishes in the dishwasher and cleans up after himself. He took the trash out. I put him to work while he was there."

Secluded from midtown's perpetual barrage of horns, sirens, and shouts, Judge savored the change of scenery. Gardner said that he and Judge didn't do much during their time as housemates: they'd sleep, get lunch, and maybe talk a little hitting on the ride to the Stadium. That was the point.

"He just wanted me to check out what was outside of New York City," Judge said. "He said, 'New York isn't all tall buildings and flashing lights.' I loved it up there. I felt like I was in a cabin up in the woods, but I had all of my stuff in New York, so I eventually had to go back. I liked them both."

The only black mark on Judge's visit to Casa de Brett was that he had helped himself to some leftover Easter candy, much to the dismay of Gardner's young sons, Hunter and Miller.

"He hasn't invited me back over," Judge said. "His boys weren't too happy about that."

Whether he was in the suburbs or the city, Judge kept slugging. He reached base safely in every June game and earned his first AL Player of the Month honors, batting .324 with 10 homers, 25 RBIs, and 30 walks in 28 games. After watching Judge hit on television, Cubs manager Joe Maddon remarked, "He's Frank Howard all over again." It was an astute observation, ripped from baseball's history books. Howard represented perhaps the best old-school comparison to what big league pitchers were now trying to handle in Judge.

It is believed that Judge was the eleventh position player in major league history to have stood six-foot-seven or taller, and only four of the previous ten played in at least 200 big league games. The best of them was Howard, who was six-foot-seven and hit 382 homers with the Dodgers, Senators, Rangers, and Tigers from 1960–1973. Other more recent notables included Tony Clark and Richie Sexson, a pair of power-hitting first basemen.

"It was going to be risk, but maybe high, high reward," said Yankees special assistant Jim Hendry, who had been dispatched to a handful of Judge's games at Fresno State in 2013. "But if it clicks, then you've got something. You always dream. You say, 'It took Richie Sexson a while, when he was struggling, then he took off.' If you told me by the end of the season that Judge was hitting .250 in the big leagues with 30 homers, we'd have been thrilled."

Though Judge seemed to be exceptionally grounded, the Yankees had concerns about the budding star's time being spread too thin. Judge wisely began to limit his availability at his clubhouse locker, relying on Zillo to filter hundreds of media requests from local and national outlets. Judge also told agent Page Odle that he was not ready to begin sorting the dozens of endorsement offers that corporate America had started to drop on his doorstep. Shortly after the season, Judge picked his first, locking in as the newest pitchman for Pepsi.

"You worry about him being pulled in a lot of different directions and how you handle that," Girardi said. "Because when you get off to starts like this and you're new and the types of home runs that he's hitting, people are going to want his attention. It's important that he stays focused on what his job is and he doesn't get pulled in too many directions."

Unlike Jeter, who was criticized by George Steinbrenner for his club-hopping bachelor lifestyle in the early 2000s, Judge preferred to save his energy. Despite a growing profile that promised to open any of Manhattan's hottest doors, Judge seemed to have little interest in experiencing the late-night party scene.

"I'd rather spend a night at home," Judge said. "If my teammates want to come over and hang out at home or go to a nice dinner and hang out, I'll do that. But I don't like to burn the midnight oil going out. It's going to take away from what I've got to do at the field."

On one occasion, Judge's parents traveled to New York hoping to view some of the city's tourist attractions. Judge said that he took them to breakfast at a diner, but begged off the sightseeing excursion, opting to take his morning easy and then get to the stadium early for the game.

"I think he's been extremely professional in how he's gone about his business, the focus being on baseball," Cashman said. "One thing Judge has always had is high leadership qualities throughout our minor leagues that were very similar to Derek Jeter's qualities. Clearly different players, and you never want to compare anybody to a first ballot Hall of Famer, but makeup side there's a lot of similarities there."

Judge's off-field weakness, if you could call it one, was a propensity to get caught up in marathon video game sessions. Judge had a love affair with his PlayStation 4 and was able to name all of the Pokémon characters, which prompted CC Sabathia's young son, Carter, to name Judge as his second favorite Yankee. Judge's gaming obsession stretched into the team's charter flights, where a Nintendo Switch proved to be as indispensable a travel item as neck pillows and comfortable clothing.

"Yeah, he's a big nerd when it comes to video games. *Big* nerd," Tyler Wade said. "He loves video games. He plays Destiny, Mario Kart, all of it. I'll go back to my room, hang out for a little bit, talk to my parents, and go up to his room and play video games. That's every night."

The adventures in those digital universes were fun, but they were no competition for what Judge was doing in the real world. On June 11, Judge hit the longest home run that the majors would see in 2017, punishing a flat slider from the Orioles' Logan Verrett for a mammoth 495-foot blast that landed in the back of the left-field bleachers at Yankee Stadium.

When Judge returned to the dugout after a second homer that day, his teammates jokingly gave him the silent treatment, pretending they hadn't noticed. Two weeks later, when his Blue Jays visited New York, first baseman Justin Smoak said that he stared at that back row of the left-field bleachers and attempted to make sense of what kind of human could reach that part of the stadium.

"I was just standing at home plate during BP and I'm like, 'I could hit a ball twice and hit it that far,'" Smoak said. "He's a big, strong man. When he gets on first base, honestly, I try to get in my crouch position. I feel like I'm a big guy, but he makes me feel like a little guy. He's got a short swing for a big guy. It's hard to do that."

Reggie Jackson once said that "fans don't boo nobodies," and Judge's rising profile made him a target for the leather-lunged. The jeers were particularly loud during a June 29 game at Chicago's unfortunately-named Guaranteed Rate Field, as a group of well-lubricated White Sox followers in right field taunted Judge through the first five innings.

In the sixth, Judge crushed his major league-leading twenty-seventh homer off reliever Jake Petricka, then shot an extended glance toward his would-be tormentors after rounding first base. Some of them applauded when Judge returned to right field for the bottom half of the inning; others seemed to have vanished altogether, shrinking into the darkness.

"I like having some fun with the fans," Judge said. "They were heckling me pretty good out there. I'm not going to say anything to them, I gave them a little peek when I was rounding the bases. Just having some fun with them."

Judge said that he had learned a long time ago to let his actions speak for themselves, recognizing that if he had turned around and said anything to the hecklers, the verbal abuse would have increased. Judge had shut them up in the best possible way, and it was a focused intensity that Mike Batesole had seen before on the Fresno State ballfields.

"That sweet kid, that big beautiful smile that you see, don't get fooled by that," Batesole said. "This kid will blow you up in a second. This kid's got a mean streak. To play in the 150-game area with the travel they go through, and still get my 100 swings in after the game, and still get my lift in, you've got to have a little bit of a mean streak to get through those times, especially late in the season. And he's got that. You think about a guy who's got his teammates' back. At some point, there's going to be something that happens with the Red Sox or somebody else. Don't get in my boy's way. He'll be right in the middle of it."

The fans only saw the side of Judge who created indelible memories by playing catch with young glove-toting fans in the front row, both at home and on the road, and who tried to take time every day to dole out handshakes and signatures before the first pitches of games.

Autograph seekers had been a constant outside the Yankees' hotels in the "Core Four" era, but in the years since Jeter's retirement, their early-morning check-ins were sometimes witnessed only by the employee working at the front desk. In July, the Yankees were greeted by an enthusiastic group while unloading their bags at the Grand Hotel in Minneapolis, despite arriving close to four o'clock in the morning. Sleep or say hello to Aaron Judge? For those fans, it was an easy choice.

Judge didn't necessarily mind, as he'd been practicing his signature in notebooks since grade school, but his celebrity now seemed irreversible. Rob Refsnyder recalled one midsummer evening in Toronto when he, Brett Gardner, Chase Headley, Matt Holliday, and Judge attempted to go out to dinner. The players' meal was continually interrupted by visitors seeking some time with Judge, who smiled and exchanged pleasantries with all. Still, the next time Refsnyder and Judge broke bread, they did so in the privacy of Judge's hotel room.

"He's charismatic. Fans are really drawn to him," Refsnyder said. "There's something about Aaron. I feel like whenever we go out and try to get something to eat, he can't really mix into the crowd. That dinner wasn't very quiet, but he's really gracious. I think he's always going to have to deal with that, being the biggest guy in the room."

Everyone seemed to want a piece of Judge, and the deep-pocketed crowd was especially willing to pony up for the privilege. In July, a rare 2013 Bowman rookie card autographed by Judge sold for $14,655 on eBay ($350 less than the sticker price to drive a 2017 Ford Fiesta off the lot). Weeks later, the jersey that Judge used in his first major league game on August 13, 2016, sold at auction for an astounding $157,366, making it the most expensive game-worn jersey from any major U.S. sport over the past fifteen years.

By the time Judge homered in three straight games from July 4 through

7, the craze was officially in full swing. He garnered 4,448,702 All-Star votes, becoming the first Yankee since Jeter in 2009 to lead the American League, and at age twenty-five was the youngest player to lead the AL in voting since a twenty-four-year-old Ken Griffey Jr. did so in 1994.

The reward came in the form of a trip to Miami for the All-Star Game, where Judge was joined by four of his teammates: Dellin Betances, Starlin Castro, Gary Sanchez, and Luis Severino, all of whom were selected to the Midsummer Classic via the player ballot.

"It's incredible," Judge said. "I get a chance to play in front of the best fans every night at Yankee Stadium. Having their support through these first couple of months has been incredible. They've really motivated our team and they've helped this team a lot. They're always supporting us, so I've got to thank them."

Arguably the game's biggest home run hitting attraction by this point, Judge paced the majors with thirty bombs, and his stunning batting practice displays made him a natural fit to participate in the Home Run Derby. Major League Baseball had invited Judge and Sanchez to take part weeks earlier, but both held off on confirming their attendance. They'd later say that they were waiting to make sure that they were actually selected to the All-Star team, though that was largely a formality in Judge's case.

When Indians bench coach Brad Mills announced the AL's lineup for the All-Star Game, filling in while manager Terry Francona recovered from a heart procedure, Mills called Judge "one of the best stories in Major League Baseball" and said that he had no choice but to hit Judge third in the exhibition. Mills, like the audience at home, wanted to see Judge bat in the first inning.

The real draw, of course, was Judge's participation in the Derby, which preceded the Midsummer Classic by a day. The events that would take place at Marlins Park on the unforgettable evening of July 11, 2017, cemented Judge's starring role on the national stage, prompting Commissioner Rob Manfred to wonder if his sport was watching a young Yankee on the verge of greatness.

"Aaron Judge has been absolutely phenomenal," Manfred said, speaking during a day-after luncheon with the members of the Baseball Writers' Association of America. "There is no other word to describe it. He is a tremendous talent on the field. A really appealing off-the-field personality. The kind of player that can become the face of the game."

CHAPTER 10

MIAMI HEAT

Aaron Judge was beginning to perspire as he anchored his size seventeen cleats into the artificial turf of a batting cage, concealed from view under the field-level seats of Marlins Park, steps away from the visiting clubhouse. As he swung his bat with lethal force, mashing ball after ball into the protective netting surrounding him, the rhythmic practice hacks were interrupted by waves of thunderous applause that leaked through the ceiling and walls.

Judge moved his eyes toward a mounted television screen, and for an instant, he wondered if the in-house ESPN feed had become stuck on a looped replay of the same drive. The on-screen graphic that charted Justin Bour's growing tally in the Home Run Derby said otherwise, and Judge allowed himself a brief chuckle.

"This is going to be tough," he told himself, "but we'll see what happens."

An annual highlight of Major League Baseball's All-Star Game celebration, the Home Run Derby matches eight of the game's top power hitters in a single-elimination, three-round bracket format. Each player is given four minutes to hit as many home runs as possible, with thirty bonus seconds awarded if a homer is hit farther than 440 feet.

The buzz leading into the 2017 event had been an anticipated final-round showdown between Judge and the Marlins' Giancarlo Stanton, a pair of hulking power hitters who seemed as though they had been crafted out of the same machine. Each featured a physique that appeared more appropriate for professional football or basketball than for baseball: Judge stood six-foot-seven and 282 pounds, while Stanton was listed at six-foot-six and 245 pounds.

In fact, as he prepared to defend a Derby title that he'd earned during the 2016 festivities in San Diego, Stanton had remarked that Judge was "like the twin you've never met."

"The resemblance is insane," Stanton said. "Everyone wants us to hate each other, but we're so similar."

Bour, a twenty-nine-year-old first baseman for the hometown Marlins, had seemed to be an afterthought in the lead-up to the Derby. When the contest's roster of sluggers lined up on a stage prior to the event, four wearing blue American League tops and four dressed in orange for the National League, Bour and Judge had literally rubbed elbows. Photographers directed Judge and Stanton to serve as towering book-ends around Bour, the Dodgers' Cody Bellinger, the Rockies' Charlie Blackmon, the Twins' Miguel Sano, the Royals' Mike Moustakas, and Gary Sanchez of the Yankees, who stood directly to Stanton's right. Most eyes in the room seemed to be focused on Judge and Stanton, including those belonging to the six other contestants.

"It's going to be awesome for all of us, but I'm excited to see Giancarlo and Judge," Moustakas said.

To the chagrin of a pro-Marlins crowd that wildly cheered every mention of their players while booing all others, Sanchez defeated Stanton with a stunning first-round upset. The eighth-seeded Sanchez slugged seventeen homers, one of which measured 483 feet. Stanton fell one shy of matching the Yankees catcher, popping up on his final swing in the bonus round.

For Judge, who had hit back-to-back with Sanchez in the Yankees' minor league lineups for multiple seasons, the power display that knocked Stanton out early came as no shock.

"I was over on the sidelines," Judge said. "Watching him kind of hit one after another after another, it was impressive. I've seen Gary do that for years now, so I wasn't too surprised. Seeing him do it there on the big stage was even better."

Judge said that he had not given much thought to facing Stanton, insisting that his focus was on "trying to get out of the first round." Stanton mentioned the difficulties that came along with serving as an All-

Star ambassador after his 5:00 a.m. arrival from San Francisco, where his Marlins had wrapped up the season's first half with a win over the Giants.

Stanton had legitimate gripes, but it wasn't as though Judge and Sanchez had been sipping piña coladas on South Beach. New York headed into the break with a 45-41 record, dropping a 5–3 decision to the Brewers before their players scattered to the winds. Five were headed to Miami, the team's largest All-Star contingent since eight Bombers were selected in 2011.

Along with Dellin Betances and Luis Severino, plus infielder Starlin Castro, the Yankees travel party touched down in Miami the night before the Derby—right around the time that rapper Pitbull was thumping a blend of hip-hop and reggaeton across Biscayne Bay from the stage of a posh, sweaty All-Star Gala at the *Pérez Art Museum Miami*. Judge said that he made no effort to explore the Magic City, choosing to get as much rest as possible.

"I was thinking about a lot of things, trying to prepare," Judge said. "I'm big into preparing. I don't like being unprepared for things, so in my mind I went through all the different scenarios, what's going on for tomorrow and the next day."

He hadn't rehearsed for a situation in which Bour stole center stage, but here the lefty swinger was, crushing ball after ball over the lime green walls. A six-foot-three, 265-pound block of a man, Bour had joked that he'd need "about 100" homers to defeat Judge, and he was making a hell of a run at that round number.

As Judge watched on a high-definition TV screen, Bour paused to chomp on a donut that Stanton had procured as a mid-round snack. Maybe the sugar rush helped Bour complete his assault, which culminated in a commanding twenty-two home run lead.

Judge wiped another lather of perspiration from his brow and took a deep breath before striding toward home plate. Ascending the dugout steps, Judge reminded himself that this was supposed to be fun, and the experience already had been; he had gushed like a nervous teenager earlier in the afternoon during a chance interaction in the stadium tunnel with Giants catcher Buster Posey.

"I grew up a Giants fan in California. I've watched him for years," Judge said. "I was coming out of the bathroom and he was walking into the clubhouse. I had to stop him and say, 'Buster, I'm a huge fan.' I've had fun watching what he's doing, the way he plays on the field, the way he acts off the field. He's the true definition of a professional. He said, 'It's been fun to watch.'"

Posey was correct. Judge's thirty homers at the All-Star break were three more than the Astros' George Springer, and four more than Stanton and the Reds' Joey Votto. He'd already shattered Joe DiMaggio's record for home runs by a Yankee rookie, with DiMaggio having hit twenty-nine in 1936. Posey's parting words to Judge had been a friendly push to keep it going. As Judge rolled his bat along his right shoulder, the twenty-five-year-old took a moment to appreciate the unfamiliar surroundings.

An abstract stucco, steel, aluminum, and glass monument placed on the site of the old Orange Bowl, Marlins Park would feel out of place in any other big league city, but somehow the mix of Miami-Deco features connect with the surrounding Little Havana neighborhood. An aquarium lined with bulletproof glass resided immediately behind home plate, its tropical tenants oblivious to the madness taking place a few feet away.

With the retractable roof and left-field windows both closed, the humid summer air was blocked off in favor of a climate-controlled seventy-two degree atmosphere, providing prime conditions to launch baseballs—some flying so far, observers would wonder if they had been stitched differently than the ones used in regulation play. The left-field foul pole sat 344 feet away, the right-field foul pole measured 335 feet from home plate, with center field residing at a distance of 407 feet.

Judge planned to clear them all, and if possible, he would take aim at the garish seventy-three-foot tall sculpture standing beyond the wall in left-center field—a $2.5 million animatronic monstrosity that celebrated each Marlins homer with flashing lasers, leaping fish, and soaring birds.

Mariners first baseman Yonder Alonso had been in the clubhouse while the American League players were trying to rest in advance of their rounds, some taking practice swings in the batting cage, as Judge had. Alonso had some National League history, having played the first six years of his career with the Reds and Padres, and some of the participants asked him about how the ball tended to fly in Miami.

"I don't think it mattered for Judge," Alonso said afterward. "He was hitting balls to right field, center field, left field. They definitely need a bigger-sized stadium for him. It's not fair. That's just crazy. I looked at him and I'm like, 'The fact you only have thirty homers, you should already have fifty by now.' He started laughing, of course."

Judge's raw power notched some homers early in his turn at the plate, but it wasn't yet translating to a scoreboard onslaught. Many of his first swings succeeded only in sending a group of Little Leaguers scrambling across the outfield grass in pursuit. Judge called for a time out with two minutes and sixteen seconds left, trailing Bour, 22–9.

This was the second Home Run Derby that Judge had ever participated in, having tried his luck in one during the 2012 College World Series. Though Judge's physique stood out, he had not yet learned how to convert his muscle into the production he would show in the first half of the 2017 season.

"I saw the guys I was going up against," said Judge, recalling that competition during his sophomore year at Fresno State. "I think I had four home runs that year. The guys I was going up against had twenty, twenty-five. I'm like, 'You guys sure you want me out there?'"

Yes, they did, and Judge won the whole thing. Down to his final out and trailing by a homer that night in Omaha, Judge had whipped a borrowed Easton aluminum bat through the strike zone to swat four long balls on four pitches, thrilling a crowd of 22,403 that included former two-sport standout Bo Jackson. At the time, it was the largest crowd that Judge had performed in front of.

Back in Miami, Betances, twenty-nine years young and somehow the old man of the Yankees' All-Star group, made his way to home plate and offered Judge a frosty bottle of Gatorade. While Judge gulped down the electrolytes, Betances tried to deliver his best impassioned pep talk over the roar of the crowd, nearly losing his voice in the process.

Judge had suspected that he might need his teammates' help to remember—in the heat of the contest—that he had a time-out available to him.

"I had told them, if you see me get out of control, wave your arms and yell at me to calm me down so I can call time," Judge said. "When you're in the box, you forget about the time-out. I was lucky I had those guys on the sidelines to help me out a little bit."

Judge stepped into the batter's box and made eye contact with Danilo Valiente. A relatively anonymous member of the Yankees' coaching staff, the graying fifty-one-year-old typically throws 400 to 500 pitches prior to every game. His taxed right arm had served up most of Judge's batting prac-

Aaron Judge has performed in two Home Run Derby competitions, and he won them both. In 2012, Judge was the champion of the TD Ameritrade College Baseball Home Run Derby in Omaha, Nebraska.

Aaron Judge's 47 total home runs (in 76 swings) during the 2017 Home Run Derby were the most ever by a Yankee and the second-most in Derby history, behind only Giancarlo Stanton's 61 bombs in 2016.

tice homers that season, including one that destroyed a television screen in a far-off concessions area at Yankee Stadium on May 2.

"He always hits my barrel in BP, so I've just got to keep that going," Judge said. "Good speed, he's got a good tempo, and like I said, he doesn't miss my barrel. Even the days I don't feel good in the cages or in my swing, he somehow finds a way to make me feel good during BP. He finds my sweet spot."

A 2014 profile in *The New York Times* detailed Valiente's unlikely path into the clubhouse. Born in Rincón, Cuba, Valiente played in the Cuban equivalent of Triple-A baseball, where players often had to toss BP to each other. Shortly after emigrating to the United States in 2006, Valiente had been heartbroken after losing his wife, Isabel, to pancreatic cancer. He approached Mark Newman, then the Yanks' senior vice president of baseball operations, interrupting one of the executive's morning walks near the team's facility in Tampa, Florida. Rattling off his credentials, Valiente asked for an opportunity to coach. The confidence impressed Newman, who agreed to permit Valiente to observe workouts at the complex.

Hired full-time in 2007, the team's minor leaguers took a liking to Valiente, and seven years later some of them asked Brian Cashman to find a place for him on the big league staff. So now Valiente was here, digging his right hand into a bucket of baseballs, plucking out two at a time and aiming to hit a spot that would invite Judge to mash a 60-mph meatball to oblivion. The ensuing display would not soon be forgotten in Derby lore.

Crushing fourteen homers after that time-out, including a 501-foot blast that cleared the home run sculpture, Judge toppled the seventh-seeded Bour and quickly won over the crowd of 37,027, turning their jeers into cheers. As he had in batting practice, Judge clipped the roof with one of his drives, a feat that had been deemed to be nearly impossible by the stadium's engineers, who utilized NASA equations when plotting out the dimensions.

The highest point of the ceiling is 216 feet above second base and as such, a ground rule was added that any ball that struck the roof would be considered "in play." No player had struck the roof in the stadium's first 5½ years of service, and now Judge had hit it twice in a single day. Judge initially believed that the roof ball had been a homer, but since it landed in the outfield grass, the ground rule determined that it did not count. With five seconds remaining, Judge was told he had only tied Bour, so he jumped into the box and easily cleared the center-field wall with his final swing of the first round.

"My adrenaline was pumping a little bit," Judge said. "I tried to use the whole field and square up every ball I could. Since there was a clock on there, you can't really take pitches and pick one out. If it's away, I try to drive it to right. If it's middle in, I tried to hit the glass out there."

In the second round, Sanchez hit ten homers but appeared to be fatigued by the exhibition, then was eliminated when Miguel Sano connected for number eleven. The battle between Sanchez and Sano was years in the making; the Yankees had scouted both as teenagers in the Dominican Republic, debating which power-hitting phenom would constitute the better investment.

Watching on television at home, director of international scouting Donny Rowland turned to his family and reminded them, "We were very close to having both these guys."

Though Sanchez retreated to Judge's cheering section, he took pride in his respectable showing, especially because Sanchez had been placed in the impossible position of defending his presence in the Derby. Rays first baseman Logan Morrison had publicly complained that he—and not Sanchez, who had hit thirteen homers after missing most of the season's first month with a right biceps strain—should be participating. Sanchez deflected the controversy.

"It's an honor to participate in the event," Sanchez said. "It's not my fault that he didn't get selected."

While Morrison stewed, Judge trounced Bellinger with a baker's dozen of homers—including blasts of 501, 504, and 513 feet—before knocking out the son of the former Yankees utility infielder with a 507-foot drive to left field. The 507 and 513-foot drives were the longest home runs ever tracked by MLB's Statcast system; no other Derby participant cleared 500 feet in the 2017 event.

"If he had a full round, he'd probably hit another twenty," said the twenty-two-year-old Bellinger, who had handicapped his chances of winning a mano-a-mano showdown against Judge at "negative twelve."

Watching from a seat in front of the dugout, Betances stood up and placed both hands upon his backward cap, screaming with disbelief. The Yankees' players knew that Judge was capable of putting on a show like this, but he was actually living up to the hype.

Gary Sanchez hit 17 home runs in the opening round of the 2017 Home Run Derby, stunning defending champion Giancarlo Stanton (16). Sanchez was eliminated by Miguel Sano in the semi-finals.

Aaron Judge celebrates his Home Run Derby title with teammates Starlin Castro, Dellin Betances, and Luis Severino. "I just think of myself as a little kid from Linden, California, getting to live a dream right now," Judge said.

"He's a kid at heart, man," Betances said. "He's a good dude. He's very deserving and I'm very happy for him. It's hard when you've got to come through with all that pressure. He handled it very well. Judge came through and he did it. It's unbelievable."

The final round seemed anticlimactic, and Judge tried to cheer on Sano, who seemed to be gassed. Judge slammed eleven homers to win it, ending his barrage with a minute and fifty-three seconds still on the clock.

"He's an animal," Sano said. "The first time I saw Aaron Judge hit BP, I could tell he was a monster."

Charlie Blackmon had hung around to watch after Bellinger knocked him out in the first round, and the Rockies star marveled at how quiet and simple Judge's approach seemed to be, remarking, "He looks like a contact hitter trapped in an ogre's body."

Stacked end-to-end, Judge's homers traveled a total distance of 3.9 miles and would have reached from home plate into nearby Biscayne Bay. In all, Judge had taken seventy-six swings and cranked forty-seven homers, the second-highest total in Derby history.

"The biggest thing is how long my barrel stays in the zone," Judge said. "The last couple of years, the path of my barrel has been in and out of the zone. This offseason, I worked on basically trying to lengthen my swing. I wanted to get the bat in the zone early and keep it in there for a long time. If I do that, my room for error is pretty large."

The first rookie to win the Derby outright (Wally Joyner of the Angels was a co-champion in 1986), Judge hit sixteen homers with exit velocities of 115 mph or harder. The performance wowed Judge's peers, including the Mariners' Robinson Cano, who won the Derby while representing the Yankees in 2011 at Arizona's Chase Field.

"I've never seen anything like that," Cano said. "Not only the home runs, but to go opposite field so many times. He made this ballpark look like nothing. I thought I'd seen it all before, but he's something else. He didn't even look tired."

A grin spilled across Judge's face as he and Valiente stood in front of home plate, greeted by Joe Torre—seven years removed from filling out his final big-league lineup card and now spending his days serving as MLB's chief baseball officer. Torre handed Judge a silver trophy that depicted two bats forming an off-center X.

"I'll tell you, Aaron, that's quite a show," Torre said. "You used every bit of the ballpark. Congratulations, and a well-earned honor right here. Nice going."

Judge shook Torre's hand and offered a wink before he and Valiente posed for photographs, with Judge chomping on a wad of gum and using his left biceps to again mop excess moisture from his forehead.

He made his way to a tiny interview room in the bowels of the stadium, where his parents proudly watched their adopted son patiently answer questions in a measured cadence that had already earned comparisons to Derek Jeter—arguably the highest praise that can be lavished upon any young Yankee.

As Judge thanked the press and stepped away from the podium, he intended to disappear into the night, celebrating his victory with Mom and Dad as though it had been a Little League game or American Legion contest in his sleepy hometown. It seemed too good to be true.

"I just think of myself as a little kid from Linden, California, getting to live a dream right now," Judge said.

CHAPTER 11

ACES HIGH

At first blush, Pedro Martinez and the Yankees should mix like water and oil, but they are inextricably linked on the sides of baseball's greatest rivalry. It was during a bench-clearing fracas in Game 3 of the 2003 American League Championship Series that Martinez instantly drew the ire of every Yankees fan in the tri-state area, sidestepping a charge by Don Zimmer before tossing the seventy-two-year-old bench coach to the infield grass at Fenway Park.

One year later, Martinez was in the bowels of Fenway when he uttered a phrase that would trail him for the rest of his life. Having been crushed by the Yankees for a second consecutive start, Martinez glumly remarked, "What can I say? Just tip my cap and call the Yankees my daddy." He'd also colorfully left no doubt about how he would have handled a hypothetical encounter with Babe Ruth.

"Wake up the damn Bambino. Maybe I'll drill him in the ass," Martinez had said.

Martinez's Red Sox got the last laugh in 2004, coming back from a 3–0 deficit in the American League Championship Series, but the Yankees prevailed when they faced a fading thirty-seven-year-old Martinez pitching for the Phillies in the decisive Game 6 of the 2009 World Series. Martinez would later claim that some of his Yankee-baiting had been for show; as a member of the Expos in the mid-1990s, he had hoped for a trade that would send him to the Bronx. Instead, Martinez settled for the role of visiting villain, and he played it well.

"The Yankees' fans are really good at that, trying to intimidate you as a Red Sox [player] when you came over," Martinez said. "They wanted to intimidate you as an opposition. But deep in their heart they appreciate baseball, they appreciate everything you do. They recognize greatness."

Given the trajectory of his career arc, the Hall of Famer never would have anticipated that he would be assigned a pivotal role in the development of the Yankees' next ace. Like most young pitchers in the Dominican Republic, Luis Severino had marveled at Martinez's tempo, his fearlessness, his willingness to pitch inside. Now, as Severino faced a career crossroads in the winter of 2016–2017, he was about to call upon his idol for help.

Through a mutual friend, Severino was able to score a working telephone number for Martinez. He dialed the digits, nervously shifting his weight as the line rang, and was thrilled when Martinez agreed to clear his calendar. The first time that they met in Santo Domingo, Martinez told Severino to meet at 2:00 p.m.; Severino was on the field at Estadio Quisqueya by noon, not wanting to miss his window.

"Pedro is a really nice guy, [being] available to work with me," Severino said. "That's very cool, very nice. I called him and he said, 'Yes, of course, I can help you.'"

Martinez had an advanced student on his hands. After Severino accepted the Yankees' $225,000 contract offer, turning down previous bids from the Marlins and Rockies, the whip-armed right-hander rewarded the investment by rocketing through the lower levels of the farm system, making his name in the organization quickly.

Debuting with the Yankees' Dominican Summer League affiliate at age eighteen, Severino recorded an unremarkable 6.3 strikeouts per nine innings against similarly inexperienced talent, but he showed good command of the strike zone by walking 2.7 per nine innings. The Yankees worked on refining Severino's game, with increased weight training and a clean delivery helping to bump his fastball to 95 mph the next spring.

They assigned Gil Patterson, then the team's minor league pitching coordinator, to instruct Severino how to throw a changeup that would keep hitters off balance at the higher levels. Donny Rowland, who hammered out the deal that made Severino a Yankee—a pact agreed upon in the dugout of the team's Dominican Republic facility—said that they'd signed the hurler based upon his fastball and slider.

"He didn't really have a change," Rowland said. "We asked him to throw it a couple of times and he had action to it, but his arm speed was still too firm. Our player development people have done a great job with changeups, so I wasn't concerned about that."

In the final days of spring training 2012, Will Kuntz—then the Yankees' director of pro scouting—made the forty-five-mile trek from Tampa to the Pirate City complex in Bradenton, Florida, intending to perform some internal evaluations as the Yankees sent out some of their youngest prospects against the Pirates' lower level minor leaguers. What Kuntz saw that afternoon had seemed largely unremarkable, and he once told the *New York Post* that he braced for more of the same when Severino walked to the mound.

Dutifully raising his radar gun, Kuntz peered at the diminutive pitcher's motion, then expressed surprise as Severino fired a fastball across the outside corner of home plate. Strike one registered at 95 mph. Kuntz turned to the person next to him, a Pirates minor leaguer charting pitches, and asked for confirmation. The prospect nodded. Kuntz rebooted his radar gun, trained it upon the field again and was rewarded with a 94 mph reading.

Severino hit 95 mph with his third pitch, then snapped off a hard slider that left the batter flailing weakly for strike three. Kuntz's eyes widened. This was a special combination of arm strength, a smooth delivery and two plus pitches with command. Even better, he was already a Yankee. Kuntz watched some more, then hustled to the privacy of his car to alert Cashman and Billy Eppler.

"I just saw our best pitching prospect," Kuntz told Cashman.

Cashman was pleased, but not completely surprised. He'd received a call from Rockies GM Dan O'Dowd about Severino earlier that spring; Colorado had pursued Severino with fervor and he was still on the organization's mind. The Yankees weren't tempted to discuss a trade, but the Rockies' interest spoke to the value that opponents saw in Severino.

After being promoted to Class-A Charleston in 2013, the nineteen-year-old found that the challenges of facing professional hitters paled in comparison to the adjustments that were necessary to live on his own in the United States. In Tampa, Gulf Coast League players are provided with breakfast, lunch, and dinner, as well as bus transportation between the ballfields and the hotel.

Severino learned that no such amenities were provided in the South Atlantic League, so he had to learn how to do his own grocery shopping. He took crash courses via FaceTime from his mother and wife, Rosmaly.

Before long, Severino and four of his teammates would take turns cooking and doing dishes, seasoning meat and rice with whatever spices they could find. Al Pedrique, Charleston's manager that year, said that despite with the improving culinary skills, Severino still had a long way to go.

"You could tell that he wasn't ready," Pedrique said. "He was a young kid playing in front of crowds, night games, stuff like that. He realized that he was basically on his own and he needed to take care of himself off the field. That's something that took him some time, to feel comfortable about taking care of himself off the field."

Pedrique said that he saw Severino gaining comfort near the end of the season. Working diligently to learn English, Severino sometimes trailed a group of his teammates to a restaurant and let the American players order first, then tried to attach the word he'd heard to the food that arrived. There were many trips to McDonald's and Burger King, and the first vocabulary words that stuck for Severino were "pizza" and "chicken sandwich."

Re-runs of *Friends* also helped; Severino is one of several big leaguers from Latin America who discovered the long-running NBC sitcom could serve as a resource to pick up on the nuances of the English language. He laughed often, identifying Matt LeBlanc's dim-witted but lovable Joey Tribbiani as his favorite character.

In 2013, Luis Severino arrived in Charleston, South Carolina, wielding a fastball that approached the triple digits and a biting slider. The prospect's biggest adjustments would take place away from the ballpark.

"How *you* doin'?" Severino would repeat.

To his teammates, Severino's electric fastball and smooth mechanics transcended any language barriers. Tyler Wade played in the infield behind Severino during his 2014 season in Charleston, and was one of many teammates who marveled at his dominance.

"I was like, 'This guy is throwing 100 [mph],' and in Low-A guys aren't really commanding their pitches," Wade said. "Playing up the middle, I could see what signs were put down, and every time he'd get a sign down, he would literally hit the glove. I was like, 'This is unbelievable.'"

In August 2015, the Yankees summoned Severino to the majors after a late-season injury to Michael Pineda. The boy who'd treasured the Yankees cap given to him by his father in the Dominican was now a young man issued a fresh New Era 59/50 model by the team, which he tugged toward his ears as he made his first walk to the mound at Yankee Stadium. Boston was the opponent that night, and thrilled by the opportunity to face fellow countrymen David Ortiz and Hanley Ramirez, Severino held his own by striking out seven over five innings in a 2–1 loss.

"That young kid, he's got good stuff, man," Ortiz said that night. "I think he's going to be pretty good. I think at the end of the game he was missing location a little bit, but other than that, his stuff is very explosive."

Making 11 starts at the end of that season, Severino experienced near-instant success, finishing 5-3 with a 2.89 ERA while helping the team reach the American League Wild Card game. That prompted the Yankees to guarantee Severino a place in the rotation at the beginning of the 2016 season, but he stumbled mightily, going 0-8 with an 8.50 ERA in 11 starts while bouncing between the disabled list, the minors, and finally the bullpen. Severino seemed to have lost trust in his changeup, and he had returned to being a more predictable fastball-slider pitcher. Opponents feasted, batting .337 off Severino in those starts.

"His command wasn't as good and people saw it, especially in our division," Joe Girardi said. "They knew who he was and they knew that he had a good fastball and a good slider, and so when you're trying to get through a lineup a second and third time, you have to incorporate more than two pitches or you'd better be really, really good at locating your other two."

The demotion was a wakeup call for Severino; instead of flying with the Yankees and staying at first-class hotels, he had returned to a world of eight hour bus rides that ended in the parking lots of the Fairfield Inns of the International League. Instructed to keep working on the changeup while with Triple-A Scranton/Wilkes-Barre, Severino went 8-1 with a 3.61 ERA in 13 games (12 starts), though he would later say that the pitch still didn't feel quite right.

The Yankees called Severino up on July 25 as a reliever, and after two more tries in the rotation, decided to keep him in the bullpen for the rest of the season. He was 3-0 with a 0.39 ERA in eleven relief appearances, striking out 25 in 23⅓ innings, but both Severino and the Yankees still believed that his future would—and should—be in the starting rotation.

"2016, in the sample that he had, it was not something that you all of a sudden just pivot," Cashman said. "This guy has the potential to be an ace and then 11 starts later, at age twenty-two, you're going to all of a sudden just throw that out the door and say that's not the case anymore? It was more of the noise that comes with being in a big market and trying to win. Development involves patience and he had to go through that process, for whatever reason."

The Yankees had some theories. Cashman said that Severino may have hit the weights too fervently in the winter of 2015–2016, costing him flexibility. Pitching coach Larry Rothschild instructed Severino to lose some of that muscle mass, which they believed bumped up the velocity on his fastball *and* his changeup, eliminating the separation that permits a pitcher to fool big-league hitters. Severino reported to spring training at 216 pounds, down ten from the previous September, and said that he intended to win a spot in the rotation.

"I didn't like the bullpen," Severino said. "I always said I wanted to be a starter, and I went into the offseason determined to work to earn a spot. You can't be a starter with two pitches. You have to have more than two pitches to be a starter."

Unlike in 2016, there would be no guarantees. Cashman said that he viewed Severino as competing against Luis Cessa, Chad Green, Bryan Mitchell, and Adam Warren to fill the final two rotation spots, and if Severino was unable to win a spot, he would return to starting at the minor league level. That wasn't going to happen. While Severino valued Rothschild's input, he also suspected that someone of Pedro Martinez's pedigree would have something useful to add.

"He figured we were very similar," Martinez told *Newsday*. "He idolized me when I was pitching and he was a kid watching me at home. And he figured we look alike a lot and he wanted to actually correct some of the things that he was doing wrong, and I was able to help him out."

The day of their first winter workout, Martinez had watched Severino throw on flat ground, then immediately dug into Severino's mechanics, mound presence, and poise. Martinez observed that Severino seemed to sometimes lose his rhythm, then coached Severino to throw his changeup from the same angle as his fastball, something that Severino had tried without success to fix during the 2016 season.

A comparison of Severino's motion between the 2016 and 2017 seasons reveals a subtle but important difference. When Severino started his motion in 2016, his arms sat belt-high, pushing both arms away from his body before moving his right arm back. In 2017, he still kept his hands belt-high, but moved his hands only slightly forward before moving his right arm back.

"I think that was the change that I made for this season, my mechanics," Severino said. "[Martinez] told me that, if I change my mechanics a little bit, I'll be more consistent in the strike zone."

When Girardi learned that Severino had tapped Martinez as a resource, he applauded the pitcher's resourcefulness.

"Pedro had outstanding command of his fastball, an outstanding breaking ball, and an outstanding changeup," Girardi said. "He had different weapons to get anyone out and he had more than one swing-and-miss pitch. I think anytime you have an opportunity to work with someone of his caliber who really knew how to pitch, that pitched inside very effectively, went deep into games—the mindset is so important in developing a pitcher like that."

That was the poised approach that Severino brought to New York to begin his first full big-league season, determined not to let this second chance slip away. After taking a no-decision in his first start of the season at Baltimore, Severino put it all together on April 13 against the Rays in New York, striking out 11 while holding the Rays to two runs and five hits over seven innings. Martinez praised Severino's slider and tempo from afar, tweeting, "So proud of this kid."

Severino had absorbed a crucial lesson: velocity might get you to the majors, but intelligence was what kept you there. In a remarkable turnaround, Severino developed into the Yankees' best homegrown starter since Ron Guidry, going 14-6 with a 2.98 ERA in 31 starts.

The twenty-three-year-old ranked third in the American League in ERA, fourth in strikeouts (230), ninth in innings pitched (193⅓), and tied for ninth in wins. His 10.71 strikeouts per nine innings were the highest in franchise history, and Severino's teammates often remarked that they were glad they didn't have to dig in against him.

"It's filthy," Judge said. "When he's on, he's got the good fastball command and his off-speed pitches are unhittable. That's what I saw in the minor leagues for so many years. It's just he's attacking hitters, using his off-speed at the right time and that's just what he does."

Named to his first career All-Star team, Severino recorded his first five career double-digit strikeout games, becoming the second AL pitcher in the last forty-one years to post a sub-3.00 ERA with at least 225 strikeouts at age twenty-five or younger. The other was Roger Clemens, who did it in 1986 to win both the AL MVP and the Cy Young Award.

"We saw a bunch of really good starts pretty early on," Girardi said. "[In 2016] he made some decent starts, but didn't get any run support and I think it frustrated and it snowballed for him. He was dominant early on, and he was using his changeup, fastball. He was using up and down in the zone, where a lot of times last year he was mostly up and that's when he was getting hit."

Rowland had to be impressed by how far Severino had come. Severino's fastball had been sitting between 89 and 93 mph on the afternoon his first professional contract was negotiated in December 2011, and now he was consistently among the hardest throwers in the majors, maintaining his strength deep into starts. In 2017, Severino equaled the highest average four-seam fastball velocity among big league starting pitchers, tying the Reds' Luis Castillo (97.5 mph).

"We projected him with two plus pitches, an average pitch and above-average control, but nobody predicted the highest velocity fastball of all starting pitchers in the American League," Rowland said. "That's Mother Nature, that's strength and conditioning, performance science, his personal work ethic, and commitment to excellence. I give him a heck of a lot of credit, I give our scouts a heck of a lot of credit. I give player development a heck of a lot of credit. It's a team effort."

Severino's sixteen starts of one run or fewer led the majors, coming in a season in which Severino defeated Chris Sale, former Cy Young Award winners Rick Porcello and Felix Hernandez, and 2016 AL Rookie of the

Luis Severino's 2.98 ERA in 2017 was the lowest by a qualified Yankees pitcher since David Cone (2.82) and Andy Pettitte (2.87) in 1997.

Year Michael Fulmer. Third baseman Todd Frazier said that one of the aspects of Severino's games that his infielders appreciated the most was the speed with which he worked.

"When he's working fast and he's getting the pitch, when Sanchez puts whatever pitch he puts down, he's like, 'Let's go, let's do it,'" Frazier said. "That's when he's more devastating. That's the best thing that can happen for us. Whether he's giving up hits or not, we're still in the game defensively because of how fast his pace is, for sure."

CC Sabathia said that while the term "ace" tends to be thrown around loosely in many instances, Severino had earned it.

"He's got the stuff. His stuff is very electric," Sabathia said. "His changeup has been a big key for him this year, throwing that into the mix. He throws 100 mph the whole game with a nasty slider and he throws that changeup in there."

When the Yankees qualified for postseason play, it spoke volumes that Girardi set his rotation to have Severino start the win-or-go-home Wild Card game against the Twins. It was the first playoff game of Severino's life at any level, and though his effort would end far too quickly, no one doubted that Severino would have more opportunities to showcase his stuff.

CHAPTER 12

THE FUTURE IS NOW

The Yankees repeatedly downplayed the suggestion that 2017 was intended to be a rebuilding year, but there was ample evidence of how young they were. Joe Girardi's lineup card for the April 2 season opener at Tropicana Field featured Gary Sanchez, Greg Bird, Ronald Torreyes, and Aaron Judge in the batting order—all of whom would still be subject to an under-twenty-five penalty fee if they had attempted to rent a car before leaving the Sunshine State.

It was the third time in franchise history that the Opening Day lineup featured four players under the age of twenty-five. In 1932, the Yankees had sent out a batch of kids: pitcher Lefty Grove, catcher Bill Dickey, third baseman Frankie Crosetti, and right fielder Ben Chapman. It had also happened in 1914 (first baseman Harry Williams, third baseman Fritz Maisel, shortstop Roger Peckinpaugh, and center fielder Bill Holden), and at twenty-eight years and 334 days, the average age of the Yanks' Opening Day roster was its youngest in at least twenty-five years.

Beginning his tenth year as the Yankees' manager, Girardi had grown accustomed to peeking around his office doorway to see a parade of established stars walking past, marching toward their round career milestone numbers and compelling cases for enshrinement in Cooperstown. Some of them, like the "Core Four," had been teammates of Girardi. Others had been opponents. This was different for the veteran manager, surveying a crowd of fresh faces who could have been asking their parents for Beanie Babies or Tickle Me Elmos when Girardi was squatting behind the plate.

"We haven't been this young in a long time, probably not since maybe 1996," Girardi said. "It was a great mixture of youth and veteran players and guys that had a significant impact, guys that the fans recognized when they came up as homegrown and fell in love with players who did wonderful things. I think it's going to be a very exciting year."

It didn't start that way. The Yankees dropped four of their first five games to the Rays and Orioles, and the mood in the visiting clubhouse at Camden Yards took another hit after the Saturday afternoon contest, when Sanchez sustained a right biceps strain after fouling off a 97-mph Kevin Gausman fastball. Their starting catcher, the AL's most dangerous bat over the final two months of the previous season, would miss twenty-one games.

The Yankees were able to pull the emergency brake in the April 9 series finale; trailing by a run in that matinee, Judge tied the game with an eighth-inning homer off Mychal Givens and the Yanks added four runs in the ninth to secure a happy flight home.

"I think the turning point for us was in Baltimore," Chase Headley said. "We had a chance to win both of the first two games there, and they came back to get us late. I thought that's where it really started and we got off to a great start at home, and really played well the whole homestand."

Taking the field for the Yankee Stadium home opener, the Bombers swept both the Rays and Cardinals in a pair of three-game series before taking two of three from the White Sox. The Yankees packed for their second road trip having celebrated their best fifteen-game start in more than a decade, fattening their record with an 8-1 homestand that blended dominant starting pitching with jaw-dropping thump from the big bats.

It had taken until the season's twenty-seventh game for the 2016 Yankees to post their tenth victory, when the calendar had already flipped into May. As the Yankees arrived in Boston for a rain-shortened two-game series later in the month, they had sent the message that they were not going to be pushovers in the AL East race.

"My brother called me after the first couple of weeks of the season and said that I sounded like I'd been shot out of a cannon," said Suzyn Waldman, the Yankees' longtime radio broadcaster. "It's really changed everything around here. You smile more. They're having fun. You're watching them learn on the field. It's just so refreshing. They laugh. They actually sit in the dugout and they laugh. They have a good time.

"I think the best part of it is they enjoy each other. For example, when I've talked to Sanchez about Severino, they talk about when they were in A-ball. I haven't heard those conversations since Posada and Mariano were making fun of the skinny shortstop who arrived in 1991. We haven't seen that. They all know each other very well. Judge and Bird, you listen to them have conversations. They go back, they're all so young. Nobody is over twenty-five in the whole group. It's tremendous fun."

Masahiro Tanaka had another statement that he wanted to make. The Red Sox's acquisition of Chris Sale had been the biggest move of the baseball offseason, popularizing the belief that Boston was going to be an unstoppable juggernaut. Cashman had wandered into that arena, opining in December that baseball had its new answer to the NBA's star-studded Golden State Warriors.

As Sale prepared to face the Yankees for the first time as a member of the Red Sox, having compiled an 0.91 ERA and 42 strikeouts in his first four starts for Boston, Tanaka privately told pitching coach Larry Rothschild that he intended to "beat the odds" against Sale.

Feeding the Red Sox a steady diet of two-seamers, cutters, splitters, and sinkers that were popped up or pounded into the ground, Tanaka out-performed Sale in a ninety-seven-pitch gem, recording his second career shutout in a 3–0 New York win. It would not be the last time that the Yankees watched Tanaka raise his game against an intimidating opponent.

"He mentioned that before the game, that he's pitching against a really good pitcher, one of the better pitchers in baseball," Rothschild said. "He was well aware of it. Any pitcher that's a veteran and has had a lot of success is going to feel that way. You just rise to the challenge. You may win, you may lose, but you're ready for it."

The Yankees could shut down teams, and they could also outslug them. The next night in New York, the Yankees rallied from an eight run deficit to stun the Orioles with a 14–11 victory, with Matt Holliday hitting a three-run, walk-off shot in the 10th inning. Judge homered twice, Jacoby Ellsbury hit a grand slam, and Starlin Castro forced extra innings with a two-run shot.

Something special was happening, and Judge voiced the opinion that the big kids had been showing their baby Bronx brothers the way.

"I think it's just the veteran squad we've got on this team," Judge said. "I've learned a lot just watching them; how they prepare for the games, how they handle themselves during the game. We've kind of fed off Headley and Castro and Holliday. The at-bats they were having were amazing and fun to watch."

The Yankees finished April with a 15-8 record, welcoming shortstop Didi Gregorius back to the lineup for the final three games of the month. Though Greg Bird was unable to recapture his spring performance before landing on the disabled list, the Yankees kept rolling.

An early May series at Chicago's Wrigley Field cemented their never-say-die nature. On a frigid forty-five degree afternoon during which the wind blowing in from Lake Michigan necessitated ski caps and scarves, the Yankees had been iced over the first eight innings by Cubs pitching. Down to their final out, Brett Gardner dug out an 83-mph Hector Rondon slider and launched it over the bricks and ivy in right field for a three-run homer, giving the Yankees a 3–2 lead.

Gardner screamed as he sprinted around the bases and Aroldis Chapman—who'd received his World Series ring from the Cubs in an on-field ceremony a few hours earlier—rapidly warmed up to lock down the save.

"I think [I started to believe] maybe in April," Gardner said. "We got off to a really, really good start without Didi, without Gary Sanchez. Seeing the way Severino was throwing the ball, seeing the start that Judge got off to, we knew we had a chance to be better than we expected to be. We lost [Michael] Pineda [to Tommy John surgery], but for the most part we've kept the majority of our team healthy throughout the course of the season."

To complete a sweep of the Cubs on May 8, the Yankees played another of their most memorable games, though it required all night to finish. Chapman coughed up a 4–1 lead in the ninth inning and the clubs played another nine innings—a videotaped Harry Caray led the fourteenth-inning stretch, singing 'Take Me Out to the Ballgame'—before Aaron Hicks finally broke the tie, sliding home safely on a Castro fielder's choice. The six hour, five minute contest featured more than 500 pitches from fifteen pitchers, with the clubs combining for forty-eight strikeouts, a new major league record.

"It showed that we're going to grind out games," Hicks said. "We're going to fight to the end. They're a great team, but we're a good team too."

Though he'd finished second in the spring right field battle to Judge, Hicks began to fulfill his five-tool promise, joining the growing crowd of cost-controllable twenty-somethings. An introspective switch-hitter with a cannon for a right arm from Long Beach, California, Hicks had landed in MLB after first envisioning his future in the PGA, spending much of his childhood driving and putting on the courses once traversed by a rising Tiger Woods.

Hicks' father, Joseph, knew the disappointment that baseball could deliver all too well, his own career having stalled out in Double-A after seven seasons in the minors with the Padres and Royals, plus one more in Mexico. Hicks was born seven years later, and when his friends urged him to join the local Little League, his father told the natural right-hander he could play only if he agreed to bat left-handed.

The challenge did not steer Hicks away from baseball, improving his skills and helping him become a coveted prospect at Woodrow Wilson High School in Long Beach. Though Hicks stopped playing golf competitively at age thirteen, he still plays often during the offseason and has drawn curious glances from other golfers when showing off his ability to hit from both sides of the tee—thanks, Dad.

After batting .191 in his first 95 games as a Yankee, Hicks turned it on late in 2016. He had struggled to adapt to a part-time role, and believed that his consistency improved because the late July trades permitted him to log regular playing time.

"I always said that this kid had a chance to be a hell of a player," said Ron Gardenhire, who managed Hicks in his first two big league seasons and piloted the Tigers in 2018. "He was just a young guy that loved to be there, but he never understood what it took to be a big leaguer. I'm happy for him. I hope he continues it."

A first-round selection of the Twins in 2008, Hicks' tendency to rely on his natural talent exasperated the organization. There were occasions when Hicks arrived at the stadium not knowing if they were facing a left-hander or a right-hander that night, an inexcusable occurrence in an era where hours upon hours of scouting video are made available to every player.

There was evidence to suggest that Hicks had been hurried to the big leagues by Minnesota. Frustrated by his struggles against right-handed pitching, Hicks had entertained giving up switch-hitting before Hall of Famer Rod Carew was summoned to talk him out of it.

"I wanted to try to something new, and I wanted to help my team win," Hicks said. "It was one of the low times of my career. Rod Carew actually called me and told me, what the heck am I doing giving up switch hitting? It's a blessing, and that I should go back and work harder at it and learn from my mistakes. And he was right. I learned from my mistakes and I'm happy that I was able to change that."

Carew and Hicks had worked out together in Southern California frequently during past offseasons. Torii Hunter, a nineteen-year big league veteran who returned to the Twins for his final season in 2015, regularly gave Hicks his version of tough love and pushed him to pay more attention to the mental side of the game.

Those flashes of progress prompted Cashman to believe that Hicks still could follow a career path similar to Jackie Bradley Jr., the talented Red Sox outfielder. Bradley hit .213 with a .638 OPS in his first 700 at-bats with Boston from 2013–2015 before breaking out as an American League All-Star in 2016.

"The talent package was recognizable and worth waiting on. Sometimes you have to walk through fire," Cashman said.

The Yankees pushed their record to 21-9 after a May 8 victory at Cincinnati, standing alone in first place by a half-game in the AL East. As the Yankees adopted Bruno Mars' funky "24K Magic" as their celebration song, thumping the track at window-rattling decibels following every victory, Girardi was ready to buy into the hot start.

"We've won in all different ways," Girardi said. "We've won in games where we haven't scored a lot of runs, we've won in games where we've scored late to take the lead. I think when you have power in your lineup like we have, you have the ability to win games and we've had to do that at times too. Our guys believe, and they should believe."

As previously mentioned, New York's June 11 matinee saw Judge hit the majors' longest homer of 2017, a 495-foot drive off the Orioles' Logan Verrett that came as part of a 14–3 victory. Judge would crush Baltimore pitching all year, and manager Buck Showalter joked that he wished the rules permitted him to position fielders in the bullpens while Judge batted.

"I can break it down all you want to, but he's a big, strong man who puts some pretty good swings on baseballs and is making guys pay for a lot of mistakes we're making," Showalter said. "I don't feel like he's picking on us. He's been doing it to everybody."

At the conclusion of the day's business, Judge led the AL in all three Triple Crown categories, batting .344 with 21 homers and 47 RBIs. Miguel

Cabrera had been the most recent big leaguer to win one, doing so in 2012 for the Tigers, but Judge said the thought hadn't crossed his mind.

"Not really, especially when you hit .179 the year before," Judge said.

After winning five of six from the Red Sox and Orioles, the Yankees traveled to the West Coast on June 12, where their record improved to 38-23 with a 5-3 victory over the Angels in Anaheim. That victory gave New York a season-high four-game lead in the AL East, but the rest of their California adventure went miserably. They dropped the next two contests to the Halos and were swept in a four-game series by the Athletics, a series marked by Matt Holliday's absence due to a mysterious illness that was later revealed to be the Epstein-Barr virus.

"The sun will come out," Dellin Betances said during the seven-game losing streak. "We haven't really been talking too much about it. We've been playing good ball. Those games, we've been close."

With Headley struggling to provide offense at third base, the Yankees thought they might have a reinforcement in Gleyber Torres, but that option was dashed by an ill-advised headfirst slide into home plate. The Yankees' top position player prospect, Torres was promoted to Triple-A shortly after vice president of baseball operations Tim Naehring passed through Trenton and reported to Cashman, "This guy is ready to go from my perspective, any time you want."

Torres continued to enjoy success against more established competition, batting .309 with two homers and 16 RBIs in 23 games in the minors' highest level, but his season ended in the fourth inning of a June 17 game in Buffalo, New York. Attempting to score from second base on a Mark Payton single to right field, Torres dove awkwardly into the plate, tearing the ulnar collateral ligament in his left (non-throwing) elbow.

The Yankees said they expected Torres to make a full recovery for spring training, but the injury dashed any chance of him making his big-league debut before 2018.

"He conquered the Eastern League for the period of time he was there, and he was starting to conquer the International League," Cashman said. "The way his trajectory was going, I think you would have seen him in the big leagues at some point. You may very well have seen him as the third baseman or the DH. It may have prevented us from trading for Todd Frazier, who knows? We never did find out, because he didn't get more time."

• • •

Ronald Torreyes delivered another season highlight on June 23, with the smallest Yankee drilling his first career walk-off hit nineteen minutes after midnight to end a 2–1, 10 inning duel against the Rangers. It was the second win in ten games for the scuffling Yanks.

The evening had featured an elite matchup between Masahiro Tanaka and Yu Darvish that was beamed to millions watching early on a Saturday morning in Japan—"Breakfast at Wimbledon; Breakfast at Yankee Stadium," Girardi had quipped. Following a 102-minute rain delay, Tanaka was ahead of the Texas lineup all night, registering two first-pitch balls. Tanaka needed an outing like that one. He'd been 0-6 with an 8.91 ERA in his previous seven starts, permitting 33 earned runs in 33⅓ innings.

"I was excited going into the game," Tanaka said, "but once the game starts, then you're not actually going against Darvish. You're going against the Texas lineup. My focus was on every batter, every pitch. I think I was able to throw with good conviction. I'm really happy with the results."

A Gary Sanchez passed ball allowed the Rangers to grab a late lead, but Gardner answered with a ninth inning homer and Sanchez atoned with a one out hit in the 10th, scoring the winning run on Torreyes' clean single to center field.

Masahiro Tanaka signed with the Yankees in 2014 after a standout career in Japan, where he was 99-35 with a 2.30 ERA in 175 games for the Tohoku Rakuten Golden Eagles.

"I just have the mindset that at any given moment, they're going to need me and I've got to be ready," Torreyes said through an interpreter.

Five days later, Miguel Andujar went from the airport to the history books, becoming the first Yankee to collect at least three hits and three RBIs in his debut as he powered a 12–3 victory over the White Sox in Chicago. Signed out of the Dominican Republic at age sixteen, Andujar still carried some questions about his defense at third base, one week after he had been promoted from Double-A. His bat sure looked big-league ready. Stepping in as the DH in place of the ailing Holliday, the free-swinging Andujar went 3-for-4 with four runs scored, collecting a double, walk, and steal.

"I'm never going to forget this day," Andujar said through an interpreter. "Going out there for the first at-bat, I felt a little nervous. It's my first at-bat in the big leagues. Following that at-bat, everything was normal again."

The Yankees got another glimpse of the future in early July when Clint Frazier was tapped on his shoulder by RailRiders manager Al Pedrique, who led the twenty-two-year-old outfielder into the visiting manager's office at McCoy Stadium in Pawtucket, Rhode Island. As the door shut, Frazier thought to himself, "This is it. I'm going up."

Then, as Pedrique rattled off a straight-faced list of things that Frazier still needed to improve upon, Frazier wasn't quite so sure about the purpose of this chat. Frazier finally exhaled when Pedrique concluded his sermon, telling Frazier that he could begin to work on those things the next day in Houston, where he would become the latest Baby Bomber to arrive in The Show.

"It was a bittersweet moment," Frazier said. "There was a lot of truth to what he was saying; that I need to continue to work my defense, my base-running, and just focus on being a good teammate in the clubhouse, and just be all ears while I'm here. Those are things that it's not bad to be reminded on. I'm glad we had that conversation."

Reflecting on the interaction months later, Pedrique said that he sensed Frazier had put too much pressure on himself early in his Yankees tenure, trying to live up to the glowing scouting reports while proving to the organization that he was ready to play in the big leagues.

"When I told Clint, 'You've got to be a better teammate,' my point was that you've got to communicate with everybody, whether you have a good game or a bad game," Pedrique said. "It's a team. My advice to him that time was make sure you communicate with your teammates. You've got to feel like you want to be in the clubhouse. That's where you spend most of your time, with your teammates, whether you're on the road or at home. That's like your second family. So you need to open up more, you need to relax, you need to enjoy the game on the field and off the field."

Frazier credited many people, including Reggie Jackson and Matt Holliday, for helping him make the necessary adjustments to wear a big-league uniform. Holliday had spent time with Frazier during spring training, developing a friendship that kept them in text message contact during the first months of the regular season. While he tried to heed Pedrique's advice, Frazier added that he still wanted his personality to shine through on the big stage.

"I think if I clip my own wings, I'm not going to be able to play the way that I want to," Frazier said. "I think for me, as long as I can be myself without being a distraction or cause harm to the clubhouse or the team, I think I'll be in good shape."

Frazier made an immediate impact, becoming the twelfth Yankee ever to homer in his big-league debut, and the first since Tyler Austin and Judge hit their back-to-back blasts the previous August. Frazier's first hit was a sixth-inning double off Astros right-hander Francis Martes that eluded left fielder Marwin Gonzalez, sparking a five run inning.

His parents, Kim and Mark, had made the trip from Georgia for the game, and Kim shed tears when Frazier's seventh-inning line drive landed in the Crawford Boxes over the left-field wall for his first career homer. Frazier said that he gave the ball from his first hit to his mom, and the home run to his dad.

"My parents are my role models, and my dad is my hero," Frazier said. "For me, to go out there and have this kind of first game for him is really special for the whole Frazier family."

Embracing his nickname of "Red Thunder," six of Frazier's first seven hits went for extra bases. He rescued the Yankees in the ninth inning of a July 8 game against the Brewers, crushing a walk-off, three-run homer in what was Frazier's sixth career game.

"It's just cool to be on the same plane as all of these guys," Frazier said. "I keep telling people, 'I went from eating Domino's and Waffle House after the games in the minor leagues and now I'm eating steak on the plane.' It's the New York Yankees, man."

As exciting as Frazier's brand of play proved to be, he had not been the Yankees' first choice to grab a spot in the outfield. That had been Dustin Fowler, whose season cruelly ended June 29 on Chicago's South Side. As he pursued a foul pop-up down the right field line in the bottom of the first inning, Fowler's right knee slammed into an exposed metal electrical box when he flipped into the seating area. He would be diagnosed with an open rupture of his right patellar tendon.

Like Archibald "Moonlight" Graham, the turn of the century New York Giants outfielder whose one and only big-league game in 1905 inspired a character eighty-four years later in the movie *Field of Dreams*, Fowler had played defense for half of an inning without having the chance to bat. Brett Gardner said it was "one of the worst things I've seen on a baseball field," and Girardi hid his tears while he called for the cart that transported Fowler off the field.

"It just makes you sick," Judge said. "It's your debut, you're about to lead off the next inning, and something like that happens. It's tough. Especially all the hard work he's done, what he's been through, to finally get a shot up here and get the call."

The next day, the Yankees held a closed-door meeting prior to their game in Houston in which the entire team had a video chat with Fowler from his bed at Rush University Medical Center in Chicago, hours removed from surgery. New York responded with a 13–4 drubbing of the eventual AL champs, which included a Gardner grand slam and a pitcher-batter showdown between Judge and outfielder Nori Aoki, who had been summoned to the mound to save the Astros' beleaguered bullpen.

As they began their ninth-inning battle, Aoki stared at Judge from the rubber and said that he thought the slugger looked "nine or ten feet tall." Aoki reared back and floated a 78-mph fastball toward home plate, which Judge took a mighty cut at and missed, prompting a loud cackle to spill through the bars of catcher Brian McCann's mask. On the next pitch, Judge lifted a towering but routine fly to center field.

"He got me on the first one, geez," Judge said. "I swung and missed. That was my first time facing a position player. That was a little different. I had Mac behind the plate laughing at me a little bit. It was all fun. It was good. I was trying to hit one to the moon and I just missed it."

Frazier walked into the clubhouse the next day, and he was trying hard to keep the focus between the white lines. Frazier admitted having put too much pressure on himself following the July 2016 trade, when he regularly checked the Indians' box scores to see if Andrew Miller had pitched the night before.

"I tried to prove that I was the guy that I got traded for and I think I struggled doing that," Frazier said. "Early on in April I carried some of that over with me and continued to try to make the big-league club out of the first month of the season. I just needed to fail more to realize there are things I need to work on to be the player that I'm capable of being."

With 11 extra-base hits in his first 16 games, Frazier joined Joe DiMaggio as the only Yankee ever to do so, and Frazier had tallied 16 RBIs through his first 20 games. That made him the fifth player in franchise history to accomplish that feat, joining select company in Hideki Matsui, DiMaggio, Mickey Mantle, and George Selkirk.

"He's going to wear you down," Judge said. "No matter what, he's going to battle, he's going to claw, he's going to scratch…I saw that fire in his eyes. As a player, man, he's the total package. He's got speed, he's got power, he can play any outfield position."

Frazier noticed that as he garnered more big-league reps, his cell phone started lighting up with calls and texts from acquaintances from days gone by. Matt Holliday counseled Frazier to keep his inner circle small, focusing on baseball and limiting distractions. It was sage advice that Frazier followed, helping him more thoroughly enjoy the opportunity at hand.

He found a place to live in Manhattan's Financial District and spent his down time wandering the city with his girlfriend, Faith Jewkes, sampling some of the finer dining that New York had to offer. As though he were counting from one to three, the product of Logansville, Georgia—where the highest-rated eatery on Yelp is a gyro joint located next to a gas station—rattled off the names of LAVO, TAO, and Bodega Negra among the memorable restaurants he'd visited.

"It's been the best time of my life," Frazier said. "I just said to her, 'I can't believe we live in New York.' It's just a really cool experience for a young kid getting to grow up and see the bright lights. I think my taste has always liked things to be bigger. I've never liked living in a small city; I wanted to live in Atlanta. I like the faster life. I'm not a country person, even though I'm from a very country area. This is the kind of environment where I want to be."

• • •

The Yanks struggled to recapture their early-season mojo, with a crushing Aroldis Chapman blown save on July 14 at Fenway Park marking their nineteenth loss in twenty-six games. The contest dropped them into third place, 4½ games behind Boston in the AL East, and Chris Sale was set to start the following afternoon. Helped by creeping shadows across the infield, Sale's performance was as good as expected, striking out 13 over 7⅔ scoreless innings before Holliday shocked Boston with a game-tying homer off closer Craig Kimbrel in the ninth.

The Yanks would have played all night to get that win, and they almost did. Red Sox manager John Farrell protested the game after Holliday embarked on a bizarre base-running play in the 11th inning (sliding back into first base feet-first on a Jacoby Ellsbury ground ball to the right side of the infield) and Didi Gregorius cracked a go-ahead, run-scoring single in the 16th, helping to end the five-hour, fifty-minute affair.

"To win that game was really big," Holliday said. "We needed that game."

With the Yankees still very much a factor in the division race, Cashman was tethered to his cell phone in advance of the trade deadline, saying that he intended to be "careful buyers" in advance of the July 31 cutoff. A frenzied eighteen-day surge of movement added six new players to the Yankees' roster, capped by the arrival of right-hander Sonny Gray, who was viewed as the top available starting pitcher in the marketplace.

Gray's acquisition highlighted a makeover in which the Yankees brought back a pair of homegrown arms in David Robertson and Tommy Kahnle, a local product in New Jersey native and third baseman Todd Frazier, and an experienced veteran in Jaime Garcia, whose grandfather once predicted that he would someday be wearing the famed pinstripes.

The first whispers were heard prior to a July 18 game at Target Field, where the Yankees were about to play the middle game of a three-game series against the Twins. In Chicago, Frazier had been a "healthy scratch" from the White Sox lineup, and speculation followed on social media that he was being traded to the Red Sox, who were seeking a replacement for underwhelming third baseman Pablo Sandoval.

Girardi had a better source of information, speaking to Cashman from the visiting manager's office. He kept his secret close to the vest, steering his team to a 6–3 victory, but trickles of information reached the dugout by the ninth inning. The Yankees were not only adding Frazier, but they had also acquired Kahnle and Robertson in exchange for four players: right-hander Tyler Clippard, left-hander Ian Clarkin, and outfielders Tito Polo and Blake Rutherford.

"It's exciting that we did something to get better," said Chase Headley, who shifted from third base to first base in order to accommodate Frazier's arrival. "We're in a tough stretch where we're not playing great and we go out there and make a move that makes it feel like the front office and the team believes in us."

The negotiations with the White Sox had opened with the Yankees' unsuccessful pursuit of Jose Quintana, as Cashman spent months attempting to land the left-handed starter, who had been an All-Star in 2016. When Quintana was dealt instead across town to the Cubs on July 13, the White Sox circled back to the Yankees to see if a different deal could be explored, eyeing the twenty-year-old Rutherford as a centerpiece.

Cashman said that it had been difficult to part with Rutherford, a left-handed-hitting high school standout who grew up with a shrine to Jeter and the Yankees in the game room of his Simi Valley, California, home. Rutherford's talents had merited a $3.28 million signing bonus after being selected in the first round in the 2016 draft, but there was also undeniable appeal in adding Kahnle and Robertson to what was already viewed as one of the league's top bullpens.

"Selfishly, you want them all to be Yankees," said Damon Oppenheimer, who directed Rutherford's selection in the first round of the 2016 draft. "You draft them, you talk to them, you develop relationships with them. You want them all to contribute to the New York Yankees and that's what they want, but at the end of the day, it's a business. We can't control where they're going to play and who they're going to play for."

The trade delighted Robertson, who had been one of Mariano Rivera's successors before signing a four-year, $46 million contract with Chicago as a free agent following the 2014 season. Until the trade, Robertson's blown save in Jeter's final home game had been his penultimate appearance as a Yankee. The thirty-two-year-old instantly sensed a different vibe in the clubhouse, where he joked that he was "the new old guy."

"It had to get younger," Robertson said. "It couldn't get any older when I was here."

Indeed, the Yankees would use seventeen rookies by the end of the regular season, including twelve who made their big league debuts: Miguel Andujar, Garrett Cooper, Dustin Fowler, Clint Frazier, Giovanny Gallegos, Domingo German, Ronald Herrera, Kyle Higashioka, Jordan Montgomery, Caleb Smith, Tyler Wade, and Tyler Webb.

Clint Frazier had been wearing uniform No. 30, but he yielded that to Robertson, allowing the reliever to reclaim the digits that he had worn during his previous tour with the Yankees. There were some laughs heard when Frazier opted for No. 77, as he'd been involved in a minor stir earlier in the season when it was reported that he had asked someone if the Yankees ever consider un-retiring numbers. Frazier said that putting on No. 77 had nothing to do with Mickey Mantle, for whom No. 7 has been out of circulation since 1969.

"I wanted a number with seven in it," Frazier said. "There's not many available numbers and Judge wears 99, so maybe go with something like 77. I hope someone else picks up 88 in the outfield. I think it's going to look cool with me and Judge on the corners."

Todd Frazier also had to find a new uniform number, having worn No. 21 in his stints with the Reds and White Sox. While not officially retired, No. 21 has been kept largely out of circulation by the Yankees since Paul O'Neill's final game in the 2001 World Series. When reliever LaTroy Hawkins tried using it in 2008 as a tribute to Roberto Clemente, the fan reaction was so negative, Hawkins gave it up by mid-April.

Clubhouse manager Rob Cucuzza issued Frazier No. 29 upon his arrival, and though Frazier initially said that he would seek O'Neill's blessing to wear the number when the team returned home from their road trip, the conversation never took place. Frazier said that he had spoken to "a couple of guys," who convinced him that it would be better to leave the number to "The Warrior." The Yankees have retired twenty-one of their numbers for twenty-two players, including all of the single digits, but there are no plans to do so for O'Neill. He is, however, honored with a plaque in Monument Park.

There were more important numbers to consider. Though Frazier was batting .207 at the time of the trade, the Yankees' analytics department speculated that some of it might be attributed to bad luck, pointing out his bizarrely low .144 batting average on balls hit in play in White Sox home games.

A 1998 Little League World Series champion who once took the field alongside Jeter at the old Yankee Stadium (Frazier said he feels sorry for how many times Jeter has been asked about that day in the years that have followed), Frazier made the eighty-five-mile commute from his home in Toms River, New Jersey, while he and his family sought a more geographically friendly place to rest their heads.

"I'll be stuck in traffic and yelling at my steering wheel the whole time, but hopefully it's after a win, so it won't be that bad," Frazier said. "To do it every day at home for a seven to ten day home stand, it gets to be a pain in the butt."

Cashman said that the Yankees insisted upon getting Kahnle, a heat-throwing right-hander who had recorded an eye-popping 60 strikeouts against seven walks in 36 innings at the time of the trade. A product of Latham, New York, Kahnle spent his first four pro years envisioning himself running through the bullpen gate at Yankee Stadium, having been selected by the Yankees in the fifth round of the 2010 draft. That dream took a detour when Kahnle was taken by the Rockies in the 2013 Rule 5 Draft, then dealt to Chicago two years later.

"It definitely means a lot [to come back]," Kahnle said. "Growing up, a lot of my family and friends were all Yankees fans. I feel like I want to do good for them. Each day, I'm just going to come to the yard, work hard and do what I've been doing."

• • •

The Yankees returned home on July 25 for the seventy-first annual Old-Timers Day, again paying special attention to the twentieth anniversary of the 1996 World Series championship club. Standing behind the batting cage underneath blinding sun, Jorge Posada said that he could hear echoes of those winning teams in these young Yankees, who were in the middle of what would be a stretch of nine victories in eleven games.

"I see guys who are hungry. They don't quit," Posada said. "Even down six or seven runs, they still give it a fight. You don't want to throw away at-bats, and I see guys grinding at-bats. That's what we used to do back then."

Though wary of putting pressure on Girardi by comparing the current squad to his own clubs, Joe Torre agreed that the Yankees seemed to have the makings of something special.

"When I spoke with Aaron Judge early in the year, he seems to have his head screwed on right," Torre said. "He has a ton of ability and seems very grounded. I know it's fun for a manager when you see young players develop, especially in the fishbowl of New York. You have to go back to giving Brian Cashman a great deal of credit for this. I'm not sure, if George was still with us, that he would have let the Yankees do some wholesale selling of some of their veterans a couple years ago. But it certainly is paying off."

With Michael Pineda lost for the season, Cashman padded the rotation by plucking Jaime Garcia from the Twins. The left-hander had pitched only once for Minnesota following a July 24 trade with the Braves; in fact, Garcia never set foot in the home clubhouse at Target Field, as both of his trades had occurred during the same road trip. No pitcher since Gus Wehling in 1895 had made three consecutive starts for three different teams.

Acquired in exchange for pitching prospects Dietrich Enns and Zack Littell, the thirty-one-year-old Garcia was viewed as an upgrade over Luis Cessa and Caleb Smith, who had made a series of forgettable starts in Pineda's absence. As a bonus, the Twins (seven games off the pace in the AL Central and appearing to give up hope on a playoff spot) agreed to assume the remainder of Garcia's salary—approximately $4 million.

"My grandfather was always a huge Yankee fan," Garcia said. "He told me when I was a kid [that] he would always see me playing for the Yankees one day. So my mom was very emotional about it because of that story. My grandfather passed away when I was thirteen years old. The family was touched by that because they were all Yankees fans."

Garcia's presence allowed the Yankees to remain mindful of the growing innings totals attached to both Montgomery and Severino. While they'd keep the gas pedal depressed on Severino through October, the Yankees eased off of Montgomery, bouncing him between the minors and the bullpen to wrap his season at 155⅓ innings. Montgomery finished 9-7 with a 3.88 ERA in 29 starts, leading all AL rookies in starts, strikeouts (144), innings, and WAR (2.7).

"You definitely think of the big leagues and you think, 'Oh, wow, it's going to be really hard,'" Montgomery said. "It's lived up to it. You've just got to settle in and trust yourself."

With those moves, the Yankees had clearly announced their intent to chase a playoff spot, so acquiring Gray from the Athletics seemed like a natural fit. Gray was already convinced that his time in Oakland was coming to an end, and he had an ideal destination in mind, as the Vanderbilt-educated native of Smyrna, Tennessee, remarked that "every kid wants to play for the Yankees."

The A's demanded legitimate talent for Gray, whose five-foot-ten, 190-pound frame generated a nasty arsenal of four-seam fastballs, sinkers, and curveballs. Cashman understood that at least one of the players he surrendered could develop into a star, but said that the team's strong play had dictated that they must "push a lot of these chips in the middle of the table and recognize 2017 has a chance to be special."

About an hour before the 4:00 p.m. ET deadline on July 31, the Yankees agreed to send outfielder Dustin Fowler, right-hander James Kaprielian, and infielder Jorge Mateo to the Athletics in exchange for Gray and $1.5 million in international bonus pool signing money. The cash was a not-so-subtle nod to the anticipated availability of the "Japanese Babe Ruth," twenty-three-year-old Shohei Ohtani, a right-handed pitcher and left-handed slugger whom the Yankees had scouted since 2012.

Cashman would say that he viewed Ohtani as a "perfect fit" given the youth movement, but Ohtani quickly eliminated the Yankees in early December, signing with the Angels, with whom he'd earn honors as the 2018 AL Rookie of the Year. Cashman was told that Ohtani had expressed a preference not to play for a large market, East Coast club. Often, New York City was a selling point; this time, it had not been.

"When players are in the marketplace like that, you do everything you possibly can," Cashman said. "In this case, we prepared with trade deadline money, acquisitions, international slot money. We put forward everything that we were about, but if it's not a fit, it's not a fit."

Two of the three players that Oakland received in the Gray trade were injured assets; Fowler was on crutches, and Kaprielian's right arm had recently been in a sling. Despite the Yankees' best efforts to protect their top pitching prospect, permitting him to pitch in only one Grapefruit League game that spring, Kaprielian experienced pain in his pitching elbow and underwent Tommy John surgery in April.

The healthy piece of the deal for Oakland was Mateo, a speedy infielder who appeared to be blocked on New York's depth chart by Gregorius and

Gleyber Torres, prompting the club to experiment with Mateo in the outfield. The Athletics viewed Mateo as a future big-league regular in the infield, and given the chance, Cashman believed that he would become one.

Still, Gray's high-end talent—and the fact that he would not be eligible for free agency until 2020—made it a gamble worth taking in the GM's eyes. Oakland's first-round selection (eighteenth overall) in 2011, Gray lost most of the '16 season to a pair of stints on the disabled list, but he seemed to be again throwing the ball with authority. In his final six starts as a member of the A's, the twenty-seven-year-old went 4-2 with a 1.37 ERA.

"I really feel like, in the last month or the last two months, it's starting to click," Gray said at the time of the trade. "You'll see it. I'm starting to feel the baseball again and make it do the things that I've always been able to make it do. The baseball feels good in my hand again."

Though they have been friends for years, Cashman and A's executive vice president Billy Beane had matched up in only four trades. The last one of significance delivered Jeff Weaver to the Bronx in July 2002, one year before the release of Michael Lewis' *Moneyball* made Beane a celebrity GM and forever changed the way MLB front offices did business. Cashman was skeptical that they could find common ground concerning Gray, a former All-Star who was pitching like an ace, but there was motivation to push forward through the tough talks.

"We just have not matched up, despite being close," Cashman said. "I think we've liked the same players. We think probably very similarly, and that doesn't create an atmosphere of matches as easy. I think opponents attract when you're trying to do business with others. So, if you're an analytical organization, you can match up easier with an old-school organization. But if you're kind of like-minded, I think you probably repel more than anything else."

Shortly after he received the official word from Beane, Gray presented a factory-fresh Yankees cap to his 2½ year old son, Gunnar, and tried to explain the situation.

"The first thing I said was, 'Gunnar, I'm not going to be playing for the A's anymore. I'm going to be playing for the Yankees,'" Gray said. "And he just says, 'Why, Dad? Why?' He doesn't know, but I know he's going to love it here."

The move fired up several of the Yankees, including CC Sabathia, who

Acquired from the Athletics on July 31, 2017, Sonny Gray compiled a 2.84 ERA over his final 17 regular season starts of the 2017 season, the seventh-lowest in the majors over that span.

remarked that they were "back to our same old Yankees—the goal is to win the World Series. We're here now."

Grinding through bone-on-bone arthritis that necessitated a bulky right knee brace to pitch and will eventually require replacement surgery, Sabathia had been one of the more vocal veterans panning the 2016 sell-off, recognizing that his own window to win another title was closing. Now, Sabathia believed that he was once again on the ground floor of something special.

"It's still the same attitude. It's still the same Yankee way," Sabathia said. "There has been turnover with a lot of us, but the guys that have come in with the rebuild—Sanchez and Judge—those guys have carried us. It's been a lot of fun to watch Severino emerge as one of the best pitchers in baseball. It's been fun to be the old guy and sit back and watch these guys do their thing."

CHAPTER 13

PLAYOFF PUSH

"All Rise" had turned into "All Sit," and the Yankees needed answers.

There have been numerous studies performed over the years to investigate the existence of a so-called "Home Run Derby Curse," attempting to prove that the intensity of the homer-hitting competition impacts a player's swing and influences a performance dip in the second half of the season.

While sparing you a detailed dive into an ocean of numbers (though that is only a Google search away, should you so desire), suffice it to say that there is no definitive link, and that the expected regression of players after their above-average first halves seems to be a reasonable explanation.

Still, Bobby Abreu (2005), Chris Davis (2013), and David Wright (2006) have been among the more notable examples of a player whose second-half performance tanked after participating in the Derby, and Aaron Judge was quickly becoming the newest "Exhibit A" for those who'd prefer to see their sluggers sit out. For what it was worth, Judge consistently rejected the suggestion that there had been any connection between the Derby and his slump.

"People talk. That's baseball," Judge said. "You're eventually going to go through those times where you're 1-for-10, 1-for-20, 2-for-10. It's just part of it."

In 84 games prior to the All-Star break, Judge had been incredible, batting .329 while hitting thirty homers and driving in sixty-six runs. Though he struck out often (109 times in 301 at-bats), that was offset by his .448 on-base percentage (66 walks) and .691 slugging percentage. But as the Yankees returned to action following the Derby-winning performance, Judge went into a six-week tailspin that prompted some fans to wonder if the amazing first half had been a mirage.

No one in the organization believed that Judge would turn out to be the second coming of early 1990s power hitter Kevin Maas, the go-to example of a Yankees rookie whose performance dipped after a promising debut. Still, in his next forty-four games, Judge replicated the performance that he had shown in his first tour of the majors, right down to the batting average—.179, those same numbers he'd tapped into his iPhone as fuel for his winter workouts.

From July 14 to August 31, Judge managed 27 hits, striking out an alarming 67 times in 151 at-bats to land on the wrong side of history. Though Judge repeatedly said that he was not concerned by the spate of strikeouts, he did so at least once in thirty-seven consecutive games, tying a major league record set by Bill Stoneman—a Montreal Expos pitcher—across the 1971–1972 seasons.

Big-swinging Adam Dunn of the Reds had set the single-season record of 32 straight games with a strikeout in 2002, and Indians manager Terry Francona said that it looked like the league had caught up to Judge.

"There's not a lot of secrets when guys get extensive at-bats or pitcher innings," Francona said. "It's like the player bursts onto the scene, then the league makes their adjustments, and then you see what the player does. It's always been that way and it's fun to watch, because the really good ones, they then make their adjustments."

That was easy for Francona to say. The Yankees relied on Judge's thunder, and his outage was coming at a time in which the lineup was lacking notable pieces in Starlin Castro, Aaron Hicks, and Matt Holliday, all of whom had played key roles in the first half. Holliday in particular had been a sizable influence on Judge over the first few months of the season, taking over the role of trusted veteran counselor that Carlos Beltran had filled in the spring of 2016.

During his extended stays on the disabled list, first with a viral infection and then with a left lumbar strain, Holliday said that he often swapped friendly text messages with Judge but little more. There was advice coming from all corners, and Holliday said that he had no desire to join the many voices who were likely trying to help Judge break out of the slump.

"I've been through what he's been through, and there's no need to panic," Holliday said. "When you look at the body of work, he's had a great season. And sure, it's been a little bit rough and it's not the production that he had in the first half, but I just know who he is as a person and I know the talent and I know that these things come and go.

"There's only one way to deal with it. You get in there and you keep grinding and you do your drills and practice. That's the mystery of hitting a round ball with round bats."

While at Fresno State, Judge had adopted a superstition in which he started each game chomping on two pieces of bubble gum, then kept working the same chaw until he made an out. The ideal outcome was for Judge to finish nine innings with a stale, unflavored piece of Dubble Bubble in his mouth. This strikeout streak meant that Judge had spent completely too much time digging into the dugout snack stash for his liking.

Too many discarded wads of gum called for a temporary switch to sunflower seeds, and Judge tried that too, hoping to snap out of his slump. He also tried swapping out his gear; Judge began to frequently wear an elbow guard with letters of Hangul, the Korean alphabet, reading '슈퍼 신 인 재판관.' It had been sent to him by first baseman Ji-Man Choi, who was now in Triple-A after a six-game cameo in the majors. Judge did not know what the characters meant, and was pleased to learn that it translated to "Super Rookie Judge."

"That's great," Judge said. "I didn't think Ji-Man would run me out there with something that was bad language or a bad word or something, so I kind of trusted him."

Reggie Jackson, who'd compared Judge to luminaries like Dave Winfield, Willie McCovey, and Willie Stargell over the last year-plus, recounted how he himself had hit thirty-seven homers for the Athletics prior to the All-Star break in 1969, then managed ten the rest of the way. Jackson believed that Judge was going through a similar "course correction," those periods of time where bat handles are too thick, the spikes of your shoes are too long, and nothing seems to feel right.

"That's what baseball is," Jackson said. "It hits you, it grabs you, it sits you a little bit. It gets you to wake up, gets you to pay attention. It lets you know who is boss, but you figure it out. You get it worked out. They figure you out, and then you figure them out. That's how that works. You have your turn and then all of a sudden, they start planning for you, taking a little more time, going over you in their meetings. You get it figured out, get it turned around, and you get on a roll again until you go into another slump."

If the skid shook Judge's confidence, he never acknowledged it publicly, but Jackson would not have been surprised if some doubts began to appear in Judge's mind.

"Yeah, but if you let them creep in, you've got to get them out of there," Jackson said. "You've got to keep going. You can't go home. You've got to come in again tomorrow. The game starts at seven o' clock, you've got to hit at 7:20. You've got to hit again at twenty after eight."

Judge repeatedly maintained that his left shoulder was not affecting him, but the Yankees did not accept that at face value. The team discussed sending Judge for a cortisone injection (though Cashman and Judge both declined to confirm if one had actually been administered) and Girardi said that he asked Judge about the shoulder a number of times. The answer was always the same—Judge wanted to play.

"You come to the ballpark, your swing doesn't feel 100 percent every day," Judge said. "Your body doesn't feel 100 percent. That's why only a few people can play this game. It's tough, it's a grind and we've just got to keep working and battling. The days you don't feel 100 percent, if you've got eighty percent, you've got to give it all eighty."

That reminded Girardi of Jeter, but his rookie right fielder didn't push back as forcefully as the more established captain had. Left out of the starting lineup for three games in late August, Judge said that he had gone "stir-crazy" during a benching that was meant to serve both as a mental and physical respite.

"He never wants to sit," Girardi said. "He's got some of those character traits of No. 2. You ask him how he is and it's always, 'Good.' Those are things that you have to read through. Maybe being around '2' so often, I learned something."

The shoulder wasn't Judge's only physical issue of note. While celebrating Brett Gardner's 11th-inning, walk-off home run to defeat the Rays on July 27, Judge was hit in the mouth by Gardner's errant batting helmet, chipping his front left tooth. The Yankees jumped at home plate, reveling in their sixth win in seven games. Judge covered his mouth with his left hand and disappeared down the dugout steps.

Later, while a member of the team's security team searched in vain for the fragment of Judge's tooth, several of the veterans examined videos of the celebration as though it had been the Zapruder film. Freeze-framing the moment of impact, Todd Frazier quickly identified Clint Frazier as a suspect in the whodunit, shouting the outfielder's name from across the clubhouse: "It was Frazier!"

The rookie darted over to see the video on a reporter's iPhone and pleaded his case, saying, "Listen, there is someone else. Austin Romine is in there." The elder Frazier dismissed the comment, warning the rookie not to point fingers.

"You just pointed [your finger] from across the distance," Frazier the younger shot back.

The thirty-one-year-old veteran settled the matter with his seniority card: "Well, I can do that. You can't."

For the record, Judge said it was no one's fault but his own; he'd spotted Gardner's helmet rolling in the middle of the pile and picked it up, fearing that a teammate could twist an ankle if they jumped on it. When Judge retrieved the helmet, it struck Gardner's back and slammed into his mouth. After an emergency dental procedure, Judge played the next night. He said that he'd snapped a pic of the ugly aftermath but opted to keep that for himself.

Despite the growing whiff totals, Judge was getting comfortable. It seemed unlikely that he would be returning to the minors anytime soon, so Judge sought recommendations from teammates about finding a more permanent place to live. After saying goodbye to the hotel staff, many of whom Judge now knew on a first-name basis, Judge found a high-rise apartment building in midtown Manhattan to his liking.

"I just kind of wanted a place that I could unpack my bags and hang up my clothes," Judge said. "Living out of a suitcase, I already do that on the road. The hotel had been where they put me when I got called up, and it was kind of the only hotel I knew, so I just kind of stayed there. It was a great fit for me at the time."

There was another big change that summer, as fans had started recognizing Judge more regularly, especially in the wake of the Home Run Derby. He'd grown used to strangers walking up to him on the street and saying things along the lines of, "Hey, you're tall, what do you play?" Now, curious bystanders were stopping him more frequently and saying, "Hey, you look like Aaron Judge." Judge said that he'd usually smile, shake a hand or two and be on his way.

"That's the cool thing about New York. Everyone's on a tight schedule," Judge said. "They don't have time to sit around and talk, and ask for this or that. They say hi, and then it's, 'All right, see ya. I've got to get going.' They've been great."

• • •

The go-for-it sheen of the July trades wore off as the team stumbled into August, falling out of first place in the AL East as they dropped six of nine on a road trip to Detroit, Cleveland, and Toronto before returning home. Gary Sanchez seemed to be in the middle of everything. Girardi seldom spoke critically of his players in public, but he raised eyebrows by openly challenging Sanchez to step up his defense on August 4 in Cleveland, after watching Sanchez's league-leading twelfth passed ball sail between his legs.

"He needs to improve. Bottom line. He needs to improve," Girardi said in the cramped visiting manager's office at Progressive Field, minutes after absorbing a 7–2 loss to the Indians. "He's late getting down. That's what I see sometimes. It's something we've been working on. We need to continue to work on it."

The tone of Girardi's words was different than they had been after a June 28 game against the White Sox in Chicago, when television cameras spotted Girardi lecturing Sanchez during the fourth inning of a 12–3 win. Sanchez had failed to snare a Masahiro Tanaka splitter that was recorded as a wild pitch. Girardi said then that the conversation had been about helping Sanchez shift his weight better, but insisted that it "had nothing to do with scolding him."

Five weeks later, Sanchez seemed uncomfortable as a pack of reporters and television cameras circled his locker in Cleveland, where bilingual media relations coordinator Marlon Abreu patiently translated questions from English to Spanish and back again. Sanchez explained that some of the passed balls had been related to cross-ups with pitchers, but in the case that pushed Girardi over the edge, Roberto Perez flashed bunt at a Jaime Garcia fastball that Sanchez lost sight of, with the pitch rolling to the screen behind home plate.

"I feel good behind the plate, but there's definitely been a couple of situations there where I haven't been able to catch the ball," Sanchez said. "It has cost us runs. Blocking is a matter of reacting quickly to the ball. I'm not going to be able to block them all, but if I set myself well, I have a good chance of blocking them."

Cashman said that he considered ball-blocking a smaller part of the game and pointed out that the other aspects of Sanchez's defense, particularly his game-calling and throwing arm, had been consistently rated as above average.

"Have there been balls that he's botched every now and then? Yeah, it's happened," Cashman said. "We were led to many championships by a player with the same kinds of questions around him in Jorge Posada, who was a great offensive catcher that had a lot of ability, but at times defensively it wasn't his calling card. We won quite a bit."

Sanchez wouldn't be the first elite offensive catcher to improve after struggling to block balls; beginning his Hall of Fame career with the Reds, Johnny Bench permitted thirty-two passed balls and saw 118 wild pitches on his watch over his first two full seasons, leading the majors with eighteen passed balls in 1968. By 1970, Bench had trimmed that number to nine, and would never permit more than twelve in another single season.

Girardi said that he had not necessarily been sending a message of tough love to Sanchez; he was trying to be honest about a way in which his catcher's game could improve.

"I think there's a ton of talent," Girardi said. "I think this is a kid who has a chance to be a perennial All-Star. I think it's a kid who has a chance to be an MVP. You don't say that about a catcher very often because of the demands on their bodies and how physical the position is. Usually, you don't put up the offensive numbers that he's put up, but I think he has a chance to be really special."

Hicks, the team's other Aaron, returned from the disabled list in mid-August to pick up where he had left off in his breakout campaign. He had carried a .398 on-base percentage, ninth-best in the majors, when he was shelved by a right oblique strain in mid-June. Hicks reminded the Yanks what they had been missing in an August 11 win over the Red Sox, crushing a two-run homer and uncorking a terrific ninth-inning throw in that cut down Eduardo Nunez at third base.

"We need to get as many wins as we can against these guys, and it showed that we're willing to fight back. That was also very important,"

Hicks said. "It feels good to be able to be around the guys and to see their smiling faces again."

The Red Sox took two of three games in that weekend series, with twenty-year-old Boston rookie Rafael Devers turning around a 102.8-mph Chapman-fastball for a game-tying home run on August 13. The Yanks lost in ten innings, and it was crushing; instead of being 3½ games back of the Red Sox, the Yankees were now staring at a 5½ game deficit, the farthest they'd be out of first place all season. Devers became the second left-handed batter to ever homer off of Chapman, joining Luke Scott, who did it for the Orioles back on June 26, 2011.

"It would've been better if it was 3½, but I've seen 5½ games go away in a hurry," Chase Headley said. "There's a lot of baseball to be played. We play them quite a few more times. We're going to need to play well against them, but this was an opportunity that we didn't take advantage of to make up a little bit of ground."

Sweeping the Mets in a four-game, home-and-home Subway Series proved to be a momentary salve, as Judge offered a reminder that—slump not withstanding—he was still capable of feats most big leaguers could only dream of.

Crossing borough lines to play at Citi Field on August 16, Judge stole the show, crushing a Robert Gsellman slider toward the third deck in left field. It was retrieved in the far-off Section 536, and Mets left fielder Yoenis Cespedes did not bother to turn his head, declining to move an inch in pursuit. Judge dropped his bat and ran immediately.

"When you hit it and you kind of know you got one, you just run the bases," said Judge, who said there was no temptation to watch the flight of his drive. "They all feel the same. Usually when you get it on the sweet spot of the bat, you don't really feel it."

Judge returned to the dugout, finding his teammates still gawking at the incredible feat, pointing and debating where the ball had actually landed. Statcast calculated the moonshot at 457 feet, a number that raised eyebrows in the clubhouse. Didi Gregorius guessed 530 feet, while Jaime Garcia said that it looked more like 550.

"If that ball only went 450, then no ball is ever going over 500 feet, because that ball was crushed," Headley said.

Since Judge preferred not to talk about his own homers, he didn't mind when his muscle was overshadowed by Sanchez's bat catching fire.

Sanchez became the sixth player in franchise history to hit 12 home runs in the month of August, and the first since Alex Rodriguez in 2005. Joe DiMaggio, Mickey Mantle, and Babe Ruth were among the bold-faced names who had also accomplished the feat, with Ruth slugging 15 in August 1929.

Maybe Alex Rodriguez and Jennifer Lopez had something to do with the surge. Following Girardi's harsh evaluation of Sanchez's defense, the catcher said that a midtown Manhattan power lunch with the celebrity couple had helped to clear his mind, with the trio huddling at the Casa Lever eatery at the corner of Park Avenue and East 53rd Street.

"We talked a lot about pretty much everything," Sanchez said. "Everything that comes from him, it's positive. We talked a little bit about defense, creating a routine, following your routine, preparing for games. We keep talking—we've had phone calls here and there. And his girlfriend was there, J-Lo. She gave me some advice. She's a superstar at what she does, she's a great singer and great actress, and Alex is a superstar in base-ball. Any advice coming from them, I will listen to them."

One-third of Sanchez's August homers came off Tigers pitching over the course of three games at Detroit's Comerica Park, and that sparked one of the team's most cohesive experiences of the year. Playing a getaway day matinee on August 24, Sanchez's fourth-inning solo drive to left-center field off Michael Fulmer proved to be the final straw for Detroit.

In Sanchez's next at-bat, he was drilled in the left hip by a Fulmer pitch. Sanchez glared as he walked to first, eyeing Fulmer as the hurler shook his hand, later claiming that he'd experienced a "zap" of his ulnar nerve. Tommy Kahnle wasn't buying it. The right-hander retaliated in the bottom of the sixth, firing a 96-mph fastball behind Miguel Cabrera, prompting home plate umpire Carlos Torres to eject Kahnle and Girardi.

The beef between the clubs actually stretched back weeks, when Kahnle had hit Detroit's Mikie Mahtook on July 31 in New York. Fulmer had responded by plunking Jacoby Ellsbury the next inning, which appeared to settle the matter—at least, until Sanchez's muscle show in Motown.

Aroldis Chapman emerged from the bullpen to relieve Kahnle, and during the on-field delay, Cabrera approached Austin Romine and exchanged words with the catcher. When Romine removed his mask, Cabrera responded by shoving Romine, landing a punch before the players wrestled on the dirt near home plate.

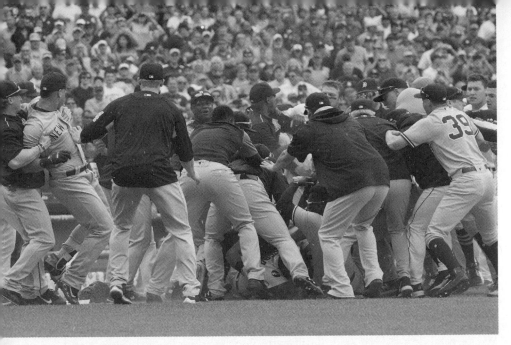

An August 24 scuffle between Yankees catcher Austin Romine and Tigers slugger Miguel Cabrera prompted both benches to clear on a wild afternoon of punches and hit batsmen at Detroit's Comerica Park.

"He said, 'You have a problem with me?' and I said, 'This isn't about you,'" Romine said, "And then he pushed me. It felt like he wanted a confrontation there, and I just tried to defend myself the best I could."

Both benches cleared, as did the bullpens, led by David Robertson's high-socked, high-stepping sprint across the grass. Members of both teams created a pile on the infield grass, and replays clearly showed Sanchez—the Yanks' DH that day—arriving on the scene, delivering at least two punches to Cabrera's body. Cabrera and Romine were both ejected.

"I have a really good relationship with Romine," Sanchez said. "At the moment of everything, instinct takes over. I went out there to defend my teammate, my team. Definitely the situation got out of control a little bit there, but at the end of it all what you're trying to do is trying to go out there and protect your team, defend your guys."

Sanchez was also captured on video punching infielder Nick Castellanos at the bottom of the pile, and Cabrera challenged Sanchez to try doing it "face-to-face" next time. Pedro Martinez was among those who wondered if Sanchez's actions would hurt his reputation, tweeting, "Cheap shots will stay around the league forever. I think Gary Sanchez could be badly remembered for this for a long time."

Girardi disagreed, defending his catcher by invoking Jorge Posada's name.

"I knew another catcher who had a lot of fire and a lot of fight in him," Girardi said. "He ended up being a great player who could one day wind up in the Hall of Fame, and his number's retired in Monument Park. And that's what we loved about Jorge. Learning how to control it as you go through in the game and as you grow up is important, but the kid plays with a lot of passion. He's going to protect his teammates. He loves his teammates, he's got a lot of fire and fight and I like that about him."

The day was not over. In the seventh inning, Dellin Betances drilled catcher James McCann in the helmet with a 98-mph fastball, clearing the benches again. Betances pleaded his case, pointing to the scoreboard, which read 6–6 at the time. With warnings having been issued, though, Betances and Yanks bench coach Rob Thomson were both ejected.

"That's the last thing I want to do," Betances said. "At that point, I felt like everything was over. I was disappointed because it was a tie game and we're out here trying to fight for a playoff spot, and for me to get thrown out there, that shouldn't have happened."

Detroit returned fire once more in the eighth, as Alex Wilson plunked Todd Frazier in the left hip. The benches cleared again when Frazier took a few steps toward the mound, with Wilson and Tigers manager Brad Ausmus both ejected. Brett Gardner was among the most incensed players on the field, shouting obscenities at Ausmus while being restrained.

The Yankees lost the game, 10–6, and it took days for Major League Baseball to sort through a mess of umpire reports and video footage. Once the appeal process had been completed, Sanchez was suspended for three games, sitting out an entire series against the Orioles. Romine was suspended for one game, while Cabrera received the harshest penalty, slapped with a six-game ban. Seven others were fined, but not suspended.

"I think, honestly, it brought us together and closer with the guys," Todd Frazier said. "You see guys come together—you don't want to see it during a brawl, but those things kind of kick-start a team and get them going."

Still jockeying with the Red Sox in the AL East, the Yankees made good use of a new weapon in right-hander Chad Green, who had quietly become the most dominant pitcher that no one had heard of. Pitching in the first game of an August 30 doubleheader against the Indians, Green

Chad Green's 13.43 strikeouts per nine innings in 2017 invited comparisons to Mariano Rivera's stellar 1996 season, when the future Hall of Famer whiffed 10.87 batters per nine innings.

became the first player in big league history to record seven strikeouts while facing eight or fewer batters in a game.

In twelve appearances from August 23 through the end of the regular season, the twenty-six-year-old allowed one run with two walks and 28 strikeouts in 17 innings. Green finished the year with a 5-0 record and 1.83 ERA, enjoying six appearances with at least five strikeouts. That invited comparisons to Mariano Rivera's lethal 1996 season, in which he had nine such games while setting up for closer John Wetteland.

"I've heard that. It's not something I can really put a finger on," Green said. "I've always been a fastball pitcher. I guess something just clicked. The location is probably a little bit better this year, I think, but other than that I'm not really doing anything too different than I've done in the past with it."

Green had garnered the Yankees' attention as a minor league starter in the Tigers system, where they ignored his 5-14 record for Double-A Erie in 2015 and instead focused on his command of the strike zone. Green was acquired in December of that year along with right-hander Luis Cessa, a converted infielder who got his start in the Mets' system, in a swap for left-handed reliever Justin Wilson. Some wondered at the time if the Yanks intended to flip the young pitchers elsewhere; no, Cashman said, they desired Cessa and Green for their own use.

"I had Chad Green as a starter, and I still think he's a starter," Cashman said. "But the way this team was set up, when we had some injuries and needs, he just kind of filled in. He's clearly a different animal out of the bullpen. In most cases, relievers are failed starters, but he's not a failed starter. He just happened to be needed in a long, multi-inning type relief period when we called him up, and then he just excelled to such a rare degree that it was hard to take him out of it."

A product of Greenville, South Carolina who left the University of Louisville as the school's all-time ERA leader (2.38), the course of Green's career had changed while he and his wife, Jenna, were returning from their honeymoon in Jamaica. The Tigers hold their spring training in Lakeland, Florida, a forty-five-minute cruise up Interstate 4 from George M. Steinbrenner Field, but Green said he sensed a different vibe in his new workplace very quickly.

"With the Yankees, winning is just kind of expected," Green said. "I came up with the Tigers and it's just different. Maybe it's more expected here in the minor leagues than other places. There's a reason that the Yankees have won twenty-seven world championships. It's not something that's discussed, but I guess you just kind of know. They preach winning in the minors so when it gets up here, it gets more natural because it's expected up here. I think it all starts down there, watching guys like Judge and Gary and those guys have success up here. Monty and Sevy, there's a lot of guys. I think it all starts in the minors with the personnel and the staff they have there."

Green traced his big-league experience to a late-night load of laundry, during which he received the call that he had waited a lifetime for. Severino had been placed on the disabled list with a triceps strain, and Green rushed to join the team, making his big-league debut by pitching four innings at Arizona's Chase Field on May 16, 2016. It went by in a blur, and if he were to watch the game video now, Green said that the rookie on the mound that day would be nearly unrecognizable.

"I didn't really know what I was doing," Green said. "You feel like you're good enough to pitch in the big leagues, but that day, that's not really how I pitch at all. The breaking ball wasn't very good, the fastball wasn't very good, I didn't think. I was working on things at the time, so looking back, it was just different."

Green had pitched out of the bullpen in college, which provided something of a model to work with. Sabathia had seen flashes of Green's talent before spring training, remarking that Green's stuff was "unreal," but the hurler's confidence didn't completely set in until the midpoint of 2017. On more than one occasion, catcher Austin Romine gushed about a disappearing fastball that was giving opponents fits.

"It just jumps on you," Romine said. "I don't know how else to put that in words. It comes in and it keeps its velocity and kind of jumps at you, instead of a normal fastball coming in. I know we're searching for an answer; I can't give you one. It gets on me, so I know it gets on hitters."

• • •

In Girardi's view, the turning point of the season came after a three-game sweep by the Indians in late August, when New York was outscored 17–7 in a Yankee Stadium series that included a long and ugly rain-necessitated doubleheader. They answered by taking three out of four from Boston in the Bronx. Severino pitched a gem in the finale before the Yanks busted open their 9–2 win with a six-run sixth inning, highlighted by Judge's 38th homer of the year.

The Yankees checked into their Baltimore hotel around 3:00 a.m., then beat up on the Orioles in a Labor Day afternoon contest at Camden Yards. In that 7–4 win (the first game Sanchez, their hottest hitter, missed as part of his suspension), Gregorius hit his 20th homer, becoming the first Yankees shortstop ever to reach that plateau in back-to-back seasons.

"We seemed to really get on a roll," Girardi said. "We probably won a game a lot of people thought we shouldn't have won when we got in so late to Baltimore. Then we just had a really good road trip. We were playing really well, we were pitching well, and everyone was contributing. It just seemed that we knew this was possible."

The Yankees thoroughly believed that they were capable of catching Boston, a team that had been on a similar trajectory to the Yanks. The Red Sox had developed a new core of talent with Xander Bogaerts, Mookie Betts, Jackie Bradley Jr., and Rafael Devers, but they had to take considerable lumps to do so, absorbing last-place finishes in 2014 and 2015.

There was a window into the future as fans delighted in contrasting Judge against budding Red Sox star Andrew Benintendi, who had been a preseason favorite for the American League's Rookie of the Year award. The lefty-swinging, shaggy-haired Benintendi emerged as a persistent thorn in the Yankees' sides and as a fresh face of the renewed rivalry.

In August, Benintendi became the first player since Jimmie Foxx in 1938 to hit a pair of three-run homers against the Yankees, both coming off Severino. When someone asked Benintendi that night if he had been trying to match Judge in his own park, he replied: "No, not at all. He's having an unreal year and he's kind of struggling right now. I went through that for two months. I'm sure he'll figure it out."

Perhaps the most bizarre "road" trip of the season took place in mid-September, as the Yankees and Rays had a series relocated to Citi Field while Hurricane Irma pounded the state of Florida. Though they were officially Rays home games, the majority of the crowd cheered for the Yankees, taking advantage of $25 general admission tickets as the Yanks took two of the three games in the Mets' house.

The Rays sent along their hype videos from Tropicana Field, creating the strange optic of having "D.J. Kitty," the Rays' unofficial feline mascot, trying to pump up the crowd on a center-field scoreboard that read, "Let's Go Mets." But the games went viral when the YES Network introduced the world to the "Thumbs Down Guy," previously known as Gary Dunaier.

A fifty-four-year-old Mets fan from Queens, Dunaier was in the field-level seats on September 11 when Todd Frazier rounded the bases for a three-run homer off of Tampa Bay's Jake Odorizzi. Realizing his voice would be drowned out by the Yankees fans surrounding him, Dunaier instead stood perfectly still and offered Frazier a displeased thumbs-down, like a relic out of the Roman Empire.

Something about the combination of Dunaier's expression, beard, teal shirt, suspenders, and red-rimmed glasses, clicked. Frazier later joked that Dunaier had seemed to "put this little pouty face on, like he'd just lost his dog or something." The clip became an Internet sensation, and when Judge spotted one of the retweets the next day, he urged Frazier to mimic the thumbs down after his next hit.

"It was pretty comical, so I thought it would be a good thing for Fraz to do, and it kind of caught on with the whole team," Judge said.

Before "thumbs-down," the Yankees had been pointing to the dugout after each knock, something that Gary Sanchez brought with him from the 2016 season in Scranton/Wilkes-Barre, when Nick Swisher insisted that the RailRiders needed a signature gesture. Judge, Sanchez, and others brought the habit with them to Yankee Stadium. The thumbs-down was a welcome upgrade.

"I think all that stuff kind of intertwines with everything," Frazier said. "A lot of stuff happens during the season. Lucky for us, we had some guy put the thumbs down and it kind of just took off. I know Didi does a lot of emoji things that people love. That kind of interaction, that makes baseball even better. It makes a team come together and it makes for a fun time coming to the ballpark."

Late in September, the Yankees began celebrating home runs with mock dugout interviews. The idea for that running gag came from Ronald Torreyes, who served as the cameraman for each "taping" of what became known as "The Toe-Night Show." Sitting in the dugout, Torreyes had been inspired by a Starlin Castro homer in a September 26 victory over the Rays, marking Castro's first homer in nearly a month.

"It was a long time coming for Castro," Torreyes said. "When he hit that home run, the first thing that came into my mind was to get the guys together and set up an interview and ask him how he felt."

With Gregorius serving as the lead interviewer, the news team assembled. Torreyes first cradled a bat as a makeshift camera, then upgraded the next day, using a bulky plastic tub of sunflower seeds. Finally, someone fashioned a camera out of a pair of shoeboxes held together with athletic tape. Gregorius, Castro, Luis Severino, and Miguel Andujar created microphones out of water bottles and paper cups, allowing the players' creativity to shine through.

"We just grabbed whatever was over there and just went with it," Gregorius said. "We're trying to have some fun, trying to keep everybody loose. We're having a really good time with it. We just ask, 'How does it feel to hit a home run?' 'What pitch?' Stuff like that. We keep it fun."

Since it was Torreyes' idea, why wasn't he in front of the camera? Torreyes explained that he'd volunteered, but Gregorius' contributions allowed the 'show' to be multi-lingual; he'd speak to Castro in Spanish after one big hit, then cleanly pivot to engage players like Greg Bird and Aaron Hicks in English.

"That's why we have Didi around," Torreyes said. "He can speak five, six different languages. That's why he's the person asking the questions."

Meredith Marakovits, who normally would be tasked with volleying those sorts of inquiries for the YES Network's viewers, said that she sensed a new looseness in the clubhouse. That served to reinvigorate battled-hardened veterans like Brett Gardner and CC Sabathia.

"It's not as regimented as it was when I first got here in 2012," Marakovits said. "You can see the pure excitement on a lot of these guys' faces when they do something for the first time, that they're experiencing it for the first time. It's almost like a childlike joy that they exude. I can't even envision, with some of those old teams, something like what Ronald Torreyes is doing with the camera. I can't imagine that."

The reporters in pinstriped pants had plenty of opportunities to approach Judge, who snapped out of his late summer funk to assemble an awesome final month that would be his best of the regular season. Earning his second AL Player of the Month award (also June), Judge hit .311 with a .463 on-base percentage and a .889 slugging percentage, crushing 15 homers and driving in 32 runs in 27 games.

Judge's 15 homers were the most by a Yankee in any calendar month since Roger Maris also hit 15 in June of 1961, when the "M & M Boys" of Maris and Mickey Mantle kicked their pursuits of Babe Ruth's single-season record into high gear. Again, Judge and the Yankees declined to say if he had gone for that cortisone injection, leaving observers to draw their own conclusions. Judge certainly appeared to be swinging without pain or discomfort.

Snapping a fifteen game homerless stretch with a September 3 blast off Boston reliever Addison Reed, Judge reached base in twenty-five straight games to complete the regular season, helping New York rattle off a 46-30 record after the All-Star break that was second only to Cleveland (55-20) among AL clubs.

"What I admire about him the most is, he's going to be the same cat every day," said Jim Hendry, a special assistant to Cashman. "He's not going to change. He didn't act any different when he was going through a tough time. He just hung in there. Not many kids who are his age with less than a year of service time go through what he went through in August, and then do what he did in September. You've got to have great makeup for that."

Having long since blown past Joe DiMaggio's franchise record of 29 homers by a rookie, Judge shattered Mark McGwire's major league rookie record for homers in a season on the afternoon of September 25, mashing his 49th and 50th home runs in a makeup game against the Royals at Yankee Stadium.

McGwire had hit 49 homers in 1987 for the Oakland Athletics, a tally that Judge equaled with a third inning blast off Royals starter Jake Junis. Kansas City had been the last remaining AL team on Judge's hit list; with that, he'd now homered against every AL club in 2017. Judge eclipsed "Big Mac" in the seventh inning, going deep off Trevor Cahill.

Like much of the baseball world, McGwire had been enthralled with Judge's pursuit of his record. Now the Padres' hitting coach, McGwire had witnessed Judge's 49th homer on live TV before beginning his drive to Dodger Stadium for that night's game. Somewhere on the freeway, McGwire heard his cell phone chime, with an alert from MLB's At Bat app informing him that Judge had gone deep again for number fifty.

Via Matt Holliday, who passed along Judge's cell phone number, McGwire reached out to congratulate Judge on the accomplishment.

"I couldn't be happier for him," McGwire said. "The future for him as a bona fide home run hitter is bright. Who knows what the number is going to be? Watch out, seventy-three. Seriously. The home run is back. It's awesome. People love seeing home runs. They love seeing the power pitcher and the power hitter. And it couldn't be any better for the game."

Thirty-three of Judge's homers came at Yankee Stadium, surpassing a franchise record for home runs hit at home in a single season. The previous mark had been held by Babe Ruth, who hit thirty-two homers at the Polo Grounds in 1921, when the Yanks shared the upper Manhattan facility with the New York Giants. By the Yanks' final series with the Orioles, manager Buck Showalter had seen enough of Judge, who hit eleven of his homers off Baltimore pitching while compiling a .429 average and 1.049 OPS.

With Clint Frazier on third base and the Yankees trailing by two runs in the bottom of the ninth inning on the afternoon of September 17, Showalter ordered closer Zach Britton to issue a two-out intentional walk to Judge, a head-scratching move that brought the potential winning run to the plate. Showalter said that he had to "pick your poison there," and he preferred to have Britton face Gary Sanchez rather than allow Judge another opportunity to inflict damage.

"It came up heads today," Showalter said. "Tomorrow it might be tails."

Judge finished the year as the second rookie in history to record at least 100 runs scored, 100 RBI, and 100 walks in a single season, joining Hall of Famer Ted Williams (1939). The slugging outfielder became the eighth Yankee (rookie or veteran) in team history to accomplish the feat, joining Hall of Famers Lou Gehrig, Babe Ruth, and Mickey Mantle, as well as Charlie Keller, Jason Giambi, Bernie Williams, and George Selkirk.

Before Judge, no player had led the American League in the three "true outcomes" (plays that only involve pitcher, catcher, and batter)—home runs (52), strikeouts (208), and walks (127)—since Mantle in 1958.

Cashman said that as high as the Yankees' scouts had been on Judge, there was nothing in the draft database that predicted anything like Judge's final 2017 line.

"I don't think we had anybody having fifty-plus home runs on his ledger, ever," Cashman said. "He's physically capable of all that stuff, and there's a lot to dream when you see the physicality, but I don't think anybody would have expected that. I'm not sure anybody would ever expect that from anybody.

"We felt, by our scouting assessments and his development, that he would be an above-average right fielder and an above-average offensive player. That would be a lethal combination for us for years to come. But an MVP candidate, especially in his first year? That moved the needle a lot more than anyone would have expected."

Judge's homer total would have been higher if he hadn't lost one to the April 16 fan-interference replay snafu that credited him with a triple, plus leaping catches by the Red Sox's Jackie Bradley Jr. (July 17), and the White Sox's Melky Cabrera (June 29). Reminded of the bizarre triple, Judge chuckled.

"I'd almost forgot about that," Judge said. "The biggest thing is winning ballgames. This is the right time to get hot. It's coming down to the wire and I'm going to try to do whatever I can to help the team be in a good position going into October."

Gardner said that there was more to Judge's game than home runs and walks, and some of Judge's most impressive work took place off the field, where he brought a positive attitude to the stadium every day. By

September, Sabathia said that he sensed Judge had already developed into one of the team's leaders.

"It's a young team. He came up with a lot of the core," Sabathia said. "I think it's just a natural thing that happened. I guess it's just the way he goes about his business and works hard every day. Guys follow that. You get in a routine, start doing your thing and guys see him having success. I guess it could be his size, but I think it's just his personality. You can talk to him. I think he's a good teammate and a good friend."

To the Yankees' frustration, the Red Sox kept pace with their splendid September. Boston answered New York's 20-9 record after September 1 by going 17-11, good enough to hold on and clinch the American League East by two games over the ninety-one-win Bombers. But for the first time in three seasons, and the second time in the last five years, the Yankees could call themselves a playoff team.

"All we needed was an invitation," Todd Frazier said.

They officially clinched with a 5–1 win over the Blue Jays on September 23, heading for a showdown with the Twins in the AL Wild Card game. With plastic sheets covering their lockers in the tight quarters of the visiting clubhouse at Rogers Centre, the Bombers gleefully doused each other while Didi Gregorius shot video with an expensive camera, dodging the droplets. Tommy Kahnle rolled his body over the middle of the saturated carpet, literally soaking up the experience.

It was a night that the youngest Yankees vowed never to forget, while some of the veterans seemed to be holding something in reserve for the future.

"I told some of these guys, 'It's a lot more fun to celebrate at home than it is here in Toronto,'" Gardner said. "Our clubhouse is a lot bigger and there's a lot more room. I think we realize that there's a lot more work to do, but I think it's important for us to celebrate and to realize that it's a big accomplishment to make it back into the playoffs. There's only ten teams that get to play in the postseason and we're going to be one of them."

CHAPTER 14

LIGHTS, CAMERA, OCTOBER

Luis Severino brimmed with confidence as he stood in front of his Yankee Stadium locker, having been informed that his next assignment was to start the AL Wild Card game against the Twins. He had never pitched in a playoff game of any type during his career, going all the way back to his childhood; the closest he had come was sitting in the bullpen, on the roster but unused, for the 2015 postseason contest against the Astros.

It spoke volumes that the Yankees were comfortable placing all of their trust in Severino with everything on the line—especially after some had suggested one year prior that the organization might be wise to cut their losses and declare Severino a reliever for life.

"It's a real honor," Severino said. "Last year they didn't trust me to start a regular game and right now I have the opportunity to open the postseason. I feel proud of myself and the team too. At the end of the season, [pitching coach] Larry [Rothschild] told me to go and work out because I was going to be a starter and fight for a spot in spring training. That's what I did."

The Yankees had home field advantage on their side, with the October 3 showdown set for Yankee Stadium because Joe Girardi's club finished with six more victories than the Twins' eighty-five during the regular season. But that had been no guarantee during New York's previous experience in a Wild Card game, and Brian Cashman said that he was far more nervous watching the two teams take batting practice than he would have been suiting up for a jump off the side of that Connecticut office tower.

"See, I *like* rappelling off the building," Cashman said. "Now I do, anyway. I don't like these nine innings, but I'm thankful to have the chance to be on pins and needles. That's what you work for. There's no safety net in the cage match."

When playing head-to-head during the regular season, the Yankees had taken four of six games from Minnesota, including polishing off a three-game sweep in an 11–3 rout on September 20 that included back-to-back homers by Aaron Judge and Gary Sanchez. Sanchez's 33 homers in 2017 set a new record for a Yankees backstop, eclipsing the 30 hit by Yogi Berra (1952, 1956) and Jorge Posada (2003).

Severino had started that game, his only career appearance against the Twins to date, but he had been worn down by an epic thirteen-pitch battle with Joe Mauer that ended with a run-scoring single. Severino was lifted after throwing forty-six pitches in the third inning, having allowed three runs and five hits in his second-shortest start of the season.

Still, the Yankees believed Severino was the right choice for the must-win game.

"Just what he's done all year; he's been dominant, he's attacking hitters," Aaron Judge said. "He's always getting in the good counts. Every time I look up there, it's always 0-1, 0-2. He's never falling behind a lot of hitters. When you've got his repertoire and his stuff and you're getting ahead of guys like that, good things will happen. He just dominates."

Managed by Paul Molitor, a Hall of Fame infielder during his twenty-one-year playing career with the Brewers, Blue Jays, and Twins, Minnesota had enjoyed a remarkable turnaround, becoming the first team in history to make the playoffs after losing 100 games in the previous season. Their young stars had fought valiantly after the front office waved the white flag in late July, approving a series of moves that included trading pitcher Jaime Garcia to New York.

The youngest Yankees pitcher to start a potential elimination game since Mel Stottlemyre in Game 7 of the 1964 World Series, Severino appeared to be cool and collected on the eve of the Wild Card game, saying that he was "not nervous" at all. That changed when he arrived at the mound on a clear sixty-two-degree evening. Severino's command was absent, and second baseman Brian Dozier crushed his fifth pitch over Brett Gardner's head in left field for a leadoff homer.

A pop out and a walk followed before Eddie Rosario ripped a line drive over the right-field wall for a two-run homer. The plan had been for Severino to give his team six good innings, then turn the game over to the bullpen, but that was not going to happen. By the time Eduardo Escobar flared a single into center field, Chad Green was already warming in the bullpen, and Girardi retrieved the ball one batter later when Max Kepler doubled.

There were boos heard among the crowd of 49,280 as Severino trudged to the dugout, leaving the bullpen to soak up the most formidable task in franchise postseason history since Whitey Ford recorded four outs in the ten-inning Game 6 of the 1958 World Series against the Milwaukee Braves.

"I tried to do too much," Severino said. "I just didn't command my pitches and was always behind in the count."

Making his postseason debut, Green and his disappearing fastball quickly turned the night around, pinning two Twins aboard with swinging strikeouts of Byron Buxton and Zack Granite. Didi Gregorius jazzed the crowd with a three-run homer off starter Ervin Santana in the home half of the first inning, and it was a brand-new ballgame.

"It was a really great feeling for me to be able to come up big, to tie the game right there," Gregorius said. "We got the fans and everybody right back in the game."

The Yankees kept coming, knocking Santana out after two innings. Gardner hit a second-inning homer into the second deck in right field, Jose Berrios served up a run-scoring Greg Bird single and a two-run Aaron Judge homer, and the Bronx bullpen was able to take it from there.

"That's what it's all about, postseason baseball," Judge said. "This is where a lot of those numbers that are hanging out there in left field, this is where they made a name for themselves, in the postseason."

No pitching staff had been asked to get twenty-six relief outs in a non-injury postseason situation since Dwight Gooden recorded one out while pitching for the Indians against the Red Sox in the 1998 ALDS. Green, David Robertson, Tommy Kahnle, and Aroldis Chapman were up to the challenge. The quartet of relievers struck out thirteen Twins, allowing one run as the Yankees advanced to the American League Division Series with an 8–4 win.

"To get through the whole postseason, you have to do it a bunch of different ways," Chase Headley said. "This is a great way to do it the first time, but you're not going to be successful using your bullpen for 8⅔

David Robertson was up for any situation after rejoining his original team in 2017, going 5-0 with a 1.03 ERA and one save in 30 appearances for the Yankees.

innings for the entire postseason. Fortunately, we have the group that can do that, but our starters will do their job."

Robertson had played the part of an ultimate team player since putting the pinstripes back on, disregarding his contract and career accomplishments to tell Girardi that he was always available for any situation. Nicknamed "Houdini" for his ability to wriggle free of tight spots, Robertson turned in a valiant effort, working 3⅓ innings and throwing fifty-two pitches, both career highs. Robertson's only longer outing as a pro came on April 26, 2008, when he threw 3⅔ innings for Double-A Trenton.

"Roles may change throughout the season, and I may be asked to do things that I'm not normally used to doing, but it doesn't mean I can't go out there and do it," Robertson said. "If it's the second or third inning and that's when I'm needed to help us win a ballgame, that's when I'll pitch. It doesn't matter to me. I just want to win another World Series."

Kahnle also retired all seven batters he faced, and the July trade with the White Sox had paid tangible dividends. As bright as Blake Rutherford's future might turn out to be in Chicago's outfield, Robertson and Kahnle had combined for 5⅔ scoreless innings in a win-or-go home postseason game. The Yankees popped champagne in their clubhouse, and Gardner had been right—celebrating was more fun at home.

"There's a lot on the line in a one-game playoff like this. Anything can happen," Gardner said. "As we found out two years ago, it can all come and go pretty quick and everything can be done. To be able to move on, it means a lot."

There wasn't much time to savor the accomplishment, as they were off to Cleveland in a matter of hours. The defending American League champions presented a formidable challenge: Terry Francona had piloted the club to 102 wins, including an epic run of twenty-two straight victories from August 24 to September 14, establishing an all-time AL record and second in major league history only to a twenty-six game streak by the 1916 New York Giants. The streak helped Cleveland easily claim the AL Central by seventeen games over Minnesota.

"They might be the best team in the American League, and last year we knew they had a really good team too," Gardner said. "We know how good their rotation can be, and offensively and defensively. We've just got to play well. If we play well, we've got a chance."

Though Francona's rotation featured one of the AL's best pitchers in Cy Young Award front-runner Corey Kluber, the Indians elected to assign Kluber to pitch ALDS Game 2 so he would be on line to start a potential Game 5 at home. Instead, the Yankees arrived at Progressive Field preparing to face eccentric right-hander Trevor Bauer, who had gone 17-9 with a 4.19 ERA during the regular season.

Bauer had earned a place in baseball's litany of bizarre off-field injuries during the 2016 postseason, when he required ten stitches after gnarling the pinky finger of his pitching hand while repairing a drone, then had to exit an ALCS start against the Blue Jays after twenty-one pitches because the gash opened on the mound. There were no such mishaps in the ALDS opener, as the twenty-six-year-old Bauer's nasty curveball made the Yankees look like a bunch that was not ready for prime time in a 4–0 Indians victory.

"He varies it. He likes to play around with it a little bit," Judge said. "He'll throw in there a little softer, and then in certain counts he'll go a little harder with it and change up the spin a little bit. He works with it. He's out there pitching. He's done a good job this year, and he did a good job tonight. Now we've got to pick ourselves up and get ready for tomorrow."

Sonny Gray struggled in Game 1, giving up three runs in 3⅓ innings.

Fireworks popped and the crowd erupted in a cry of "Bruuuuuce!" after a two-run homer by the Indians' Jay Bruce, a left-handed hitting outfielder whom Cashman had entertained acquiring during the summer months. Ultimately, Cashman balked at the Mets' request to absorb the remaining $4.2 million of Bruce's $13 million salary; the thirty-year-old slugger went to Cleveland instead. Bauer shut down the Bombers, holding them hitless until Aaron Hicks doubled off the left-field wall with one out in the sixth inning.

"We were in the game the whole time," Todd Frazier said. "We were within grand slam range, but we just couldn't get on base at the right time. If you get three hits, there's no chance you are going to win a game like that."

Bauer settled for 6⅔ innings of scoreless, two-hit ball, striking out eight, as Judge and Sanchez combined to go 0-for-8 with five strikeouts. Cleveland hurlers tipped their hands at the scouting report on the Bombers duo; twenty-one of the thirty-five pitches they saw were curveballs. Judge in particular had struggled to make solid contact with hooks since the All-Star break, hitting .104 (7-for-67) on breaking balls put into play.

"They need to beat us three times," Dellin Betances said. "They've got great pitching, but at the same time we believe in the guys we have here. We've always fought back when we're down."

Kluber loomed large for Game 2. Nicknamed "Klubot" for his stoic, robotic demeanor, the thirty-one-year-old righty had held the Yankees to three runs and six hits over seventeen innings (0.86 ERA) in two dominant regular season starts, striking out eighteen against two walks. New York was countering with its stopper, CC Sabathia, who'd gone 9-0 with a 1.71 ERA in ten starts immediately following a team loss during the regular season.

Sabathia shrugged that off as a statistical quirk, saying that he had never been one to look too deeply into the numbers, but the Yanks knew they could count on the big man to empty the tank. That was especially true in Cleveland, where he'd made his name after being called up to the big leagues as a celebrated twenty-year-old prospect.

"I've pitched here a lot," Sabathia said. "I played here parts of almost eight years, so I'm very familiar with the city, a lot of the fans. A lot of who I am as an adult, as a male, as an adult man, Cleveland kind of shaped that. Three of my kids were born here. I have a lot of history in the city."

He was about to write more, and perhaps the calendar—Friday the 13th—should have indicated that the contest would be anything but mundane. The plan to force Kluber into deep counts worked with aplomb, as Gary Sanchez and Aaron Hicks each homered off the ace, sending him to the showers after 2⅔ innings in arguably the worst start of his career.

Sanchez hit a two-run homer to dead center field in the first inning and Hicks hammered a three-run shot in the third, chasing Kluber. Greg Bird's two-run homer off Mike Clevinger in the fifth inning seemed to seal the deal, putting New York up 8–3 at the time.

"At 8–3, we were comfortable with that and we feel confident, but anything can happen," Bird said. "There was still a lot of game left."

Sabathia had allowed three runs in the first two innings before settling in, and had retired twelve of the last thirteen batters when Joe Girardi walked to the mound in the sixth inning, lifting the starter after seventy-seven pitches. Girardi wanted the game in the hands of the bullpen and his choice was Chad Green, who recorded the second out of the inning on an Austin Jackson flyout, then got ahead of Yan Gomes 0-2 but couldn't put the catcher away.

Gomes dented the left-field wall with a line drive double, and Francona sent up the left-handed Lonnie Chisenhall to pinch-hit for Giovanny Urshela. Green again worked the count to 0-2 before zipping the seventh pitch of the at-bat inside, a 95.7-mph fastball that home plate umpire Dan Iassogna believed had clipped Chisenhall's right hand.

The ball caromed sharply into Gary Sanchez's glove, and Sanchez immediately yelled, "Foul! Foul!" while looking into the visiting dugout for help, believing that the pitch had hit the knob of Chisenhall's bat. If so, it would have registered as a foul tip and an inning-ending strikeout, since Sanchez caught the ball.

"I definitely heard something," Sanchez said. "I wasn't sure if it hit the bat. I didn't think it hit him because he never reacted to that. He stood still there."

Chisenhall later said that he felt vibration in his right hand and trotted to first base, believing that replay would sort out the issue one way or the other. From the bench, Chase Headley also shouted for a replay, believing Chisenhall's actions were not consistent with a player who had been hit by a pitch. Girardi hesitated.

Brett Weber, the Yankees' video coordinator, frantically refreshed his replay screen, but the super slow-motion video that would be seen in living rooms across North America did not arrive in time for Weber to make a definitive call. It wasn't until the next batter was already walking to home plate that Weber was able to report what had actually happened, and Girardi was spotted reacting with frustration to the news.

"Slowly it trickled down that it didn't hit him, and now everybody is like, 'We should have done something different,'" Headley said. "But in the heat of the moment, those types of things can happen. That turned out to be a huge play. It's the biggest play of the game. I think when you get word that the call was right, why would you challenge it?"

After the game, Girardi said that he had already gone beyond the thirty seconds allotted for managers to issue a challenge, though he later acknowledged that he—not the umpires—had motioned for play to continue. Since the use of replay was expanded in 2014, Girardi's philosophy had been not to waste challenges on inconclusive replays, and the Yankees' seventy-five percent success rate in 2017 was the best in the majors.

Though Girardi understood that he had two challenges remaining, he added somewhat confusingly that, being a former catcher, "I think about rhythm and never want to take a pitcher out of rhythm, and have them stand over there [for] two minutes to tell me that he wasn't hit."

Given the eventual outcome, Green would have preferred to have his tempo altered. Two pitches later, Green snapped off a backdoor slider that Francisco Lindor clanged off the right-field foul pole, trimming Cleveland's deficit to 8–7. Green said that as Lindor rounded the bases, it hadn't occurred to him that the Yankees could have been out of the inning with a challenge.

"For me, it didn't even register that it would have been a foul tip and strike three until after," Green said. "It was an important part of the game, but it just didn't work out in my favor."

Bruce tied the game in the eighth with an opposite-field homer off David Robertson, who seemed to be running on fumes after the fifty-two-pitch outing in the Wild Card game, and the night stretched into extra innings. New York wasted a gift error by third baseman Erik Gonzalez in the 11th when pinch-runner Ronald Torreyes was picked off second base on a snap throw by the catcher Gomes. In the Yanks' dugout, Todd Frazier fired a paper cup at the wall in frustration.

"The plan right there was for [Gardner] to bunt and me to go to third. I was trying to be aggressive there," Torreyes said. "I wanted to make sure that I had a good lead. I tried to get back, I did everything I could to get back as fast as I could. But I couldn't make it."

Two innings later, Gomes knocked home the winning run with a single down the third base line off Dellin Betances, who was beginning his third inning of relief. The mood in the visiting clubhouse was one of stunned disbelief, with the players trying to comprehend that they were now down 0–2 in a series that could have—should have—been tied.

"When you go in somewhere and you can split the first couple of games, you kind of feel like, 'Mission Accomplished,'" Headley said. "We had an opportunity to do that, and to let a big one slip away was disappointing. But I think guys were confident that we could beat these guys."

Girardi became an instant scapegoat. In the early morning hours immediately following the loss, Aroldis Chapman "liked" an Instagram comment by another user that read, "Let's hope Joe's contract is not renewed after the season. He's a complete imbecile." The next day, Chapman apologized to Girardi; since Girardi does not use social media in any form, the manager required a primer on what Instagram was and how it works.

"I really believe it was an accident. We talked about it," Girardi said. "He came in and apologized. He was concerned about it that night. He had conversations with people, not me, because it was two or three in the morning. I had to ask how it works because I don't know how that works. I guess it's easy to hit a button when you're scrolling. I really believe him, I take his word for it that it was an accident and we move forward."

Girardi had bigger fish to fry. As anticipated, he was roasted in the tabloids and on sports talk radio for his blunder, warning his family that they should prepare to hear him get booed before Game 3 at Yankee Stadium. As the team returned to New York for a workout day, Girardi delivered a cleaner version of the press conference that he had held in Cleveland, admitting that he had "screwed up" and was feeling "horrible" about it.

"Let's just see what happens tomorrow and as we move forward," Girardi said. "That will probably determine the severity of it."

The contest was played ten years and one day to the date of what Joe Torre would later call his greatest regret in a dugout, which happened to take place on the same patch of turf. In Game 2 of the 2007 ALDS at what was then called Jacobs Field, Torre believed he should have pulled the Yankees off the diamond when a swarm of Lake Erie midges enveloped pitcher Joba Chamberlain. New York lost that game and the series, marking Torre's final tour as the team's manager.

It seemed that if the Yankees were to save Girardi from a similar fate, they needed to win the next three games and end Cleveland's season. A window into the players' thinking came courtesy of Gary Sanchez, who whipped out his iPhone and tapped out a tweet that would generate thousands of likes and retweets: "Every great story happened when someone decided not to give up."

Girardi's warning to his wife and children was prescient; when players from both teams were introduced prior to Game 3, an extended, loud boo trailed Girardi from the dugout to the first-base line. Hours before, as part of a ten-minute session with the team's beat reporters in his Yankee Stadium office, Girardi touched upon the uncertainty concerning his future as the team's manager. It seemed like an odd topic to discuss so freely before a must-win playoff game.

"I think an organization has to do what they're comfortable with, right?" Girardi said. "And it may not always agree with the person that is either being fired or however it goes. But I think that's Hal and Brian's decision. Whatever their decision is, you know, I'll live with."

Girardi had addressed his team briefly before Game 3, apologizing for what had taken place in Cleveland while reminding his players that he had believed in them since the first day of spring training, and he still did so. Todd Frazier had been the first to speak up, shouting, "Let's go!" as he led the Yankees out of the clubhouse and toward their dugout.

"He talked to us for a little bit, had a quick meeting," Gregorius said. "He admitted to it. It just shows everybody is united. Everybody has accountability. That's the best thing. If you made a mistake, you admit it. You pass it on. That's in the past. All he told us was, 'Hey, let's play one game at a time right now, and that's all we can control right now. Whatever happened in the past happened in the past.' We, as a team, we always have each other's back."

The Yankees had the house on their side, having played exceptionally all season at Yankee Stadium, where they owned a 51-30 record at home that rated as the best in the American League. Now, with thousands of pairs of stomping feet making its triple decks quiver and liquids flying through the air anytime something positive happened on the field, many observed that the building was finally beginning to look, sound and feel like the old Stadium.

"I've never been a part of something like that," Judge said. "I heard stories about the old Yankee Stadium, what it was like during the playoff runs then. What I've experienced in the couple of home games in the playoffs is out of this world. It's a jungle out there. They're behind us every pitch. It's a real home field advantage."

Todd Frazier agreed; for a moment, he said that he was transported to 1995, when he'd been a nine-year-old in the far reaches of the upper deck for New York's fifteen-inning Game 2 ALDS win over the Mariners.

"It was crazy. I remember telling my dad, 'Hey, man, are we going to be all right up here?'" Frazier said. "He's like, 'Yeah, we'll be all right.' They're exciting. You can hear the crowd playing a big part. We appreciate them and the way they're getting after it, man. We're having fun. It's just a great place to play, and with the crowd behind us 100 percent, seems like every pitch, it helps out that much more."

Mariano Rivera had pitched the final 3⅓ innings of that epic against Seattle, and he was an appropriate guest for Game 3 of the ALDS, firing a cutter over the outside corner for a ceremonial first pitch strike. Wearing a pinstriped No. 42 jersey over a collared shirt, the forty-seven-year-old Rivera looked like he could still get big league hitters out, but so could Masahiro Tanaka.

Claiming the mound from Rivera, Tanaka fired what he called "probably the biggest win that I have gotten since I came here," handcuffing the Indians to three hits over seven scoreless innings by getting them to flail regularly at his lethal splitter over the course of a ninety-two-pitch effort.

The bright lights and pressure-packed atmosphere were exactly what Tanaka had envisioned when an eight-person contingent of team officials traveled to Los Angeles in January 2014, going up against at least nine other interested clubs to sell the Japanese standout on why he should accept $155 million of the Bombers' cash.

"I came here to pitch in these types of games, and to be able to help the team win in these types of games," Tanaka said. "As a player, those are the moments that you want to go in there and shine the most."

Judge's large frame saved two runs and potentially the season in the sixth inning, leaping at the right-field wall to deny Lindor's bid for a Yankee Stadium special. Chants of "M-V-P!" echoed throughout the crowd of 48,614, and Judge's glove-work made it easy to look past his three strike-outs and a walk, as he remained hitless in the Division Series.

"I wasn't making any contact at the plate, so you've got to make an impact on the game somehow," Judge said. "Luckily, I was able to do it on defense."

Indians right-hander Carlos Carrasco shut down the Yanks through 5⅔ innings, and Greg Bird provided the only offense of the night, turning on a 96-mph Andrew Miller fastball for a majestic seventh inning homer that landed in the second deck of the right field seats.

It was the kind of moment that had kept Bird sane and focused through what seemed to be an interminable series of doctors' waiting rooms, abbreviated minor league assignments, and finally a mid-summer surgical procedure. Bird screamed and pumped his fist as he began to run to first base, then repeatedly thumped his chest when he returned to the dugout. Gary Sanchez said that it was the first time he could remember ever seeing the stoic Bird so animated.

"I'm not impressed. That's Greg Bird," Judge said. "That's what I expect out of him. That's what he's shown me through the minor leagues, the short time he's been up here. He's a fantastic hitter, probably our best hitter, and he's proving it right now."

Sanchez also earned plaudits by sacrificing his body throughout Tanaka's effort, with the most meaningful blocks coming after Jason Kipnis' one-out triple in the fourth inning. Tanaka was confident enough in his splitter to use it repeatedly, striking out the next two hitters, and Girardi applauded Sanchez's bruising effort.

"Really good. Really, really good," Girardi said. "As I've said, this is our catcher. There's going to be times where he has a bad day, like anyone else, like any other catcher. But he was really, really good tonight."

One day after apologizing to Girardi for his social media faux pas, Chapman gave the Yankees something that they could truly "like," pitching around a pair of ninth inning singles to convert a five out save. They still needed one more win to force the series back to Cleveland, and that would give Severino his chance to atone for the poor outing in the Wild Card game against the Twins.

Earning serenades of "Sev-er-ino!" from the sellout crowd, the Dominican righty hurled seven strong innings while leading New York to a 7–3 victory in Game 4, becoming the youngest Yankees starter to notch a postseason victory since Dave Righetti in 1981. He struck out seven, the last of which was a 100-mph fastball that froze Chisenhall for the second out of the seventh inning. After that pitch, Severino pumped his fist and screamed.

"I was feeling great," Severino said. "The location on my pitches was great. Of course I heard the stadium calling my name."

Seeing Bauer for the second time in the series, the Yankees were ready to pounce on the right-hander, whom Francona brought back on short rest. Bauer lasted 1⅔ innings as the hitters patiently built up his pitch count before striking for four unearned runs.

Cleveland played sloppy defense, committing four errors—two of them by third baseman Giovanny Urshela, who was smoked on the left ankle by a Starlin Castro line drive, setting up New York's big second inning. After a passed ball advanced Castro to second base, Todd Frazier ripped a Bauer curveball into the left-field corner for a run-scoring double.

"A lot of two-out RBIs, those are huge," Frazier said. "That's where you make your money. And that's what we were able to do. Put the pressure on them early."

Aaron Hicks and Brett Gardner followed with hits before Judge finally notched his first hit of the ALDS, a two-run double that one-hopped the fence in left field. Judge slid into second base, clapped his hands and pointed both index fingers toward the first-base dugout. Judge had been fed a steady diet of breaking balls and fastballs above the catcher's mask during the series, but on the eighth pitch of the at-bat, Bauer challenged him with a 96.3-mph fastball that he could drive.

"It felt good," Judge said. "I'm not getting those mistakes. When they throw it over the middle of the plate, I've got to do damage, and I haven't been able to do that. It's been a grind, but we keep winning, and that's what is most important."

Sanchez extended New York's lead in the sixth inning with an opposite-field homer off Bryan Shaw, greeted at home plate by a leaping biceps bash from Bird. That cushion came in handy when Dellin Betances' control issues resurfaced in the eighth inning. The right-hander was searching for answers when he threw eight of twelve pitches out of the strike zone, but Tommy Kahnle bailed out his teammate by completing a six-out save in what Kahnle said was the most important outing of his career to date.

"You always have to have it in the back of your mind that one day you might be on a team that is in this situation," Kahnle said. "My whole life, I've been waiting for this moment."

The Bombers had prevented the Indians from celebrating on their turf, bailing out their embattled manager in the process. In fact, Cleveland hadn't held a lead in the series since they picked up their room keys in New York. As the Yankees walked into Progressive Field, it was impossible not to note the shift of emotions that had taken place since their departure. Gardner observed that, for whatever reason, these Yanks seemed to respond to dire circumstances.

"I just know the guys in this room," Gardner said. "They're going to fight and not give up and keep going until the end. With our backs against the wall, we seem to play a little bit better."

They needed that to hold true in Game 5 against Kluber, a meeting which represented their fourth potential elimination game in a span of eight days. This was the possibility that Francona had prepared for by having Kluber go in the series' second game instead of the opener, and the stars seemed to have aligned perfectly for the Tribe.

Indians fans packed Progressive Field once more, waving their red towels in anticipation of seeing the Klubot emotionlessly dismantle the Yankees and pitch Cleveland to the next round. Didi Gregorius ordered a re-write of the script, silencing all but a small pocket of Bombers fans with a solo homer in the first inning and a two-run shot in the third.

Gregorius had been 1-for-13 in the ALDS, but he pounced on a 94-mph Kluber fastball for the first homer and then teed off on an 86-mph curveball for the second. Saying that they were probably the biggest hits of his career to that point, Gregorius thought about the daydreams he'd once lapsed into while taking in Curacao's mountainous vistas, many of which had involved succeeding on a stage like this.

"As a kid, we always want to play in a big situation," Gregorius said. "I wanted to be a major league player when I was growing up. Then I worked for it. Now that I'm here, being in this unbelievable, unbelievable organization, all the history and everything, it's the best thing because everybody is together and the team is really united."

Kluber was dispatched to his second early exit of the series, lasting 3⅔ innings. Francona said that Kluber was "fighting a lot" to be on the hill, and while Kluber refused to elaborate, Cashman later said that Kluber hadn't been in top form for either outing. Kluber had missed all of May with a lower back strain, prompting speculation that he was also ailing in the postseason.

"It doesn't do any good to go into details," Kluber said. "I was healthy enough to go out there and try to pitch."

Sabathia, meanwhile, seemed to be on his game. Savoring the atmosphere, he rolled the clock back by going as hard as he could before burning out, retiring the first nine Indians and thirteen of the first fourteen—including leaving a divot in the turf as he fell to his knees, charging his 300-pound frame toward home plate to snare a third inning bunt attempt by Roberto Perez. Sanchez thumped Sabathia on his left chest, and the big man grinned widely.

Four straight hits chased Sabathia in the fifth inning, but Robertson bailed Sabathia out of the jam, needing two pitches to induce Francisco Lindor to hit into an inning-ending double play. As Gregorius fielded the grounder, stepped on second base, and fired to first base, Sabathia screamed with joy, smashing his palms onto the padded railing of the dugout.

CC Sabathia continued to lend a valuable veteran presence to the Yankees' clubhouse in 2017, going 14-5 with a 3.69 ERA in his seventeenth big league season. Saying that there is "unfinished business" with the Baby Bombers, Sabathia plans to retire after the 2019 season.

"It's incredible. The best [bullpen] I've ever seen," Sabathia said. "We've got four or five closers down there. We have a lot of confidence they're going to get the job done."

Robertson pitched 2⅔ scoreless innings to pick up the win. Brett Gardner provided two key insurance runs with a ninth inning single that ended an epic twelve pitch battle with Cody Allen, and Chapman converted a six-out save as the Yankees became the tenth team to advance after losing the first two games of a best-of-five postseason series.

"We moved on for a reason—because we played better than they did," Gardner said. "They had a better team than we did over the course of 162 games, but I said all the time in September, it's not about how good of a season you had. It's about playing the best at the right time."

In the first-base dugout, Girardi celebrated with his coaches and rushed onto the playing field, granted the sweetest of reprieves. Amid the champagne-soaked celebration in the visiting clubhouse, Todd Frazier declared, "This one's for Joe!" In hindsight, most of his teammates seemed either hesitant or uninterested when reporters provided opportunities to further discuss that storyline.

Standing in the hallway outside a kitchenette area, safely out of spraying distance from his players, Brian Cashman gave no indication that a managerial change was in the recesses of his mind. Saying that the ALDS victory "turns the page" on what would have otherwise been an ugly chapter in Girardi's career, Cashman preferred to focus his attention upon what his players accomplished in those last three games against Cleveland.

"Coming back against this particular team, it's a pretty impossible task," Cashman said. "That's a special team, run by a special group of people, from their front office to their manager to their coaching staff. This is as perfectly run of an organization as you can have right now. They're someone that all of us are trying to emulate, the way they go about their business both on and off the field. It seems like every move makes sense and is a stroke of genius.

"This was an extremely well put together team. I would call this a super-team, actually. That's why you've got to play the games out. I've produced 100-win teams that got knocked out in the first round, too many times. That's why you don't bet on baseball and you've got to play the games out, and play your best in October. A lot can change really quickly, as we've just seen again."

CHAPTER 15

TAKE IT TO THE LIMIT

The fifth episode of *Seinfeld*'s seventh season was "The Hot Tub," featuring a storyline in which Yankees employee George Costanza (Jason Alexander) is tasked with entertaining a group of visiting Astros executives. While taking the Texans out to a New York City watering hole, Costanza picks up the habit of casually swearing. The gag culminates in a scene where Costanza is overheard by a superior on his Yankee Stadium telephone, screaming to his new buddies: "You tell that son of a bitch that no Yankee is *ever* coming to Houston!"

That episode aired in October 1995, two years before Major League Baseball instituted interleague play, and eighteen years before the Astros shifted to the American League West after spending their first fifty-one summers in the National League. The Yankees and Astros shared some quirky history: Mickey Mantle had hit the Astrodome's first home run in an April 1965 exhibition, Yogi Berra joined the Astros as a coach after George Steinbrenner fired him as manager sixteen games into the 1985 season, and six Houston pitchers combined to pitch a no-hitter in June 2003 at Yankee Stadium. Roger Clemens and Andy Pettitte headlined the list of notable players who had suited up for both franchises.

With apologies to Costanza, the Yankees were indeed heading to Houston, as a result of the Astros having steamrolled the Red Sox in the other half of the ALDS. As the Yanks went through airport security in Cleveland, they did so in anticipation of an American League Championship Series that would feature a head-to-head showdown between Judge and second baseman Jose Altuve, the leading candidates for the AL MVP award.

The award is voted on by members of the Baseball Writers' Association of America, and since ballots must be cast by the final day of the regular season, nothing that transpired in the ALCS would influence the outcome. In the court of public opinion, supporters on both sides held strong views.

Altuve won his third AL batting title in 2017, slashing .346/.410/.547 with 24 homers, 81 RBIs, and 32 stolen bases. Judge batted .284 but finished with a higher OPS (1.049) and more RBIs (114), leading the league in homers (52), runs scored (128), walks (127), and strikeouts (208). It was a terrific example of baseball's equality; you couldn't have two more different players in terms of size (Altuve stood five-foot-six) and style of play, yet they were both able to make crucial contributions for their respective teams.

"He goes 100 miles an hour for nine innings," Brett Gardner said of Altuve. "I can appreciate that."

As the hours ticked down to ALCS Game 1, Altuve was asked who he would vote for if offered a ballot. He and Judge had spent some time talking during the All-Star Game in Miami, and Altuve recalled the young Yankee as being wide-eyed, seemingly incredulous that he had been invited to participate in the festivities. Altuve laughed, telling Judge that he had come to the Home Run Derby specifically to watch the rookie slugger hit.

"He was so humble and was like, 'No, no, no, I'm happy to be here with you guys,'" Altuve recalled. "And if he wins the MVP, I think that it couldn't happen to a better guy, because he works really hard and I like the way he plays. He hits all his homers and he doesn't even—you know, never enjoy it. And I was like, 'Wow, this guy is so good and he's so humble about it.' Maybe in another life I want to be Aaron Judge and hit all those homers."

Judge appreciated the compliments, but downplayed attempts by reporters to paint the ALCS as the 'Altuve vs. Judge show.'

"It's about the Astros and the Yankees: who's going to go to the World Series," Judge said. "It's just about the team right now. I think the fans are more excited about two great teams getting an opportunity to play. But I've talked to him a little bit—what a great guy. You see what he does on the baseball field, but the type of person he is, you see the passion he has for the game, and it's pretty fun to watch."

With stifling heat outdoors, MLB kept the roof sealed drumtight at Minute Maid Park, producing perfect conditions as the Yankees prepared to battle against Dallas Keuchel. The bearded left-hander had ended their 2015 season with a gem on short rest in the Wild Card game at Yankee Stadium, but only Gardner, Chase Headley, Greg Bird, and Didi Gregorius remained from the lineup that Girardi sent out that night.

The Yanks' number three and five hitters from that game—Carlos Beltran and Brian McCann—were now wearing Astros orange, yet the new-look-lineup produced results that appeared much the same as they had two years prior. Taking advantage of a generous strike zone, Keuchel and his array of spinning pitches were again mystifying, as the twenty-nine-year-old struck out 10 over seven scoreless innings to pitch Houston to a 2–1 victory.

"He just lives on the corner," Judge said. "He doesn't miss his spot. If you go through the whole game, there weren't a lot of pitches in the heart of the plate. He likes to live on the edges and commands it well. He mixes speeds well and keeps you off-balance."

The Yanks managed four singles off Keuchel and only one runner reached second base against him. That was in the fifth inning, when Bird singled and advanced to second on an Altuve error. Bird's best attribute had never been his speed, and three months removed from right ankle surgery, that seemed to be especially true.

Keuchel hung a slider that Judge rifled into left field for a clean single, and Bird was waved home, having made contact with the third-base bag at the moment left fielder Marwin Gonzalez scooped the ball. Gonzalez uncorked a one-hop rocket to catcher Brian McCann that arrived in time to cut down Bird. Girardi signaled that he wanted to challenge the call, but the review clearly showed that McCann had applied the tag to Bird's legs before he reached home plate.

"Well, we thought he was out," Girardi said. "But God knows I'm not doing *that* again."

Though Bird was in motion on the 3-2 pitch, he had hesitated before getting into his secondary lead, mindful that Keuchel might whirl for a pickoff attempt. Every step counted. Girardi said that if Bird was ten percent faster—five percent, even—he would have scored.

"I'm too slow. I wish I was a little faster," Bird said. "That's baseball. I was running. I feel like I did what I could do there. What are you going to do? He made a good throw, put a good tag on me. So be it."

Tanaka was charged with the loss despite holding the Astros hitless into the fourth inning, permitting two runs and four hits over six innings. Bird broke up the shutout with two outs in the ninth inning, dinging the right-field foul pole off closer Ken Giles. Despite the one run loss, Bird said that he believed the Yankees were proving that they could hang with the big boys of the American League.

"I said it after Cleveland, you've got to beat good teams and good pitchers if you want to get to where you want to be," Bird said. "We were in that game the whole way, really. We didn't get some hits or didn't get some runs in, but really, we were in that game."

It was a fairly quick turnaround for Game 2, with the first pitch thrown after 3:00 p.m. local time, and the score would be the same as Game 1—Astros 2, Yankees 1.

This time, it was Justin Verlander stifling the Yanks' bats, with the thirty-four-year-old going old-school by striking out thirteen in a complete game, 124-pitch effort. Todd Frazier's fifth inning RBI knock to left-center field, which wedged between a chain-link fence and the wall padding for a ground-rule double, accounted for New York's only run off Verlander. Gardner had been thrown out trying to stretch a double into a triple earlier in the game, a dare that proved costly.

"[The losses] are both tough to swallow," Frazier said. "We know what we're capable of. It's just going to take one thing and one little spark to get us going. I think in two days we're going to find that."

Carlos Correa touched Aroldis Chapman for the decisive hit of Game 2, a ninth inning double into the right-center field gap that scored Altuve all the way from first base. Judge fielded the ball in front of the warning track and threw to second base, where it was cut off by Gregorius. Girardi said that getting the ball to Gregorius had been the right play, describing him as "the guy on the field with the best arm."

"We were playing deep. We didn't want anything to get by us, especially with Altuve at first," Judge said. "Anything that gets to the wall, Altuve scores on. I just tried to get it in to Didi, because I thought if I got to him, I'd have a shot at the plate."

With third base coach Gary Pettis aggressively waving Altuve home,

Gregorius had no time to set his feet. He was still able to get off a throw while firing around Correa, who was executing a pop-up slide into second base. Gregorius said that the play was clean on Correa's part, though he acknowledged they did make contact. Girardi spoke with the umpires immediately after the play to ensure they had not seen interference.

Gregorius' throw skipped and Gary Sanchez could not handle the short hop, with Altuve swiping his left hand across home plate with the winning run. Resting on one knee, Sanchez allowed himself an extra beat before dutifully trudging over to pick up the baseball, which now rested a few feet in front of the right-handed batter's box.

"Bottom line is, if I catch that ball, he's going to be out," Sanchez said. "I dropped the ball. It was a small bounce, but that's a play that I know I can make."

In the Houston clubhouse, Brian McCann came to Sanchez's defense, saying that he thought it was a tough play and that his former teammate should not be blamed for the loss. On the contrary, McCann could speak to the hours required in the video room to throw the gear on and handle the Yankees' variety of pitchers, having done it one year prior. For a twenty-four-year-old in his first full season, McCann believed that Sanchez was doing fine.

"That is not an easy staff to catch," McCann said. "Guys that have splits, and they're throwing for strikes. You've got to frame them and then they bounce them. It's really hard to block a split-finger fastball, especially when they throw them for strikes as well."

Overshadowed by Sanchez's drop was the fact that Severino had been removed from Game 2 after four innings, having allowed a Correa homer that clipped the glove of a young fan perched in the first row behind the right-field wall. While it appeared to be a health-related exit, there was relief when it turned out there had been no injury to speak of.

As Girardi detailed later, there was concern when Severino appeared to flex his pitching shoulder in the fourth inning, and someone in the dugout told Girardi that Severino seemed to be "pushing the ball." Girardi visited the mound after a changeup to Marwin Gonzalez, and though Severino insisted that he was "100 percent," Girardi opted to err on the side of caution. Including the playoffs, Severino was now past 200 innings after having thrown 151⅓ between the majors and minors in 2016.

"I think it is my responsibility to protect this kid," Girardi said. "He's very young. He gave us a great effort, but I felt that I couldn't take a chance."

Severino simmered over the early exit, and it took him a while to cool off. Two days later, Girardi greeted Severino by asking him, "Do you still hate me?" The answer, Severino replied, was no. Girardi smiled, saying that it represented progress.

"I didn't agree with that. I wanted to go over there and pitch," Severino said. "I was feeling good. Even though I didn't strike out anybody, I was feeling good. I was getting outs…I'm a smart guy. If I feel something, I'm going to tell them. I'm not going to go over there and hurt myself."

If the Indians thought Yankee Stadium had been loud during the previous playoff round, the Bombers' home crowd took it to a new level when the ALCS shifted to New York, the first time in five years that a battle for the World Series had been played in the Bronx. The building was thumping before Sabathia threw the first pitch of Game 3, creating flashbacks to the Cleveland series as the players put on their pinstripes with the assignment of erasing an 0–2 series deficit.

"Everybody's heads were still high," Todd Frazier said. "We've been there before, that kind of thing. I think that kind helped us on the plane ride home. We're still playing some cards and getting going. We were coming home, we've got three home games here, and we know we've got a good shot."

The next nine innings served as a showcase for Judge to enjoy a post-season performance for the ages, crushing a three-run homer off reliever Will Harris and contributing several splendid defensive plays—the best of which was a fearless fourth inning crash into the right-field wall, sacrificing his body to take an extra-base hit away from Yuli Gurriel.

"He had a bead on it and he was going hard after it," Gardner said. "I knew that if he could get to it, he'd reel it in. That was a big play. He made another great play coming in and diving. He's an athlete out there. I know he's a big guy, but he covers a lot of ground and makes a lot of plays. He makes a difference on both sides of the ball."

Judge's chest also thudded hard against the turf in the fifth, when he dove to steal a hit from Cameron Maybin on a sinking line drive. That aggressive play looked more like a wide receiver trying to pick a pass off the turf, and confirmed what Mike Batesole had told Judge in his freshman year at Fresno State: if he could run down a football, he could do the same with a baseball.

The Yankees rolled to an 8–1 victory, and though Judge had been 2-for-27 with nineteen strikeouts in the postseason, he said that there had been no temptation to shake up his routine. Andy Pettitte, whom the Yanks summoned to throw a ceremonial first pitch during the ALCS, said that the approach that Cleveland and Houston pitchers were employing against Judge was easy to decipher.

"I would try to not throw it in the strike zone, try to make him expand the zone for sure, and I think that's what you're seeing," Pettitte said. "You're also running into a lot of great arms in the postseason. Every time he gets in situations like this and has an opportunity to be here, I believe that he'll get better and better at it and be able to control his emotions at it. You've got to remember, he's six-foot-seven, also. It makes you realize how special of a talent he is, to be able to do what he's done at that size."

Frazier also hit his first postseason homer, flicking his bat to connect with a low and outside Charlie Morton offering for a three-run shot to right-center field. As Frazier rounded the bases, he glanced down at his left wrist, as though he were checking a timepiece.

"I put my arm out and say, 'What time is it?'" Frazier said. "Just a little thing I do. I've been doing it forever, but I guess TV just finally caught onto it. I'm saying, 'What time is it? It's my time.'"

The Yanks tagged Morton for seven runs in 3⅔ innings, supporting what Sabathia called his "smoke and mirrors" attack plan, generating soft contact while limiting the Astros to three hits and four walks over six scoreless innings. Girardi tried again to allow Dellin Betances some slack to figure out his mechanical issues, but Betances walked both men he faced and Tommy Kahnle had to finish off the victory while Chapman got loose in the bullpen.

"I can't keep putting my teammates in those situations," Betances said. "My job is to go out there and have a clean inning and the next thing you know Kahnle has to clean up my mess like last time. Aroldis had to warm up. That's what upsets me the most. I know I'm better than that."

As Girardi mulled his lineup card for Game 4, run prevention was on his mind. Though he had lauded Sanchez's progress behind the plate, Sonny Gray's spinning arsenal had banged up the backstop in Game 1 of the ALDS against Cleveland. With that in mind, Girardi assigned backup

Austin Romine to catch Gray's simulated game prior to the ALCS opener, then teamed them for Game 4.

"It just looked like more of a comfortable mix. It happened with me as a player," said Girardi, who recalled that Joe Torre initially was reluctant to pair him with Pettitte. "I can't tell you sometimes why one guy might handle one guy better than the other. It just seems to happen for whatever reason. These two have worked a little bit better together."

The swap seemed to work acceptably, as Gray held the Astros to one hit over five-plus innings, but the Yankees couldn't get into gear against Lance McCullers Jr.'s curveball-heavy mix. Prior to the first pitch, Girardi had remarked that he would be "shocked" if McCullers reversed course and tried to pump gas by hitters, drawing laughter when he referenced Rocky Balboa's strategy in a (fictional) 1979 rematch against Apollo Creed.

"It's his DNA. It's how he gets people out," Girardi said. "Don't tell him I said that. It's like when Rocky switched from left to right and went back. It worked out pretty well for Rocky."

A twenty-three-year-old left-hander whose father, Lance Sr., pitched in sixty-three games for the Yankees in 1989 and 1990, McCullers threw forty-three curves in eighty-one pitches. The scouting report was dead on. The Yanks' issues were best represented by Judge's bizarre fourth inning sequence on the basepaths that left many scratching their heads. With one out, Judge took off on a shallow Sanchez fly ball to right field, then was forced to reverse course when Josh Reddick tracked it down for an out. Reddick threw to first base, where Judge was ruled out for an inning-ending double play.

Girardi challenged that call, and though replay indeed showed that Reddick's throw had arrived too late, it also gave the Astros ample time to look at the center field scoreboard and see in high definition that Judge had failed to touch second base on his way back to first. The Astros planned to appeal at second base, and so when play resumed and McCullers stepped off, Judge broke for second base immediately and was caught stealing to end the inning.

"The screen is as big as the state of New York," Astros manager A.J. Hinch said. "We could see that he didn't touch second base on the way back. They saw it, as well. Judge knew. As soon as the ball was put back in play, Judge was going to be out either way, so why not try for an easy base?

If he gets to second base safe, then we can't appeal, because that play is a live play."

Houston struck in the sixth, as Gray was chased by a leadoff walk and a catcher's interference error charged to Romine. With one out, Yuli Gurriel gave the Astros a 3–0 lead with a bases-clearing double off David Robertson, and Houston extended that lead to four runs in the seventh thanks to an error by Starlin Castro.

New York was nine outs away from having to face Dallas Keuchel with their season on the line. The most powerful Baby Bombers answered, beginning with Judge, who sparked the comeback with a long homer off McCullers that smacked into the restaurant glass over Monument Park. McCullers didn't bother to look, flipping his right arm with disgust.

"We've been in that situation a lot this year," Judge said. "We get down, but we keep fighting, keep putting out quality at-bats. We're never out of a game with the kind of offense we have."

Gregorius followed with a triple, scoring on a Sanchez sacrifice fly, cutting the deficit to 4–2. The Yankees pushed for more in the eighth, stunning the Astros by sending ten men to the plate with a furious four run rally. Todd Frazier and Chase Headley started the inning with hits off right-handed reliever Joe Musgrove, and Headley slipped as he touched the first-base bag, momentarily dropping to his hands and knees between first and second bases.

Headley's elation at having delivered a pinch-hit line drive instantly transformed into panic. Astros shortstop Carlos Correa threw to first base and Headley scrambled, slamming his left hand into second base ahead of Altuve's tag.

"I knew that Correa wasn't looking at me, so I knew he was going to be getting yelled at to throw the ball to first base," Headley said. "As soon as he made the throw, I'm going the other way and hopefully I can sneak in there. You've got to make the best out of a bad situation."

Brett Gardner knocked home New York's third run with a ground ball to the right side of the infield. Recognizing that a fly ball would have tied the game, Ken Giles threw four straight sliders to Judge, running the count to 2-2 before Judge fouled off a fastball. Giles went back to an 86-mph slider, but he left it up enough for Judge to launch a game-tying double, which was touched by a fan hanging over the auxiliary scoreboard in left field.

"That ballpark is alive," Judge said. "It was unbelievable. That stadium was rocking, the fans were going crazy. That's why we play this game, for a moment like that."

Didi Gregorius kept the line moving with a single that brought Sanchez to the plate. Giles fell behind Sanchez with two sliders out of the strike zone, then challenged with a 98-mph fastball right down the middle. Hitless in thirteen ALCS at-bats to that point, Sanchez punished the heater, blasting a two-run double to right-center field that gave the Yankees their first lead of the night.

"When I got to second base, my emotions were through the roof," Sanchez said. "When I looked around and saw the fans cheering and screaming, it's nice to see all their support to come out here. It's amazing."

The electric Yankees had come all the way back for six unanswered runs, securing a 6–4 victory. Gardner said that the four-run eighth was "one of the most fun innings I've ever been a part of," and as the Bombers

Aaron Judge and Greg Bird wait for Didi Gregorius to cross home plate during the eighth inning of the Yankees' improbable comeback win in ALCS Game 4.

remained undefeated at home in the 2017 postseason, a new feeling pervaded their clubhouse—one of confidence.

They'd still need to find a way to defeat either Dallas Keuchel or Justin Verlander to advance, but the emotional high of the last two games erased any fear of those matchups. Bring 'em on.

"I thought about it, 'Oh man, it's going to be a really uphill battle,'" Frazier said. "But once that gets in your mind, you have to think positive after that. I thought we still had a chance. We were still in grand slam range. Things started cooking. The fans were perfect for us today. They never stopped. They just keep pushing for us and we got something crazy going."

In Game 5, the Yankees finally solved their Keuchel bugaboo, moving nine good innings away from what would have been the forty-first World Series in franchise history. Bird, Judge, Sanchez, and Gregorius all contributed run-scoring hits to back a dominant Tanaka effort as New York sent the Astros to the airport with a 5–0 victory.

Bird got the party started, stroking a second-inning RBI single that represented the first run they had scored off of Keuchel in 14⅔ postseason innings. Judge ripped a third-inning RBI double down the left field line—remarkably, the first ground ball extra-base hit of Judge's big league career—before Sanchez and Gregorius contributed back-to-back run-scoring singles in the fifth, sending Keuchel on his long walk to the dugout.

It was later revealed that Bird, Castro, Gregorius, Judge, and Sanchez had all made an important adjustment to take some of the bite out of Keuchel's late-breaking arsenal, moving up in the batter's box so that they could catch the pitches a few inches in front of home plate.

"Getting on a great pitcher like that early is key," Bird said. "You try and take advantage of those situations. Getting on there, getting in scoring position, it puts pressure on him early. It doesn't let him settle in."

Tanaka ensured that the Astros were not able to get off the mat, leaning heavily on his slider to generate ten outs on the ground and eight via strikeout, limiting Houston to three hits and a walk over seven scoreless innings. Sanchez tacked on with a seventh-inning homer off righty Brad Peacock, and the Yankees clearly appeared to be the better team at that moment in time; they'd outscored the Astros, 19–5, and outhit them, 25–12, in the three games at Yankee Stadium.

"They played well, man," Houston outfielder George Springer said. "This is a tough place to play and they feed off that energy. Ideally, it would have been great to come out of here with a win or two but that's not the case. We'll see what happens."

As he fielded questions in front of his Yankee Stadium locker for what would turn out to be the final time as a rookie, Judge was asked if it had sunk in that he was one win away from playing in the World Series.

"Not yet. We're not going to think about that yet," Judge said. "We don't want to get ahead of ourselves. We've still got a job to do in Houston."

Including the postseason, the Yankees won nineteen of their final twenty-two games at Yankee Stadium, and now they needed to win one at Minute Maid Park. Constructed on the former site of the city's Union Station, the ballpark's most distinctive feature is the 800-feet of railroad track above the left-field wall upon which a train rolls, blowing its horn and ringing a bell when an Astros player hits a home run.

It would be up to the Yankees' pitching staff to keep that locomotive stationary and silent. The team took a later flight and opted to give their players a full day off between Games 5 and 6, with Girardi and Severino conducting dial-in conference calls with the media instead of heading to the ballpark. There were a few players in the clubhouse who would have liked to take the field, viewing their travel to the Space City as the equivalent of a football team icing the opposing kicker by calling a timeout.

"I think probably everyone would have probably rather played today," Girardi said. "When you're on a roll, you never want to stop playing."

The deep freeze in Game 6 had more to do with Verlander, who was once again sharp on his way to securing ALCS MVP honors. The Yankees had their bags packed for Hollywood, as the Dodgers had dispatched the Cubs in the NLCS one day prior. In the visiting manager's office at Minute Maid Park, Girardi said that he'd watched some of Los Angeles' 11–1 win over the defending World Series champs, though he'd eventually flipped off the lopsided action at Wrigley Field in favor of the Memphis-Houston college football matchup.

Verlander ensured that the Yankees kept their feet planted deep in the heart of Texas, firing seven scoreless innings while holding the Yanks to five hits. With fiancée Kate Upton cheering from a luxury suite, Verlander struck out eight, including Todd Frazier, who exhibited one of the worst swings of his career when he flailed comically at a nasty curveball.

"He buckled me. We all saw it. I looked silly," Frazier said.

Severino had said that his excitement level for the start was "about

100," and he matched Verlander through four innings on a hit and a walk before coming unraveled. Severino walked two of the first three batters in the fifth inning before McCann ripped a double that one-hopped the right-field wall, giving Houston a 1–0 lead.

Two batters later, Altuve smashed Severino's first pitch into left field—out of the reach of a leaping Frazier at third base—to drive in another two runs.

New York threatened in the sixth inning, getting two men on against Verlander, who fell behind Sanchez in a 3-0 count. Given the green light to swing away, Sanchez was sitting on a fastball but instead said he was "surprised" by a slider, weakly nubbing it to Correa at shortstop. Another rally stalled in the seventh as Verlander walked Greg Bird, then hit Starlin Castro with a pitch to put runners at first and second with none out.

Hicks prepared to drop his bat and head to first base after watching a 95-mph fastball tail outside with a 3-1 count, but home plate umpire Jim Reynolds rang Hicks up for strike two. Four foul balls followed, including a deep drive down the right field line that momentarily hushed the crowd, before Verlander struck out Hicks with the tenth pitch of the at-bat.

"I felt like that pitch was outside," Hicks said. "I'm getting ready to walk to first base and the next thing you know, he calls a strike. Now I've got to battle 3-2 against a very good pitcher. Sometimes it doesn't go your way."

Frazier followed by barreling an 0-1 fastball to the 404-foot marker in left-center field, where it was reeled in by George Springer, who jumped against the padded wall to secure the deep drive for a long, loud out. Watching from the mound, Verlander raised both of his arms in celebration of Springer's play.

"Right off the bat, I could've sworn it was going out," Frazier said. "If you play long enough, you basically know if it's going to go or not, and it was one of the best balls I squared up this whole postseason. I guess it just died and I didn't get enough."

Challenged by a 93-mph Brad Peacock fastball, Judge hit his fourth homer of the postseason, a titanic eighth inning shot that carried toward the train in left field. That cut Houston's lead to two runs, but David Robertson picked an inopportune time for his roughest outing of the year. Houston pulled away for a 7–1 victory as Robertson allowed hits to all four men he faced, including a homer that Altuve one-handed over the left-field wall.

It was now win or winter for the Yankees, who had named Sabathia as their probable starter in the event of a Game 7. Houston hadn't taken that liberty, and it wasn't until the Yankees had showered and were dressing at their lockers that they learned Charlie Morton had been tabbed as the Astros' starter. Morton had been solid during the regular season, going 14-7 with a 3.62 ERA, resurrecting his career with some velocity gains after middling results in Pittsburgh and Philadelphia. It didn't matter who was on the mound; if A.J. Hinch had activated Nolan Ryan or Mike Scott for Game 7, the Yankees needed to hit them.

"I'm excited. What an opportunity," Judge said. "We wouldn't want it any other way. We've been in this situation before. Wild Card games, in Cleveland, same kind of thing. Nothing changes. The mindset is still the same. Go out there and fight, prepare the same way we've been doing all year. We've had our backs up against the wall. Just continue to do that."

There was no rah-rah speech prior to Game 7; Girardi trusted his players to know what they needed to do, and did not believe the Houston fans would rattle them, pointing out that they had experienced hostile crowds within the division all year long. Though the Yankees were playing in their fifth potential elimination game of the postseason, Girardi acknowledged that it was different knowing that the World Series was on the line.

"You feel like you can almost grab hold of it," Girardi said. "And it can be snatched away from you really easily, too."

The decibel level spiked as soon as Morton fired a 96-mph fastball over the plate for a strike to Brett Gardner, and it took one of the finest plays ever made in a postseason setting to quiet the crowd. That took place in the second inning, when Aaron Judge robbed Yuli Gurriel of a possible homer, leaping and slamming his left wrist into the top of the right-field wall before tumbling to the warning track. Judge nonchalantly pulled the baseball out of his glove and flashed it to right field umpire Jim Reynolds while his teammates waved their caps and applauded.

"That's why you play. I wish every game was like that," Judge said. "That's why you grind through 162, for this opportunity and this moment. There's nothing like it. The crowd is into every pitch. It's what you dream of."

Judge's daring effort helped Sabathia evade trouble through the first three frames, but the lefty's luck ran out when Evan Gattis slammed a slider over the wall in left-center field leading off the fourth inning. Girardi turned the game over to his bullpen, calling upon Kahnle, who needed one pitch to escape a two on, one out jam in the fourth.

Greg Bird opened the fifth with a solid double to right field off Morton,

Aaron Judge's six-foot-seven frame came in handy during ALCS Game 7, as the future AL Rookie of the Year memorably stole a home run from the Astros' Yuli Gurriel.

and the Yanks sensed that this was their chance. Castro struck out, but Hicks worked a four pitch walk as Morton's curveball skipped away from catcher Brian McCann, allowing Bird to advance to third base. As both teams learned in Game 1, speed was not among the attributes that Bird had been blessed with, but Todd Frazier walked to the plate knowing that a fly ball would tie the game.

Frazier's eyes widened when Morton threw him a 95-mph fastball down in the zone, but instead of lofting a fly ball, the hack generated a two-hopper to the left side of the infield. Bird broke on contact, and third baseman Alex Bregman ranged to his left, fielded the ball and delivered what Bregman would later call "a Peyton Manning dime" to McCann, who dropped his glove in exactly the right place to catch Bird's spikes in front of home plate.

"The play was on the ground, so you go," Bird said. "Generally, when that's the case if it's a slow roller, you shut it down. But it was kind of a 'tweener and I went. You've got to score a run, so I went. No regrets."

Morton then induced Chase Headley to hit a ground ball to the right side that was fielded on the outfield grass by Altuve in the Astros' over-shift, stranding two men on. That was it for the Yanks; Altuve homered and McCann blasted a two-run double off Kahnle in the fifth to open a 4-0 lead.

The Astros handed over the pitching to Lance McCullers Jr., who snapped off curveball after curveball—twenty-four of them, in fact—to hold the Yankees scoreless on one hit over the final four innings. To borrow Girardi's analogy from earlier in the series, it was *Rocky II* all over again: Balboa was leading with his left and Creed was headed for the canvas. In the visiting clubhouse, CC Sabathia shed tears, something he said that he had not done for a very long time. Others stared silently, refusing to remove their uniforms.

"We were one game away from the World Series," Bird said. "It just sucks to lose, plain and simple. We were close. We did a lot of great things this year. There are a lot of things we can reflect on and say we did well, but we can get better."

If you had to boil the ALCS down to a single sentence, the most damning reason that the Yankees were pointing their charter flight east instead of toward Los Angeles was that they had managed no more than one run in any of the four games at Minute Maid Park. They drowned their sorrows that night in Houston, then flew to New York the next afternoon.

"The closer you get, the harder it hurts when things are over," Gardner said. "ALCS Game 7, that's about as close as we can get to the World Series without getting there. I'm disappointed in the way things ended up, but not disappointed in the way the guys fought this year, the hard work that we put in all year long. We tried as hard as we could, we just came up short. We ran into a really good team and some really good pitching."

The Yankees' 2017 season had started on February 24 with the opener of their thirty-four-game exhibition schedule. The clock read 10:19 p.m. Central Time as Bird lofted a McCullers curveball toward center field, where George Springer camped underneath it, securing the ball as red streamers began to rain down from the roof. Including spring training, this had been game number 209 in 239 days for the Yankees, and they returned to their lockers wishing that they could play one more.

"We'll be thinking about this night until spring training of next year," Judge said. "We're going to fight and try to get better in the offseason. We'll rest a little bit, but then we'll try to get better every day. We didn't win the World Series, so you're not really satisfied. That's what you want. That's why you play and why you train in the offseason. It's all for the opportunity to win the World Series and we came up short."

2017 SEASON EPILOGUE

The clubhouse doors remained closed for a few extra minutes after the Yankees vacated the visiting dugout at Minute Maid Park, and Joe Girardi gathered his team for what would be his final address as the team's manager. Saying that he understood how much it stung to get so close to the ultimate goal and fall short, Girardi urged his players not to hang their heads, telling them that they had a great deal to be proud of.

"He just said, 'This team has fought the whole year,'" Aaron Judge said. "Through injuries, ups and downs, this team always came to play every day. It's something that as a rookie seeing the veterans do that, I had a lot of fun playing with them. Watching older guys prepare like [Matt] Holliday, CC [Sabathia], [Chase] Headley, Gardy [Brett Gardner]. What a crew we had."

A few minutes later, Girardi made the long walk to the press conference room on the first-base side of Minute Maid Park, ignoring the revelry taking place while the Astros turned their diamond into a raging all-night dance party. Girardi had been enthused about the roster's potential when they left spring training, believing in their clubhouse leadership and ability to score runs.

Yet, in his most optimistic moments, Girardi couldn't have predicted that Judge would unanimously win the AL's Rookie of the Year Award, that Gary Sanchez would lead all catchers in runs, homers, RBIs, and slugging percentage despite missing a month of the season, or that Luis Severino would finish third in the AL Cy Young race after being banished to the bullpen and minors the year before.

"It is pretty special how quickly they came," Girardi said. "I believe that there's more and there's more talent down below that are going to continue to push people. It was a lot of fun to manage this group, it really was. I'm as proud of this group as I've been of any team I've ever managed."

On the Monday morning after ALCS Game 7, Brian Cashman spent most of the afternoon on the telephone in his Yankee Stadium office, speaking with managing general partner Hal Steinbrenner. During that lengthy conversation, Cashman officially made a recommendation that had been percolating in the GM's mind for a considerable amount of time.

Speaking of issues that he had seen firsthand and investigated concerning communication and connectivity with the players, Cashman suggested that they should allow Girardi's contract to expire and begin the search for a new manager.

Steinbrenner replied that he not only would accept that recommendation, but despite a decade in which Girardi averaged ninety-one wins per season while leading club to six postseason appearances and a World Series title, he had also warmed to the idea of having a fresh voice in the dugout.

Joe Girardi averaged 91 wins over his 10 seasons as the Yankees' manager from 2008-17, but general manager Brian Cashman cited "communication and connectivity" as areas in which he believed the former big league catcher was lacking.

"You've got to consider the fact that you've got a young team, and that maybe a different type of leadership perhaps is needed for a younger team than it is for a veteran team," Steinbrenner said. "This was not a decision that we took lightly, and not a decision that had to do with two or three weeks. It had to do with two or three years, observing things and hearing things."

Making it to the ALCS in what was widely expected to be a rebuilding campaign had been an unexpected treat, with the Baby Bombers developing into legitimate contenders ahead of schedule. With Judge, Sanchez, and Severino, the Yankees were the third team in history to have a 200-strikeout pitcher and two 30-home run hitters, all age twenty-five or younger, in the same season. The others had been the 1961 Giants (Juan Marichal, Orlando Cepeda, and Willie McCovey) and the 2009 Brewers (Yovani Gallardo, Ryan Braun, and Prince Fielder).

Acknowledging that the easy, safe decision would have been to "plug-and-play" for more years with Girardi, Cashman also voiced his doubts that Girardi's clenched-fist intensity would be the best fit for the young roster. A World Series victory, Steinbrenner said, might not have been enough to bring Girardi back for another year at the helm.

"I'm sure there would have been more pressure," Steinbrenner said. "It would've been a more difficult decision to make, but I still believe I would have made it because I felt that was what was best for the organization going forward."

The August clash with Gary Sanchez, in which Girardi publicly called out the catcher's defense as needing "to improve, bottom line," and his subsequent benching of Sanchez for the same reason stood out as one very public example of Girardi having an issue connecting with a younger player. Sanchez never complained publicly, but Girardi's actions seemed out of character for a manager who often went to great lengths to defend players from outside criticism.

"There wasn't one specific circumstance," Cashman said. "There wasn't one very specific issue."

So there would be a new Yankees manager for the 2018 season, with Girardi joining John Farrell of the Red Sox and the Nationals' Dusty Baker as those to be dismissed during the 2017 postseason. The news broke on a Thursday morning in October, after Girardi had been spotted exiting

Yankee Stadium on back-to-back days, a glum expression on his face as he pointed his sport utility vehicle south on River Avenue.

The Yankees employed two managers over twenty-two seasons, with Girardi's decade-long run following Joe Torre's twelve-year shift at the post. That was an unprecedented run of stability in the Bronx, considering that George Steinbrenner cycled through twenty managers before finally landing upon Buck Showalter in 1992. Steinbrenner used three different managers in 1982 alone, canning Bob Lemon after fourteen games in favor of Gene Michael, then turning the team over to Clyde King in August.

The next Yankees manager would have to be someone on the younger side who could handle the New York media crush while remaining in tune with a growing emphasis on analytics. The team was among the heaviest investors in the field, and the job responsibilities would be handed to someone who was able to distill those advanced numbers and have it make sense to the players, while using it to influence and defend his in-game decisions.

Part of the reason that Girardi had been hired over Don Mattingly in 2008 was that he was open to embracing the wave of big data, whereas Mattingly had seemed to be more of an old-school type out of the Torre mold who preferred to manage based upon gut decisions. Cashman did not have a specific replacement in mind, but he desired someone willing to take on the numbers while exhibiting more warmth than Girardi had.

While most of the current Yankees offered positive words or remained silent following news of Girardi's dismissal, retired Bombers first baseman Mark Teixeira offered a candid opinion, saying that Girardi's personality had worn thin with some members of the team.

"Everyone loves Joe, everyone respects Joe," Teixeira told the *New York Post*. "He is a good manager, he is a good man. But with baseball the way it is played today, and the need for a manager to be a better communicator and communicate with the front office the reasoning for doing things and to be a little bit more relaxed—especially in a place like New York, where the pressure is everywhere—he just wasn't the best man for the job anymore."

After being named the AL's Rookie of the Year (he'd finish second in the MVP balloting to Altuve, who received twenty-seven of thirty first-place votes), Judge said that he had a "great relationship" with Girardi.

"He was my first manager in the big leagues. He stuck with me in good times and bad times," Judge said. "He always had my back, always stayed positive with me. I thought we communicated well. My goal is to go out there and play, and that's what I focus on. I'm excited to see who we get, but I have a lot of respect and love for Joe and what he did for me my first year."

Over the five weeks that followed Game 7 of the ALCS, Cashman and his lieutenants compiled a list of men whom they believed might be worthy of becoming the thirty-third manager of the New York Yankees. Cashman acknowledged that there was no perfect candidate who would check all of the necessary boxes, so the team cast a wide net, inviting a diverse group of candidates to Yankee Stadium for lengthy interviews.

Yankees bench coach Rob Thomson, former Indians and Mariners manager Eric Wedge, Giants bench coach Hensley Meulens, former big league infielder and ESPN analyst Aaron Boone, Dodgers third-base coach Chris Woodward, and recently retired slugger Carlos Beltran comprised the six who made the final cut. The sessions in the Bronx were intensive, often spanning more than six hours and involving many different departments.

Each candidate spent time going over strategies and scenarios in a conference room, surrounded by a group of high-level executives that included Cashman, assistant GMs Jean Afterman and Mike Fishman, vice president of baseball operations Tim Naehring, senior director of player development Kevin Reese, assistant director of professional scouting Dan Giese, director of quantitative analysis David Grabiner, director of mental conditioning Chad Bohling, head athletic trainer Steve Donohue, and vice president of communications Jason Zillo.

Cashman said that while each man delivered valuable insights, Boone was able to distinguish himself, overcoming the fact that he had no previous coaching or managerial experience. No Yankees manager had taken the reins in that fashion since Hall of Famer Bill Dickey in 1946. Though Steinbrenner had said his preference would have been to hire a manager with a tangible track record, those concerns were relaxed after hearing how Boone had won the room.

"There was a difference of opinion among the participants as to who their number two or number three choice was," Steinbrenner said, "but there was little to no difference of opinion as to who their number one choice was. It wasn't even close, in their words."

An affable forty-four-year-old from La Mesa, California, who held a reputation as one of the best clubhouse influences in the game during his twelve-year playing career, Boone had been somewhat surprised when Cashman reached out to gauge his interest in flying to New York for a managerial interview. Boone's response to Cashman had been, "Heck yes!"

It helped that Boone's name conjured sweet memories for an entire generation of Yankees fans, having hit one of the most memorable homers in postseason history, a deciding blast off knuckleballer Tim Wakefield that defeated the Red Sox in Game 7 of the 2003 American League Championship Series. Boone's middle name happens to be John, but like Bucky Dent, he will forever carry a different one in New England because of one swing.

"It's certainly something that I'm known for in my baseball life, and in some way probably is a contributor to me being here today," Boone said. "Not a week goes by that I'm not reminded of how big the New York Yankees are or how big their reach is. I've had hundreds of stories told to me about where people were or what side of the ledger they were on."

Boone said that, in a way, he has been preparing for the job since childhood. The former corner infielder is part of the first family in history to produce three generations of big league players; Boone's grandfather Ray (1948–1960), father Bob (1972–1990), and brother Bret (1992–2005) all played in the majors, while his father managed the Reds (1995–1997) and Royals (2001–2003). He's also a descendant of the legendary 1700s American pioneer Daniel Boone.

"I feel like my job is getting the most out of these players, especially the young players," Boone said. "I think everyone that goes into this, we all desire and thirst for the championship. I feel like we have all the tools and potential to get there. Now it's on us to get the most out of it."

Cashman lauded Boone's intelligence, open-mindedness, and communication skills as having been factors in the Yankees' decision. Boone's character and honesty also were mentioned; Boone had been forthright after blowing out his left knee in a pickup basketball game following the 2003 season, setting off a sequence of events in which Boone was released and the Yankees traded for Alex Rodriguez.

Though Boone only played a half-season with the Bombers, Steinbrenner said that he was pleased his new manager at least had some prior experience in New York, which should allow him to understand the demands of the market.

Aaron Boone was introduced as the 33rd manager in Yankees history on December 6, 2017, and said one of his priorities would be to bond with catcher Gary Sanchez. "I understand what I signed up for. I understand what the expectations are," Boone said.

"It's clear in talking to him that he realizes, the way we all should, that there's always more to learn and the willingness to do it," Steinbrenner said. "His calmness, patience, confidence. I just think with a young, young team that's only going to get younger…he's going to be good for this particular group at this particular time."

On the afternoon that Boone was formally introduced to the media at Yankee Stadium, the baseball world seemed to agree that Giancarlo Stanton would not be wearing a Marlins uniform in 2018, though his next destination remained uncertain. The Cardinals and Giants had worked out separate trade agreements to acquire the reigning NL MVP, who led the majors with 59 home runs but expressed reluctance to be part of what Derek Jeter had warned him would be a cost-cutting effort in Miami.

"I thought our lineup was legit and we needed help with our pitchers, and we needed to add rather than subtract," Stanton said. "The way they wanted to go was to subtract, so I let that be known that I didn't want to be part of another rebuild, another losing season."

The problem for Jeter and the Marlins was that, because the previous ownership group issued a no-trade clause as part of Stanton's record-setting thirteen-year, $325 million contract, the leverage had shifted to the player's side. Stanton provided the Marlins with four contenders to whom he might approve a deal, listing the Astros, Cubs, Dodgers, and Yankees. He wanted to put someone over the top. In eight seasons, Stanton's Marlins had never managed better than an 80-82 record.

"He feels like he has no more time to waste in his career, because life is fleeting for him," said Stanton's agent, Joel Wolfe. "You can get hit in the face and have your career almost come to an end at any point. That almost happened to him [in September 2014]. I'm not equating it with a near-death experience or anything, but it was a near career-ending experience. That gave him a lot of humility. Because he feels that way, he wanted to win, right now."

During a meeting with Jeter and Miami GM Michael Hill, Stanton said that he was told that if he did not approve a trade to St. Louis or San Francisco, he would have to play the rest of his career in Miami. It was an empty threat, as Stanton's contract includes an opt-out clause after the 2020 season, and the twenty-eight-year-old slugger saw it as such. Stanton reiterated that he had provided Miami with four teams to whom he would consider a deal, and urged Jeter and Hill to call those clubs again.

"You can't say that and expect me to jump at what's there, if that's not the right situation for me," Stanton said. "You're not going to force me to do anything."

Cashman had spoken with the Marlins briefly in November, but his focus at that time had been split between the managerial search and preparing for the expected availability of twenty-three-year-old Japanese standout Shohei Ohtani. When Ohtani eliminated every club east of the Mississippi River except the Cubs, then selected the Angels, Cashman pivoted and re-engaged with the Marlins. Steinbrenner was intrigued when presented with a scenario in which the Yankees could add Stanton's contract while still keeping payroll under $197 million in 2018.

The Marlins, a money-losing franchise for years, were now desperate to clear Stanton's salary off their books. Hill contacted Cashman on December 7, and the GMs stayed up well past midnight trying to find an acceptable deal. The Yankees agreed to send infielder Starlin Castro, right-handed pitching prospect Jorge Guzman, and infield prospect Jose Devers to Miami, while promising to take on all but $30 million of Stanton's future salary.

After years of renting, Stanton had finally decided to buy a mansion in the Miami area following the 2017 season. He was in the process of designing his home gym and picking out furniture when Wolfe sent him their special alert code, which told Stanton to drop everything and call right away. As Wolfe brought Stanton up to speed on what was happening, Stanton said that he cut his agent off before he could complete the word, "Yankees." Yes, he'd approve the deal.

Stanton was urged to sleep on his decision, but it hadn't been necessary. He flew to Tampa, Florida, on a Saturday morning to undergo an extensive physical exam with the Yankees' medical staff, avoiding the main gate at Miami International Airport so as not to be spotted. Meanwhile, Cashman called Judge, explaining why the Yankees were about to trade for another power-hitting right fielder and how they could both be part of the team's success in 2018.

On the morning of December 11, the trade was officially completed. Stanton tried on the pinstripes for the first time during a 2:00 p.m. news conference at the Walt Disney World Swan & Dolphin Hotel in Lake Buena Vista, Florida, buttoning his jersey over a white dress shirt in front of the national media during the opening day of the Winter Meetings.

Stanton delivered a few swipes at the Marlins on his way out the door, remarking that there had been a "circus" atmosphere with "no structure" during much of his time in Miami. He advised Marlins fans to "watch from afar, if you're going to watch," then said that he was elated for the challenges and packed houses that awaited in New York.

"That's what I've always dreamed of," Stanton said. "You always want to be in competitive games that mean something, and your performance means something to the team and the city."

The 2018 Yankees featured Giancarlo Stanton (59 homers in 2017) and Aaron Judge (52 homers in 2017), joining the 1962 Yankees as the only team ever to have two players with 50 or more homers the prior season. That year, Roger Maris (61 homers in 1961) and Mickey Mantle (54 homers in 1961) anchored the Yanks' lineup.

In particular, Stanton was looking forward to joining Aaron Judge and Gary Sanchez in the heart of the batting order, as that trio promised to comprise a modern-day right-handed installment of the Yanks' fabled Murderers' Row lineup. Judge and Stanton spoke shortly after the trade, and said they looked forward to making each other better.

"They strike from everywhere, they're well balanced, and they're hungry," Stanton said. "The city's been waiting for another World Series and a playoff run, and they got close enough this year. But hopefully with my addition, we're going to advance and be a better team."

• • •

Cashman often repeated that "pitching is the key to the kingdom," and as the Yankees prepared for the 2018 season, they had assembled a promising group that boasted Albert Abreu, Domingo Acevedo, Chance Adams, and Justus Sheffield as rotation candidates. Miguel Andujar, Clint Frazier, and Gleyber Torres were among the position players poised to jump from a strong farm system in which the Yanks' eight domestic affiliates combined to win 60.2 percent of the time in 2017, with seven of those clubs qualifying for the playoffs.

"I keep saying this, but the depth of our farm system is insane," Frazier said. "I know everyone ranks the Braves number one, but I don't think one of their teams made it to the playoffs in the minors and every one of ours did, with a couple playing for championships."

Adams, the team's top pitching prospect, went 15-5 with a 2.45 ERA in 27 minor league starts, spending most of the season with Triple-A Scranton/Wilkes-Barre. While the organization resisted the urge to call Adams up and start his service clock, instead preferring to allow the converted reliever some additional time to polish up parts of his game in the International League, manager Al Pedrique said he saw exciting signs of improvement.

"This kid showed me a lot of composure on the mound," Pedrique said. "Each time out, he was getting better at slowing the game down. Definitely, he's got a great arm. Great fastball, the command of his changeup got better as the year went on. This kid has a bright future and if he stays healthy, he's going to be a bulldog. He's not afraid to challenge the hitters. This is a guy, for me, that you want to have on the mound in big games."

Touted left-hander Justus Sheffield made his big league debut in September 2018, then anchored the Yankees' offseason trade for Mariners left-hander James Paxton.

A fifth-round pick in the 2015 draft, Chance Adams rose quickly through the Yankees' system, making his big league debut against the Red Sox at Fenway Park in August 2018.

Perhaps the highest ceiling talent in the system is Estevan Florial, a left-handed hitting outfielder from Haiti who will turn twenty before Opening Day. The speedster's relatively brief rise in the ranks was marked by some controversy: he'd played under the name Haniel d'Oleo while registering for school in the Dominican Republic and had been declared ineligible for one year when MLB discovered the discrepancy.

After verifying Florial's actual birth certificate, the Yankees signed him in March 2015 for $200,000, which was perhaps one-tenth what he might have received otherwise. The investment was rewarded by a solid showing in 2017 that included a trip to the All-Star Futures Game, and Florial's name came up early in that season as vice president of baseball operations Tim Naehring came through Charleston.

"I called Cashman just to check in and I said, 'This kid Florial is a pretty exciting young man. I think your phone is going to start to light up here close to the deadline with people recognizing the intriguing tools that this guy brings to the table,'" Naehring said. "Sure enough, there's no telling how many organizations called on him during the deadline and basically asked how available a Florial type would be in a potential trade.

"He's probably one of the higher evaluated players that I've written up in my scouting days. Is he close? No, he still has some work to do on the development side, but when you look at the interesting dynamic of this young man, he has a chance to be an above-average defender that has speed, arm strength, raw power to all parts of the field and intangibles like a sense of urgency with his work ethic that is unparalleled."

Especially after the Stanton trade, it seemed possible that the 2017 Yankees might be looked upon as having been the team's weakest group for the next four or five years, a season in which they had only started to touch upon the greatness to come. In short, they hope to follow the path forged by the Cubs in 2015, an exciting, rebuilt Wild Card-winner who'd advanced to the LCS before winning it all the next season.

Asked if he believed this was the best that the farm system has been in his time with the organization, Cashman demurred, saying that it was difficult to compare anything to the chain that produced Derek Jeter, Andy Pettitte, Jorge Posada, Mariano Rivera, and Bernie Williams.

"We're trying to reset the clock and move forward," Cashman said. "This group—whatever it's going to be—we're just trying to win one. That group, 1996, 1998, 1999, 2000. That group had a lot of crazy success that typically it's hard to come by. We're just trying to get one."

One of those Core members was willing to make that leap, though.

"I see where you could compare that; just some great talent," Pettitte said. "All they're going to do is continue to go out and play and they're going to get better. All they're going to do, if they're able to get back to the postseason and play in games like this, is feel more comfortable. You see a lot of talent. You believe that it's not going anywhere, as long as they're able to stay healthy. You'll see success for a long time."

That positivity was contagious. Why not dream on what was still yet to come? Cashman was presented with the names of Adams, Andujar, Florial, Frazier, Sheffield, and Torres, and he enthusiastically added to that list by rapid-fire rattling off the names of Domingo Acevedo, Domingo German, Kyle Higashioka, Billy McKinney, Dillon Tate, and Tyler Wade.

Outfielder Jake Cave, right-hander Freicer Perez, right-hander Matt Sauer, and infielder Nick Solak have also been cited as possessing the talent and winning pedigrees to help down the line.

"It's nice to have the young guys pushing up," Cashman said. "It's nice to have the older guys hear the footsteps."

More than ever, it is realistic to envision a night in the near future where these "Baby Bombers" will hoist a championship trophy that signifies the franchise's twenty-eighth World Series championship.

"I believe, as the Yankees did for us, they'll continue to surround these guys with great talent," Pettitte said. "We wouldn't have been able to do what we'd done when we were younger if the Yankees didn't stick the talented players around us like they did. Every year I'd feel like they would rebuild and they would put great players around us. That's what made us have success.

"I think the Yankees have a great idea of how and what to do as far as keeping this thing going."

CHAPTER 16

GREATEST SHOW ON DIRT

Seven months had passed since Aaron Judge and Giancarlo Stanton shared the spotlight for the 2017 Home Run Derby in Miami, and as the sluggers prepared to claim the dimensions of another Florida diamond as a personal playground, they freed their factory-fresh bats from boxes and acknowledged each other with a nod.

Judge and Stanton sported confident struts through the tunnel that leads toward home plate at Steinbrenner Field. Everything about their attitudes in the moment seemed to suggest, "Go ahead, try not to watch this. We dare you."

Sixty players marched through the clubhouse doors on that February morning, but only Judge and Stanton had every move analyzed and scrutinized. Hacking at fastballs for the first time as teammates, each swing prompted audible reactions from a crowd of about two thousand—a tantalizing preview of the rock-star atmosphere that would follow the tandem all summer.

"The moment we touched the dirt, they were buzzing and ready for us to get in the cage," Stanton said. "That was really cool, like nothing I've ever experienced in the spring."

Though he led the American League with fifty-two home runs during his Rookie of the Year campaign, Judge was content to settle into something of a little-brother role behind Stanton. Their birthdates were separated by nine hundred days between November 1989 and April 1992, precisely spanning the time difference between the fall of the Berlin Wall and Tony Danza's final episode of ABC's *Who's the Boss?*

In other words, they were closer in age than it appeared. Stanton had signed professionally out of his Sherman Oaks, California, high school, making his big-league debut at age twenty with the Marlins, while Judge's decision to attend three years of classes at Fresno State had pushed back his minor league debut until age twenty-two, accounting for the discrepancy.

They'd soon learn how much they had in common. Three weeks before the team's first full-squad workout, Judge and Stanton were seated together at the front of a hotel ballroom, part of the dais at the Baseball Writers' Association of America dinner at the Sheraton Times Square in midtown Manhattan.

There was actually a cooler party in town—Judge and Stanton had been invited to attend the Grammy Awards, being held a few blocks away at Madison Square Garden—but it would not have created a great optic for the American League Rookie of the Year and the National League MVP to pass on receiving their own prestigious honors.

During the black-tie, $275-per-plate event, Stanton leaned over to tell Judge, "Hey, I'm excited to get into the cages with you."

"That was one of the first things he said," Judge said. "'Hey man, when we get down to Tampa, let's spend some time in the cage and pick each other's brains.'"

Judge loved the idea of having another big-bodied, right-handed slugger a few locker stalls away, someone who understood how pitchers tried to attack a hitter with that immense size. Stanton said that he and Judge were "pretty much identical in terms of levers, how people pitch us and what it's like when we step into the box." It had been amazing to watch one of them; what would two be like?

"I wish I could feel what they feel when they hit a baseball, and be able to hit it like they do," Brett Gardner said. "It's pretty humbling for me to get in there sandwiched between those two guys."

Stanton was blessed with athletic gifts, but he also had a tremendous work ethic. Teammates frequently marveled about Stanton's meticulous routines in the cage and the weight room. While Judge typically allowed himself one BP round to crush the ball over the scoreboard, Stanton attempted to slice the ball to right field, focusing on backspin rather than trying to drop jaws in the crowd.

"I know they're here for the entertainment, but we've got to get our work in, too," Stanton said. "That's my usual approach in BP. That's what got me to this point. It's not going to change."

After eight losing seasons in Miami, Stanton said that he was looking forward to the challenge of playing in a larger media market. Everything would be new again for him, though for returning players who had still not digested the result of Game 7 of the American League Championship Series against the Astros, the fresh vibes would be coming from the manager's office.

Introduced as Joe Girardi's successor in December, Aaron Boone was assembling his coaching staff when general manager Brian Cashman alerted him to the blockbuster trade, having pried Stanton from Derek Jeter's payroll-slashing Marlins. Coming off a season in which they sped up their timetable, the Yankees were now less of a feel-good story. Stanton's acquisition had restored them to juggernaut status.

Houston celebrated its first World Series championship and the Red Sox claimed the American League East by two games over New York, yet some believed the reinforced Yankees were good enough to go all the way. In a closed-door, first-day address that lasted no more than two minutes, Boone encouraged his players to embrace that. "Expect to be great," he said.

"A lot of these guys tasted success last year," Boone explained. "One of our things as we stepped into spring training was that we were going to embrace those expectations, and we understood that those expectations from outside were higher. The reason for that is that we have guys capable of delivering. We're not going to run from that, we're going to embrace that."

Following his shift from big-league infields to the broadcast booth, Boone seemed prepared to tackle the greatest challenge of his professional career; taking the reins of a storied franchise without a single day of coaching or managing experience to his name. An easygoing Californian who frequently referred to his players as "dudes," Boone spoke of hoping to be regarded as a smart, prepared manager who made solid decisions.

He added that he intended to oversee a winning culture "where players are allowed to be themselves." He never criticized his predecessor, but that comment hinted at the divide between the styles of Boone and Girardi. As for the pressure of dealing with New York's demanding fans and media, Boone had handled worse.

While in spring training with the Astros in 2009, Boone underwent open heart surgery to repair a defective aortic valve. He was born with two aortic valve leaflets instead of the normal three, the flaw having been identified during a routine physical during his college days at the University of Southern California.

The procedure—bicuspic aortic valve aneurysm surgery—was scheduled at Stanford University Hospital in California. Though Boone was confident in the medical team's assurances and in his faith, he wrote letters to his then-pregnant wife, Laura, his children, and parents, then gave them to a trusted friend just in case of the unspeakable. They remained unopened.

Boone returned to play ten emotional games with the Astros that September before announcing his retirement, moving to ESPN as an analyst for *Baseball Tonight*, where he delighted with spot-on impersonations of Alex Rodriguez and Joe Torre, among others. Boone is believed to be the first (and to date, only) major leaguer to return to the field after open heart surgery.

"It's more of a physical thing that needed to be taken care of," Boone said. "I was aware of it most of my life. I follow up every couple of years and do the due diligence that I have to do with it, but it's no issue."

Days before the Yanks' first exhibition game, Boone was asked what a realistic goal should be for the roster that he had inherited. He quizzically raised an eyebrow and replied, "Winning the last game of the World Series."

With an offense like the one he controlled, that optimism was supported. If the 1927 Yankees of Babe Ruth, Lou Gehrig, and Tony Lazzeri had been the original Murderers' Row, then this squad might be Version 2.0. Boone frequently would have inspiration strike while sitting in traffic or lying in bed, reaching for a pen and pad to scribble potential lineups.

Though general manager Brian Cashman expressed concerns in the pitching department, scoring runs was not going to be an issue. If Judge, Sanchez, and Stanton played to the backs of their bubble-gum cards, the 2018 Yankees were a good bet to shatter the single-season mark of 264 home runs held by the 1997 Mariners, who had featured Ken Griffey Jr. (56), Jay Buhner (40), Paul Sorrento (31), and Edgar Martinez (28) as their big boppers.

There was also youth on the horizon; offseason trades of Starlin Castro and Chase Headley created a pair of infield openings, and Boone hoped to use the spring to gauge if touted prospects Gleyber Torres and Miguel Andujar were ready to take over.

Though Cashman ultimately made moves to fill those vacancies, signing free agent Neil Walker at a deep discount and executing a three-team trade to land Brandon Drury, Boone said that it was "not lip service" when he had remarked how high the Yankees were on the pair. Andujar and Torres would finish second and third, respectively, to the Angels' Shohei Ohtani in the AL Rookie of the Year vote.

"I love who they are," Boone said. "They come to work and you can tell they enjoy being out on the baseball field. You can tell they're confident in their ability, the way they move around, yet there's a humility about both of them. They have a chance to be impact players for a long time in the big leagues."

After an ill-fated slide cost him a likely call to the big leagues the previous year, Torres was among the earliest arriving players for spring training, slugging batting practice homers and turning double plays while gleefully reporting that his left elbow seemed to have healed following Tommy John surgery.

The prize of the July 2016 swap that sent closer Aroldis Chapman to the Cubs, Torres had lobbied to play winter ball, but Cashman flashed a red light, preferring that the organization's most celebrated prospect focus on taking the field for spring training at 100 percent.

"I feel like a little kid with a new toy," Torres said. "After my recovery, I wanted to play winter ball. I wanted to see some pitches and see how my arm felt. But they said, 'You need to rest.' I took my rest. I had eight months in the weight room. I stretched; I felt like a pitcher."

Torres's time on the sidelines had an unintended benefit. He focused on honing his command of the English language, progressing to the point where Torres could comfortably bypass the services of interpreter Marlon Abreu and conduct interviews with the press.

"I want to explain how I feel or what I want to say," Torres said. "I think it's important for the fans and the media. Sometimes I feel embarrassed because my English is not perfect, but I practice to have perfect English to explain how I feel and what I want to say."

Torres looked rusty on both sides of the ball during the spring, managing four hits in 25 at-bats before being optioned to Triple-A. Boone and Cashman urged Torres to remain patient. The slow start saved the Yankees from a messy decision regarding Torres's service time. Twenty extra days in the minors were enough to delay his potential free agency until the offseason of 2024-25.

"[The year 2017] was not an easy year for me," Torres said. "Tommy John surgery is not good, and the recovery is a slow recovery. It was the first surgery of my whole career. I think with that experience, I saw a lot of games at home. But I stayed focused, believing in what I want. I just trained and prepared mentally for the next year, and I got ready for the next opportunity."

It was more difficult to send Andujar down. The Yankees believed in the twenty-two-year-old enough to nix him from discussions with the Pirates about right-hander Gerrit Cole, who went instead to the Astros, but most scouts judged Andujar's defense to be substandard.

Andujar zeroed in on his fielding during his workouts in the Dominican Republic, which continued into the dewy spring mornings on back diamonds of the Steinbrenner Field complex with instructor Carlos Mendoza.

"I've been wanting to be more focused, be more consistent on that side of the game," Andujar said. "I work hard with the coaches, go through the routines and the drills to help me be more consistent and keep repeating the good stuff."

No one expected Andujar to approximate Graig Nettles' Gold Glove defense at the hot corner, but his loud bat threatened to break down any doors keeping him from a big-league career. That was true even after the Yankees anointed Drury as their Opening Day third baseman, acquiring the more experienced infielder from the D-backs in late February.

While the Pirates' request for Andujar had been rebuffed, Cashman had been willing to include Clint Frazier in the talks. Less outspoken one year after the length of his hair made waves, Frazier spoke optimistically about forcing his way to New York, but otherwise made a conscious effort not to offend.

"I stepped on people's toes and I'm not going to do that this year," Frazier said. "I needed to go through that. I needed to get my feet wet in a sense and see that things that I do can cause distractions not only to myself, but to the team. Overall, I needed to grow as a person."

Frazier faced tough competition to punch a ticket north. Judge,

Stanton, Brett Gardner, and Aaron Hicks were all assured roster spots, and Stanton gamely agreed to take fly balls in both outfield corners, relegating Jacoby Ellsbury to a projected role as an expensive reserve. Injuries would ultimately cost Ellsbury the entire season, but Frazier was still on the outside looking in during the second exhibition game in Bradenton, Florida.

Tracking a second-inning drive off the bat of the Pirates' Ryan Lavarnway, Frazier completed a leaping, tumbling catch in left field, then slammed the back of his head into a chain-link fence. He played three more innings without complaint, but experienced a cloudy sensation later that day and was diagnosed with a concussion.

Frazier joked at the time that he was not worried because "there's not too much going on in my head," but the injury was no laughing matter. After a few close calls behind the wheel, he needed to be driven to the ballpark, and experienced sensitivity to fluorescent lights. At times, Frazier said that he had difficulty identifying his cats, Papi and Phoenix.

"It was a life-changing moment that I went through," Frazier said. "It altered every part of my day, not just baseball but my outside living situation. It was tough to battle back because I didn't know where the finish line was going to be. There were days I woke up and was like, 'Is it going to end or is it not?'"

While the Yankees attempted to correct Frazier's issues, he received advice from an unlikely source. That week, Seattle Seahawks quarterback Russell Wilson dressed a few lockers away, having been invited to join the roster for a taste of spring training. Wilson advised Frazier to chug bottles of water, claiming that it works for players in the NFL. Experts disagreed, but Wilson wasn't there for his medical acumen.

A one-time second baseman in the Rockies' system who attended camp with the Rangers in 2014 and 2015, Wilson was passionate about taking on a full slate of activities during his week in camp. The Super Bowl champion turned double plays with Didi Gregorius, slugged BP homers, and shared tips on leadership and preparation. His reward was a pinch-hit at-bat on his final day in camp; he struck out against the Braves' Max Fried.

"The coolest part for me was talking to him and asking him, 'Hey man, how do you prepare every week?'" Judge said. "You're getting beat up on Sunday. For you to recover, get your reps, get your body feeling well enough to do the same thing another Sunday, what's that like? He never wastes a minute. Every minute, everything he does is for a purpose."

Judge rarely shied away from a conversation, and that chatty nature earned him a slap on the wrist after a mid-March game in Sarasota, when he told the Orioles' Manny Machado that he would "look good in pinstripes" in 2019. Deputy Commissioner Dan Halem contacted Cashman, concerned about the optics of having superstar players involved in what could be construed as tampering.

"Cashman called me briefly. We spoke about it," Judge said. "He gave me a refresher that the MLB is sensitive to that kind of stuff. It just kind of came up in passing. Now I know. I got a little refresher. You learn something new every day."

Packing their passports, the Yankees traveled to Toronto for the season opener. Boone said that before boarding a 10 a.m. bus to Rogers Centre and handing the ball to his scheduled starting pitcher, Luis Severino, he had sought words of wisdom from his father, Bob, and his mother, Susan.

"He was like, 'Good luck, have fun,'" Boone said. "And my mom sent me a lot of emojis, a lot of hearts, prayers, the whole bit. So that was nice. I've got a nice balance there. My mom fires off emojis and my dad is just chill."

Facing J.A. Happ, Stanton provided Severino and his rookie manager with a near-instant lead, slugging the second pitch of his first at-bat over the fence in right-center field for a two-run shot. Stanton added a run-scoring double in the fifth and belted a solo homer in the ninth, leading New York to a 6-1 victory.

"I've never seen a debut like that," Dellin Betances said. "I've never seen anything like that. Those balls were hit out in less than two seconds. The guy just has massive pop."

The Yankees split that season-opening series in Toronto, weathering injuries to Aaron Hicks and rookie Billy McKinney that pressed Judge into emergency duty in center field. McKinney crashed into the left-field wall chasing a hit, which prompted the Yankees to call up Andujar. He would remain on the roster the rest of the way, taking advantage of the opportunity presented when migraines and blurred vision sent Drury to the disabled list.

"This was Brandon Drury's job," Boone said. "Andujar came in, just took the job and ran with it. He was incredibly consistent for us. Miguel Andujar, start to finish, was just a hitting machine. A lot of people questioned whether he was ready to play defensively at third. He handled himself capably and made strides, and he showed a lot of people that he's going to be able to play the position on a long-term basis."

After the Yankee Stadium home opener was delayed a day by snow, Didi Gregorius sparked a sizzling first month by going 4-for-4 with three runs, a double, two homers, eight RBIs, and a walk in an 11-4 rout of the Rays. That contest included a five-strikeout Platinum Sombrero by Stanton, who was booed in his first game wearing pinstripes (and in far too many games thereafter, as fans piled on).

"A lot of things were different for me, and that's life," Stanton said. "That's coming to a new team. The Yankees are more magnified than most, but you're aware of that going in. You adjust for things that you didn't think about or process before."

As Stanton settled into his new surroundings, he had a familiar face to block out the negativity and guide him through Gotham. Stanton shared a Manhattan apartment with Mets reliever A.J. Ramos, a former Miami teammate. Their salaries were disparate; Ramos earned $9.5 million in 2018 to Stanton's $25 million, but Stanton said that they had agreed to split the rent.

"We've roomed together for our career, pretty much," Stanton said. "It's a cool situation that we're in the same city. We decided, 'Why not?' We're not in the same town too often, but it doesn't matter. It's something cool to do."

Stanton, Judge, and Sanchez all went deep in the Yanks' second home game, and they'd be happy to have those big bodies on their side a few days later, when a visit to Boston prompted fireworks. After splitting the first two games of the series, Tyler Austin was drilled on the left elbow by a fastball from reliever Joe Kelly.

Austin slammed his bat on home plate and Kelly removed the glove from his left hand, beckoning for the score to be settled in the center of Fenway Park. Both benches and bullpens cleared as The Rivalry rolled the clock back about fifteen years, with the Boston players incensed over a hard Austin slide earlier in the game.

"My slide into second base was a clean slide," Austin said. "I play the game hard. I thought there was absolutely nothing wrong with that slide. I had no thought that they were going to throw at me."

Austin and Kelly threw punches; Kelly left the field with his jersey torn and spots of blood on his neck, while Austin sported a split lip. Judge had sprinted to the center of the pile, where he yanked Kelly off of Austin. Though Judge was there as a peacemaker, he was ready to mix it up if anyone dared challenge him, as Fresno State head coach Mike Batesole had once presciently predicted a year prior.

While the Yankees had their fight night at the Fens, Torres was swinging a hot bat at Triple-A, starting the countdown for his anticipated promotion. That call came during a game against Toledo on April 21, and when manager Bobby Mitchell told Torres that he was being removed from the game, Torres initially feared that he was being punished for showing frustration and jogging to first base following a groundout to the mound.

"Any player who plays baseball dreams of playing in the big leagues," Torres said. "For sure, it's my dream."

Reporting to Yankee Stadium the next day, Torres proved to be a good luck charm as the team took off, fueled by youth. On the date of Torres's big-league debut, they fielded an entire lineup of players younger than thirty, the first time that the Yankees had done so since September 29, 1989, against the Tigers. That 5-1 victory over the Blue Jays opened a span of seventeen wins in eighteen games, marking their best eighteen-game stretch since 1953.

"Gleyber gets called up at some point in April and we were kind of finding our way a little bit," Boone said. "He comes in right away and is a difference maker. The offensive production he brought right away, the defense he played in the middle of the diamond…the game comes very easily for Gleyber Torres, on both sides of the ball. There's just an ease that he plays the game with, and he's only going to continue to grow."

Over the stretch, they outscored opponents 110-45 and out-homered them 25-13. Gregorius in particular seemed to be unstoppable, memorably receiving a curtain call on the road. Summoned to take a bow after delivering a deciding homer in a wild ten-inning, 4-3 win in Anaheim, Gregorius was named the AL's Player of the Month for April after leading the majors with 10 homers and 30 RBIs, ranking second with a .739 slugging percentage.

"I do have a lot of home runs, but it's not like I'm going out there and trying to hit them," Gregorius said. "I'm not the power guy like Judge or Stanton, guys who hit 50 to 60 and up. If there's one year where I hit five, then you'll ask me where that power went. I'm not that type of guy. I try to hit line drives. It's not like I'm going up there trying to hit deep fly balls."

Contributions were spilling from all areas; Gregorius, Judge, Sanchez, and Stanton compiled at least 10 home runs through the first forty games, making them the fastest quartet in franchise history.

New York grabbed a share of first place on May 8, then briefly took sole possession the next day, part of a stretch in which they posted nine straight victories against teams owning at least a share of first place: three at Houston, three vs. Cleveland, and two vs. Boston. To be the best, you have to beat the best, and they were doing that.

"It goes back to us taking it one day at a time, especially the production we've been getting out of the bottom of our lineup," Judge said after a 9-6 victory over Boston on May 9. "Guys like Gleyber, Andujar, Walker coming through the past couple of games. It's been incredible."

During that span, Andujar had collected a walk-off hit in a May 4 win over the Indians and Torres became the youngest player in franchise history to hit a walk-off homer, doing so on May 6 against Cleveland. It appeared that the newest wave of "Baby Bombers" was here to stay.

"We started the year in the minors, but the intensity of training never changed," Andujar said. "Now we're here and we're playing good baseball and we're happy doing that. As long as we keep getting the opportunity, we're going to go out there and give the best we have."

CHAPTER 17

GROWING PAINS

Aaron Judge tapped out a text message from the chair in front of his Yankee Stadium locker, stood, and sighed. A group of reporters was approaching, seeking any morsel of news regarding his fractured right wrist. He'd learned this much over the last few weeks: if there was anything that he hated more than the injury that was keeping him from playing, it was talking about it.

Even if Judge had been in the mood to fill notebooks, there was precious little news to provide. He had sustained a chip fracture of the ulnar styloid bone in his right wrist after being drilled by an errant fastball from the Royals' Jakob Junis on July 26 at the Stadium, temporarily freezing his statistics. He had a .285 batting average, 26 home runs, and 61 RBIs in 99 games, not that they were doing the Yankees any good from the bench.

While rabid fans blitzed Junis' social media accounts with acidic messages, prompting the apologetic pitcher to engage his privacy settings, team physician Christopher Ahmad estimated that Judge would be able to return to facing live pitching within three weeks. That proved to be laughably optimistic; it would be more like seven-and-a-half weeks. His wrist still hurt like hell, and probably would until the offseason, meaning that facing big-league pitching would create a pain tolerance issue. Judge always thought of himself as tough, and now he was going to have to prove it.

"Especially down the stretch, being in the hunt for the division—you never want to be sitting out for stuff like that," Judge said.

Losing Judge had a profound effect on the Yankees, who owned a 65-36 record on the evening that the slugger was shuttled to New York-

Presbyterian Hospital for a CT scan and MRI on the injured wrist. He had remained in the game for one more at-bat, legged out an infield single, then was replaced by Miguel Andujar at DH. The Yanks went 26-22 during Judge's DL stint, and their right fielders batted .187 with a .652 OPS over that period.

"When we're talking about Aaron, not only is he a special player, but he's a special presence on our club," Boone said. "I do believe there's more impact there than just his outstanding performance."

The Yankees had been largely fortunate on the injury front through the season's early months, though first baseman Greg Bird continued to experience issues, sidelined until the middle of May after yet another surgical procedure at the end of spring training—this time, to remove a broken bone spur from his troublesome right ankle.

"One of the more challenging things for me has been dealing with injuries," Bird said. "It's not being able to [play a full season] yet. In '15, I thought I'd come back and the next year be ready to go. I wasn't. '16, same thing, '17, I put in a lot of work. I have always wanted to do that: get out there, play, and show what I can do."

Bird's absence permitted Tyler Austin to grab a roster spot, and the slugger delivered big knocks, slugging eight homers—not to mention the hits that landed on Red Sox skulls during the Fenway fracas. Upon Bird's return, he was unable to generate the production that had prompted the Yankees to view him as one of the best pure hitters in the organization.

"This year, in a lot of ways, was a lost season for him," Cashman said. "Starting out and getting hurt again and having to have surgery, that was a tough blow. In some ways, he never got all the way back physically. We've never lost sight of the fact that, when he's right, this guy can really hit."

In early May, left-hander Jordan Montgomery underwent Tommy John surgery on his pitching elbow, having opened the year with a 3.62 ERA in six starts. While rookie Domingo German stepped in as a sport starter, the prolific offense kept storm clouds from gathering. From May 8 through July 1, the Yankees owned at least a share of first place for thirty-three of fifty-six days.

An 11-1 rout of the Red Sox on July 1, in which Aaron Hicks hit a career-high three homers (going deep from both sides of the plate), marked the latest in a season in which they possessed the league's best record since

2012. They didn't experience their first three-game losing streak until June 22-24 at Tropicana Field, prior to which they had owned a 50-22 record.

Win No. 49 had come on a Giancarlo Stanton walk-off homer to topple the Mariners, marking the establishment of Stanton's so-called "Yankee moment." As Stanton's drive sailed toward the loading dock in left-center field, Seattle right-hander Ryan Cook bent at the waist, cursing the dirt of the Yankee Stadium mound.

"It's just cool, man. It's a fun moment," Stanton said. "It's good future memories. That's what you always want, man. You help win a game and you've got the whole team waiting for you."

The Bombers featured four All-Stars at the Midsummer Classic at Nationals Park in Washington, D.C., with Aroldis Chapman, Aaron Judge, Luis Severino, and Gleyber Torres all named to the squad. Chapman and Torres could not play due to injuries, and Judge declined to participate in the Home Run Derby, which was appropriately won by the Nationals' Bryce Harper.

Judge had said that because it would be difficult to top the performance he enjoyed in Miami, it would likely be his only turn on that stage. Judge said that he would rather not say if the Derby impacted the left shoulder injury that required surgery after the season, but he did acknowledge that the shoulder was a problem around the 2017 All-Star break.

"I did it once, enjoyed it, loved the experience. I was able to win it," Judge said. "It was such a cool experience. One and done is good for me."

The Yankees had been 29 games over .500 when they scattered for the break, and no one was more eager for the resumption of play than Gary Sanchez, who had been on the disabled list for three weeks with a right groin strain. After slugging 33 homers in 2017, Sanchez was enduring a perplexing campaign, hitting .190 when he winced crossing first base in a 7-6, twelve-inning loss to the Rays at Tropicana Field on June 24.

Returning to the same facility on July 23, Sanchez re-aggravated the injury in much the same fashion, thrown out at first base easily on a ground ball that ended New York's 7-6 loss to Tampa Bay. Initially, it appeared that Sanchez had loafed after a first-inning passed ball that prompted a heated dugout exchange with pitcher Luis Severino and again on the final play of the game.

Boone summoned Sanchez for a postgame meeting, seeking explanations; Sanchez mentioned the groin issue at the end of that conversation.

Even with the injury, Boone said that Sanchez "felt like he certainly could have given more and should have given more [of a stronger effort]."

"I'm going to bet on the player and the guy," Boone said. "He's not a finished product yet, but we're all going to be a part of helping him get there. When he does, we'll have a special player, a special person. I know deep down he really cares about his craft, his teammates."

At least the Yankees had tangible reasons with which to understand Sanchez's drop-off, both offensively and defensively. In addition to the groin issues, he had been receiving cortisone injections for a left shoulder injury that would eventually require surgery.

"It's tough when you're injured and you're in a position like that," Sanchez said. "You watch the games and there's nothing you can do. You want to get back, you want to help, you want to play. At the same time, you keep watching and you keep rooting for your teammates. Nobody wants to be injured."

No simple explanations existed for Luis Severino, who had transformed from Cy to Sigh without warning. Through his first 19 starts, Severino was dominant, pitching to a 14-2 record and 2.12 ERA. Opponents batted .198 against the righty, who scattered 88 hits in 123⅓ innings while walking 29 and striking out 143.

Severino took a small step backward in his final start before the All-Star break, allowing four runs and nine hits in a five-inning no-decision at Cleveland, though the Yankees pulled out a 7-4 win. His performances dropped precipitously to begin the second half, as the Rays and Royals thumped Severino for six earned runs in consecutive starts.

There were flashes that inspired confidence, but Severino was unable to recapture the magic that had made his starts must-see events during the first half. Over his final 13 regular season outings, Severino was 5-6 with a 5.69 ERA. Opponents hit .301 against him and he surrendered 85 hits in 68 innings. The Yankees later speculated that Severino was tipping pitches.

"It's obviously an area of focus that we'll continue with and battle through," Cashman said. "No matter who you are, [even] if you're as talented as him with the type of electric stuff he has, if they know what's coming, then you're going to be very vulnerable. It's something we have to fix and get better at and contain."

One of Severino's roughest starts came on September 5 at Oakland, where he experienced communication issues with Sanchez and was charged with six runs (five earned) over 2⅔ innings, throwing two wild pitches. Sanchez also had two passed balls in that ugly outing.

"I think it was a miscommunication between us," Severino said. "I think we didn't set the right signs and stuff like that. But we talked about it. We figured it out, and after that, I think everything was great."

A more significant problem was that the Red Sox refused to lose, having found their stride on their way to a historic 108-win campaign and—eventually—their fourth World Series championship since 2004. Boone frequently glanced at the out-of-town scoreboard and was dismayed to see that, yet again, Boston was on top. Even when the Yankees won, they couldn't make up ground.

"I see that they win every day, but I don't really worry about it," Boone said. "I'm worried about us playing our best. If we do that, hopefully we'll get to where we want to go."

Cashman addressed some of the roster needs in advance of the trade deadline, triggering deals to bolster the squad. Seeking to learn if Judge's preseason prognostication held firm, Cashman attempted to see how Orioles star Manny Machado would look in pinstripes, but was unable to come to an agreement with Baltimore.

Machado landed in Los Angeles instead, taking over shortstop for the World Series-bound Dodgers, but the last-place Orioles' exploration of the Yankees' system greased the way for a trade involving left-handed reliever Zach Britton, who arrived in exchange for three pitchers; Dillon Tate, Cody Carroll, and Josh Rogers.

"They had a chance to assess our franchise top to bottom," Cashman said. "We had a chance to understand and listen and be aware of the players that they valued. It put us in a much better position to know where we may be going on this."

Two days later, Cashman acquired veteran left-hander J.A. Happ from Toronto, swapping out infielder Brandon Drury and outfielder Billy McKinney. Andujar's emergence rendered Drury expendable. Other moves included acquiring right-hander Lance Lynn from the Twins for Austin and minor league pitcher Luis Rijo, and shipping right-hander Adam Warren to the Mariners for international bonus pool money.

"We did a lot of different things for a lot of different reasons," Cashman said. "It doesn't have to be splashy, it just has to work. That's all that matters. We certainly checked every color of the rainbow, so to speak, whether it was a high-end talented player who went another direction versus a lot of low-level, low-hanging fruit. We did the full baseball operation circuit."

Saying goodbye to Austin was difficult, considering the bright fashion in which he had opened his career, slugging back-to-back homers with Judge on that memorable afternoon in 2016. However, he would be out of minor league options after the season and needed an opportunity to garner regular at-bats.

When Austin joined the Twins and delivered a few big knocks, his father, Chris, tweeted: "Tyler has more hits with the Twins in a week than Bird has in a month with the Yankees." Austin apologized to his former teammate, saying that he was embarrassed by the situation, and the tweet was deleted.

There was one other move made during that flurry of transactions, a head-scratching swap with the Cardinals that largely zipped under the radar. Little could the Yankees have known that the most impactful hitter moved at the deadline was not named Machado. And that person was on his way to New York.

CHAPTER 18

THE BEST IS YET TO COME

Luke Voit's name had been circulating in the Yankees' offices for more than a year, as members of the analytics department were fascinated by the impressive minor league statistics that kept appearing on their glowing monitors. The numbers practically smacked them in their faces. Was this guy for real?

A husky first baseman in the Cardinals organization, Voit seemed to have done everything within his power to force an opportunity in the big leagues. Though he had been an avid Redbirds fan while growing up in Linwood, Missouri, Voit happened to be wearing the wrong uniform. His path to regular duty at Busch Stadium was blocked by three-time All-Star Matt Carpenter and big-swinging rookie Jose Martinez.

As Greg Bird continued to struggle near the midpoint of the 2018 schedule, general manager Brian Cashman gambled on the twenty-seven-year-old that he had been pestered about from assistant general manager Michael Fishman, as well as analysts Theo Feder and Justin Sims. The asking price was reasonable; St. Louis requested pitchers Chasen Shreve and Giovanny Gallegos, neither of whom figured prominently in New York's future plans. Voit was on his way to the Big Apple.

"This has been the craziest year of my life," Voit said months later. "Going up and down with St. Louis, I spent a lot of time at Triple-A. It sucked, but I had to stay mentally strong, and luckily Brian Cashman gave me a chance to come over here. I wanted the challenge of coming to New York City. It's a lot, but I'm having the time of my life with it."

A barrel-chested, boisterous figure who taped posters of Mark McGwire to the walls of his childhood bedroom, Voit dreamed of playing college football, having excelled as a high school fullback and middle linebacker before two significant shoulder injuries pointed him toward the baseball field. While his younger brother, John, went on to a decorated Army football career, Voit found a different way to hit hard and make fans cheer.

Joining the Yankees in early August, Voit's initial audition offered little excitement, produced hits in 16 at-bats before he was sent back to the minors. He was pressing to prove that he belonged in the big leagues, scarred from perpetual bronze finishes on the Cardinals' depth chart that stalled his career in Triple-A Memphis.

As he played seven games with Scranton/Wilkes-Barre, Voit made a promise to release that anxiety. If the Yankees gave him another chance, Voit told himself, he would relax and let his talent flow. That opportunity came in late August, as Voit joined the big league squad and made it impossible for the Yankees to keep him out of the lineup.

"When I first came up, I thought I was trying to do too much, trying to create and show everyone what I've got," Voit said. "It was nice to hit the refresh button when I got sent down. I know I can hit; I've always hit. I've got to stay within myself and use my hands instead of trying to hit 500-foot home runs."

Cracking three homers among eight hits on the club's August 21-26 road trip to Miami and Baltimore, Voit enjoyed the first multi-homer game of his career in an August 24 win over the Orioles at Camden Yards, mashing a game-tying homer in the fourth inning and a two-run shot in the 10th as part of a four-RBI performance.

"To see the Luke Voit show roll on, it has been terrific," Boone said. "He's got a little confidence, a little swagger. I think he comes in with an anticipation that he's going to be successful. Regardless of the situation, I think he's a guy that believes he can hit. He believes he can hit in this league. With his opportunities so far, he's shown it."

Standing out among his teammates for his preference to keep the top button of his jersey unbuttoned with no shirt underneath, Voit hit go-ahead homers on August 30 against the Tigers and on September 4 against Oakland, part of a surge in which he homered in three consecutive games.

Yankee Stadium fans took to serenading Voit with chants of

"LUUUUKE," reminding him of his days on the high school gridiron. The sport had changed, but Voit was still making crowds roar. He led the AL with 14 homers while hitting .351 from August 24 through the end of the regular season, delighting teammates with enthusiastic outbursts that were a bizarro combination of Nick Swisher and Jason Giambi.

"The big thing for me is, I try to be that upbeat guy in the locker room," Voit said. "Maybe it's that football guy in me. That was my sport growing up until I had some injuries. If I'm not out there having fun, then take me away from this game. I want to bring enthusiasm. Why not?"

Long-time Yankees observers had seen something like this before. Voit's out-of-nowhere burst recalled the performance that outfielder Shane Spencer enjoyed toward the end of the 1998 season, when Spencer mashed 10 homers in fifty-four games, including three grand slams. The ball "was looking very juicy" at that time to Spencer, and Voit nodded knowingly when that suggestion was raised.

According to Spencer, now a field coordinator and minor league manager in the Korean Baseball Organization, the difference is that Voit did it while his team was fighting for playoff position. By the time Spencer emerged on the '98 squad, Joe Torre had them on cruise control. Spencer's job was to offer breaks to veterans like Darryl Strawberry, one he did with aplomb.

"I did a little research [on Voit]," Spencer said. "It was kind of fun, just to see the similarities. It happens all the time, but doing it in New York is a little bit different. It gets blown out of proportion a little more, but if you're going to do it, you might as well do it there. They'll never forget about it."

How key were those contributions? When the Yankees secured their Wild Card spot later that month, Aaron Judge hugged Voit and told him, "We wouldn't be in this position right now if it wasn't for you." No one disagreed with the sentiment.

While Voit offered a power surge, Judge was moving closer to reclaiming his spot in the lineup. Judge received clearance to take swings during a West Coast trip, performing his rehab on site because the minor league season was ending. The progression started as Judge stood in for a Masahiro Tanaka bullpen at the Oakland Coliseum, tracking pitches with a bat on his shoulder, and advanced to taking swings off a tee and hitting soft-toss.

When the Yankees arrived at Minneapolis's Target Field, Judge advanced to batting practice on the field, fielding grounders and fly balls in right field before making throws to third base and home plate. It was not perfect, Judge allowed, but it was close enough.

"The pain is not gone. It's still broken," Judge said. "I knew I was going to be back in some meaningful games here down the stretch. I'm just excited to get closer. I'm getting one step closer every day to that moment and getting back on the field."

On September 14, Judge thrilled the robe-wearing fans in The Judge's Chambers by jogging to right field to play the final two innings of defense in an 11-0 win over the Blue Jays. Even though no balls were hit in Judge's direction, the visual of having No. 99 on the field—and knowing that he'd soon return to full duty—served as a confidence boost for the club.

"I finally got to watch him and Stanton take batting practice," said Andrew McCutchen, a former MVP and five-time All-Star outfielder who was acquired from the Giants in late August, in part because of Judge's extended absence. "I saw some pretty impressive stuff. I know for people who have been here all year, to them, it's probably normal. It's not normal. It was awesome."

Judge's name appeared in the lineup when the Yankees opened a September 18 series with the Red Sox at the Stadium, representing their last chance to make a statement. New York won the first two games of the series, but a loss in the finale clinched the American League East for Boston.

The Red Sox had a muted celebration on the field, then enjoyed a wet and wild one in the visiting clubhouse. Knowing that Boston was partying in their building was upsetting for the Yankees, but they swiftly turned their attention to securing their own postseason entry.

"They've had a solid year. We can't deny that," Stanton said. "You never want it to be here that they get it, but we gave it what we've got. They can celebrate now and we've got time to celebrate later."

The Yanks punched their ticket in a September 22, 3-2 victory over the Orioles, as Aaron Hicks laced a run-scoring, 11th-inning double that assured that their season would extend into October.

"It's awesome," said Hicks, who also hit a second-inning homer in the contest. "That's the whole point of spring training, is to get to this point in the year where you're fighting for something and you get yourself in the postseason. That's what we're here for."

It was a game that nearly came at a significant cost. As Didi Gregorius scored the winning run, sliding headfirst and swiping his left hand across home plate, the shortstop's right hand snagged underneath his ribcage.

Gregorius sensed little discomfort as he celebrated with his teammates that night, gleefully spraying champagne in the clubhouse, but his wrist throbbed the next morning.

An MRI revealed a small cartilage tear, placing Gregorius' availability for the postseason in doubt. Hicks also battled left hamstring tightness, but after spending extended amounts of time in the office of head athletic trainer Steve Donohue, both were reinstated to the active ranks for the season-ending series in Boston.

"Those two players are so important to us and are such quality two-way players in the middle of the diamond," Boone said. "When it first happens, obviously it's frustrating and you worry about it a little bit, but you also understand that it's next man up. We're capable of doing things and we have to make it work."

Having established home field advantage over the Athletics for the Wild Card game and the Red Sox awaiting the winner of that contest as their Division Series opponent, the Yanks' visit to Boston was far more muted than the Joe Kelly/Tyler Austin Fight Club experience in April. The pursuit of a home run record highlighted the weekend.

They had hit three long balls in a 12-1 win over the Rays at Tropicana Field on September 27, needing four in three games to equal the 1997 Mariners' total of 264. They cracked them all in the series opener, with Gary Sanchez, Hicks, Voit, and Judge clearing the walls in an 11-6 win over the Red Sox.

"We've got a lot of guys on this team with a lot of thump," Judge said. "They've been doing it all year, especially once we added Voit, what he's been doing for us has been huge. We talked about [the record] once we started getting closer, especially early in the year when we looked at our lineup and what type of firepower we had."

Boone didn't realize they had tied the record until there was an on-field scramble to retrieve Judge's home run ball, which struck near the flagpole in center field and dropped to the turf.

"The fact that it's come from so many different people, I think that has been the cool thing," Boone said. "If you would've told us we were going to break that record at the beginning of the year, you probably would've thought Giancarlo is hitting 50 or 60, Judge is hitting 50 or 60. Because of injuries and different things, that hasn't been the case. We've gotten a lot of production from a lot of different people who have had a big hand in that."

The next day, Gleyber Torres whipped the swing that allowed the Yankees to stand as history's most powerful lineup, connecting for homer No. 265, a two-run shot into the Boston bullpen off left-hander Eduardo Rodriguez. Torres pumped his right fist as he rounded the bases, recognizing that he had achieved something special.

"I feel really good. Really happy," Torres said. "It's not just me; all the guys did a really good job. I'm happy for the opportunity to hit the homer. All season, we did a really good job. Everybody does something. I'm happy for us and we enjoyed that moment."

Stanton extended the record in the seventh inning, a blast that was returned to the field by a fan atop the Green Monster, clipping Stanton on a bounce near the right biceps. Stanton laughed off the fan's effort to emulate Henry Rowengartner, the main character in the 1993 movie *Rookie of the Year*, joking, "That could be a special ball. We needed it anyway. I think he lost some money on it."

It was a record-breaking afternoon for the Baby Bombers. One inning after Torres's shot, Andujar drilled a two-run double off Brandon Workman, marking Andujar's 45th two-base hit of the season. That surpassed a franchise record for rookies set by Joe DiMaggio (44) in 1936.

Andujar finished the year with 47 doubles, tied with Fred Lynn of the 1975 Red Sox for the most by an American League rookie. The big-league record is held by outfielder Johnny Frederick of the 1929 Brooklyn Robins, who legged out 52 two-baggers three years before the franchise would adopt the Dodgers nickname.

"Just to have my name associated with Joe DiMaggio, it feels good," Andujar said. "I feel good for that. I'm looking forward. You want to keep on moving to better things. I want to have a long career. That being said, the work doesn't stop. You've got to keep going. You've got to try to keep getting better."

Voit hit the Yankees' 267th and final homer in the season's last game, completing their 100-62 campaign. It marked their most victories since the 2009 club won 103 contests on their way to securing the 27th World Series championship in franchise history, and represented the third-best mark in the majors. Yet it felt somewhat hollow, as they finished eight games behind Boston in the AL East and would again do battle in a one-game playoff.

"We were a playoff team that won 100 games, but people forget that over time," Cashman said. "We want teams that are not forgotten and the only way to do that is to be the last team standing and raising a championship flag."

Hosting the Athletics for the Wild Card game, the Yankees ensured that they remained alive past the third day of October by following the same blueprint that they brought into the year. Luis Severino showcased his high-octane arsenal and handed the game off to the vaunted bullpen, waiting for Judge and Stanton to crush balls out of sight. It resulted in a 7-2 win, the Yanks' second consecutive year surviving the win-or-winter contest.

"That Wild Card game is no joke. It takes years off of you," said Judge, who hit a two-run homer nine pitches in against A's starter/opener Liam Hendriks. "We were prepared, just like Oakland. It was a tough game, a fun game; you live for those moments. You enjoy those situations. You enjoy the pressure. Your back's against the wall; that's what this team is all about."

Showcasing crackling velocity and sharp bite on his slider, Severino rewarded Boone's belief that the right-hander represented the correct choice to start the winner-take-all contest, holding the A's hitless into the fifth inning while striking out five of the first seven men he faced.

Severino fanned seven, though his pitch count escalated quickly due to deep counts and four walks. He found an extra gear when he needed one, firing a 99.6-mph fastball past Marcus Semien with the bases loaded for the final out of the fourth inning. Severino's eyes tilted skyward and he unleashed a primal roar, thrilled by his ability to handle the challenge.

"I think last year, my first time in a playoff game, I was too excited," Severino said. "I was going to go to the mound and treat it like a regular game, hitting my spots and trying to get batters out."

After dousing one another in bubbly and beer, the Yankees rode the rails to meet the Red Sox for the Division Series. Judge's early homer in the Wild Card game had sparked chants of "We Want Boston!" among pockets of the crowd of 49,620, and that wish would be granted. They loved their chances with J.A. Happ on the mound, as the veteran had gone 7-0 with a 2.69 ERA in 11 starts since being acquired in July.

"We want Boston. They took the division from us," Voit said. "We want to take it back from them."

Despite a solid track record of regular-season success against the Red Sox, Happ's first such assignment in a postseason setting fell flat. J.D.

Martinez hit a three-run homer early and Happ endured a third-inning knockout. Though the Yankees clawed back late, coming within a run on Judge's ninth-inning homer, they absorbed a 5-4 loss in Game 1.

The Yankees responded to even the series in Game 2, as Sanchez erased the disappointment of his underwhelming season with a two-homer performance that included a staggering 479-foot blast. The big bats broke out for a 6-2 victory as Judge cracked his third homer in as many playoff contests, extending the nightmare that had been Price's postseason career to that point.

A .186 hitter during an injury-marred regular season, Sanchez started the second inning with a blast that cleared the wall in left, marking his sixth home run in 14 career at-bats against Price. That prior success had been a topic of conversation between Sanchez and Dellin Betances as they carpooled to Fenway Park on Saturday afternoon.

"[I told him], 'Everything will be erased if you have a couple of big games in the playoffs,'" Betances said. "'This is where it counts.' I had a good feeling he was going to have a good day. I spoke to him before the game. He was feeling good before the game."

McCutchen's RBI single in the second chased Price, who was booed lustily by the crowd after recording just five outs. By contrast, Masahiro Tanaka gave his club exactly what it needed, limiting the Red Sox to Xander Bogaerts' solo homer over five innings before handing the ball to the bullpen.

Sanchez had a contentious exchange with reliever Ryan Brasier in the fifth, as the hurler gestured toward Sanchez and yelled at him to get back in the box before striking him out on a heater. Payback came against Eduardo Rodriguez in the seventh, when Sanchez connected for a three-run homer that gave the Yankees a five-run lead. Yogi Berra is the only other Yankees catcher to enjoy a multi-homer postseason game, having done so in Game 7 of the 1956 World Series.

"We all know he's capable of that," Boone said. "That's kind of what we've been waiting on, where he can take over a game on offense. He was huge."

The Yankees' confidence oozed out of the visiting clubhouse that night. They had split the series in Boston and were returning home for two games at the Stadium, where they had won 53 of 81 games that season, plus the Wild Card game over Oakland. As Judge rolled a portable speaker past the

Red Sox clubhouse, blasting Frank Sinatra's "Theme from New York, New York" to accompany his trek to the bus, he had no intention of returning to Boston.

The music selection could not have been not accidental. Each playlist that Judge authored as the Yankees' self-appointed clubhouse DJ was meticulously crafted for a specific situation, whether it be to mellow teammates out before batting practice, pump them up twenty minutes prior to first pitch, or to celebrate another win at ear-splitting decibels. This time, it was to send a message.

"It's a good song," Boone said, stifling a grin. "And Aaron, he's one of our resident DJs, so he's got a pretty extensive playlist. I guess that's the one that was going. We like to hear that song sometimes when we win a big game. I think it's fun. It's something to talk about."

Sinatra was not in the regular arrangement for Judge, who typically thumped a blend of Drake, Calvin Harris, J. Cole, and Cardi B after each victory. Fenway's red-brick corridors muffled the tune for any lingering players in Boston's clubhouse, but several Red Sox players said they learned of Judge's stroll when a clip circulated on social media. Infielder Dustin Pedroia brought it to the attention of manager Alex Cora, who mostly shrugged it off.

"I just like music," Judge said. "I feel like music affects people's moods. If you have a good music tone of the day, it puts everybody in the right mindset."

Judge had assumed DJ duties following his call-up to the big leagues in 2016, when he said that there had been little to no music playing before and after games. Without much resistance, Judge took over for CC Sabathia and Aaron Hicks, then maintained the role throughout 2017.

"One day, it must have been the first week, I think Hicks or somebody put music on," Judge said. "We won that day, so the next day I came in and there was still no music on. I was wondering, 'What's going on?' We won. I think CC and Hicks just got tired of me complaining about not having any music on. They said, 'You know what? Screw it. You go take over.'"

That would prove to be the day that the music died. A 16-1 blowout in Game 3 saw Severino rocked for six runs over three-plus innings. The possibility of tipping pitches and a general lack of sharpness seemed to be responsible for the frequent hard contact, more so than a minor controversy stirred by TBS announcer Ron Darling, who speculated about Severino potentially warming up late for the 7:40 p.m. start. Television cameras spotted Severino setting foot on the bullpen mound a mere eight minutes before he threw his first pitch to Boston's Mookie Betts.

"I think that's a little bit blown out of proportion," pitching coach Larry Rothschild said. "In the playoffs, the routine is always [different] because of introductions and everything. He does a lot inside and he comes out a little bit later than most starters. Before I went out, I walked through the training room and told him, 'Introductions are at 28 and the first pitch is at 40.' No, he was perfectly clear with that."

The chase for a 28th World Series title paused on October 9, as Boston celebrated a 4-3 victory in Game 4. Most of a sellout crowd of 49,641 was still packing the house as the Yankees mounted a final threat against closer Craig Kimbrel, who struggled to protect a three-run lead. Judge worked a four-pitch walk and Gregorius singled before Stanton drew groans with a strikeout. Voit worked a free pass and Neil Walker was hit by a pitch, forcing home a run.

Sanchez lifted a deep drive to left field that, had it been a half-inch lower on the barrel, could have erased all memories of the catcher's .186 batting average and league-leading 18 passed balls. Instead, the ball sputtered on the warning track, good for a sacrifice fly that brought New York within a run.

"I've seen him swing for years," Judge said. "The way he hit it, I knew it was going to be too high to get out. He just missed a couple there."

With the decibel level spiking, Torres made the final out of the Yankees' season, a soft grounder that third baseman Eduardo Nunez charged and whipped across his body. A celebration was delayed while officials reviewed the play, but Torres said that he believed that he was out. They didn't know it at the time, but for a second straight year, the Yanks' season had been ended by the eventual World Series champions.

"Kimbrel is a really good pitcher," Torres said. "I tried to be focused and help my team. That at-bat, I tried to get a base hit and do my job. I didn't do my job. I feel really sad about that. I'm ready for next year and another opportunity."

As they partied in the Stadium's visiting clubhouse for the second time in two-and-a-half weeks, the Red Sox returned serve on Judge, blasting Sinatra. They'd do the same at Dodger Stadium after the clinching Game 5 of the World Series, gleefully singing along with Ol' Blue Eyes for a final parting shot. For the Yankees, the sting of being outplayed on the biggest stage by their rivals bled into the winter.

"Honestly, it's taken me a while," Betances said in November. "I'm kind of not over it. I have a lot of people that I know that are Boston fans. Growing up in New York, there are a lot of Boston fans, believe it or not. You hear about it a lot. You've got to give them credit; they had a hell of a year. It definitely left a bitter taste in my mouth. I'm just hoping that we have the chance to get to where they are."

As Cashman and his department assembled for the 2018-19 offseason, they were freed of the managerial search that had delayed their entry into the free-agent market a year prior. Though Boone earned high marks for how he handled the situation, Hal Steinbrenner said he was tired of rolling the dice in the Wild Card game, expecting the team to win the division and more in 2019.

"Look, the objective in October is to make it to the World Series and win a world championship," Steinbrenner said. "That is what we failed to do. You're never going to hear me call a season a failure, because I just think that's illogical. There are things to be proud of. We won 100 games. We scored a lot of runs. Our offense set a couple major league records. But there's no doubt that we let our fans down."

After re-signing clubhouse staples CC Sabathia and Brett Gardner to one-year contracts, Cashman triggered a trade to acquire left-hander James Paxton from the Mariners, upgrading the starting pitching which had been deficient during the postseason. The thirty-year-old Paxton came at the price of top-rated southpaw Justus Sheffield, right-hander Erik Swanson, and outfielder Dom Thompson-Williams.

It was difficult for the Yankees to part with Sheffield in particular; he'd been one of the prizes of the July 2016 Andrew Miller trade, advancing through the system to make his big-league debut in September 2018. Cashman rationalized the deal with the understanding that a pitcher like Paxton gave them a better chance to win now, recalling that the initial purpose of rebuilding the team in '16 was to fight for another day on which the Yankees could be crowned as champions.

"No one cares about windows. They just care about championships," Cashman said. "We have a window of opportunity because we have a collection of talented players that need to stay healthy and they need to perform as a group. To some degree, they have. To certain levels, they have.

But the ultimate, they haven't. And we haven't. So there's a door there we want to pound open.

"We've done it before, and a lot of people have been along for that ride. We want to taste that success again. There's levels of success, but the Yankees are about championships. We want to be about championships and we want to push that. We believe in it and the constant challenge is finding ways to be that last team standing. It's special to be a part of it."

ACKNOWLEDGMENTS

Thanks first to my beautiful wife Connie for her love and support throughout this project. You are the most important part of my life, and without you, none of this would have been possible. During the 2017 season, Connie and our one-year-old daughter Penny tagged along for spring training and to various American League outposts, attempting to turn the Yanks' scheduled trips to Baltimore, Boston, Chicago, Cleveland, Tampa, and Toronto into something resembling family time. The life of a baseball reporter is a strange, wonderful ride, and Penny has to be among the youngest fans in history to have already checked off each AL East city.

It meant the world to be able to share a breakfast or lunch with the girls before games, especially since Connie had a talent for finding the best eateries around, making each trip feel like a homestand. No matter what happened in that night's nine innings (and, in the case of that eighteen inning game at Wrigley, sometimes much, much more), it provided great joy to know that as I sent my final copy, they were snuggled in a Marriott bed and hopefully had not done too much damage to the room service bill. In 2018, we welcomed another baby girl, Maddie, to our traveling road show. I love you all more than words can express.

Thanks to my parents, Fred and Dorothy, for inspiring my dual loves of baseball and writing, while understanding that an unorthodox career path had taken root in my childhood bedroom. As a high school freshman in 1996, in the Wild West days of the Internet, I launched a website called *Mets Online* that was essentially a precursor to a blog. It predated Mets.

com by three seasons and gained a following that opened doors into the journalism world, including an internship with the team that placed me in the Shea Stadium executive offices on the night Mike Piazza flew out to Bernie Williams to end the 2000 World Series.

Most parents probably wouldn't understand why their teenage son needed to lug a Compaq desktop computer up a flight of stairs during a family vacation to Disney World, then use the hotel telephone line to dial into Prodigy or AOL. They got it, and for that, I am forever grateful. Thanks also to my younger brother, Shawn, a United States Navy helicopter pilot who is one of the bravest people I know—and not only because he never flinched at the errant curveballs that spun out of my left hand on a Sloatsburg, New York, sandlot. The sacrifices that he and his wife, Jaclyn, have made to serve our country while welcoming Julia and Seth into this world are an ongoing inspiration.

Thanks to my in-laws, Ray and Eileen, for welcoming me into your amazing family. There's a saying that you never get a second chance to make a first impression, but my second impression was probably worse, huffing off the subway before a 2009 game and spotting them waving at me from a bench outside Yankee Stadium's press gate. "They must be big Yankees fans," I thought, oblivious to the fact that they were my then-girlfriend's parents. Penny is so lucky to have you as her Puddin' and Pops, and I have treasured our dinners with Joan and Ick, breaking down the latest news from the Bronx. It is a blessing to have added Brian, Griffin, and Raymond as brothers, Joanna as a sister, and to be an official part of the Clymer crew and the Schwab mob. When it comes to cheering for their beloved Yankees, the Long Island Schwabs are as legit as they come. Thanks for your feedback and friendship.

The team at MLB.com has been incredible throughout this project, beginning with Dinn Mann and Matthew Leach, who swiftly gave their blessing to having one of their beat reporters add another challenge to his plate. 2018 marked my twelfth season covering the Yankees, and working at MLB.com has been a dream. No one covers this game better or more thoroughly from coast-to-coast on a minute-by-minute basis. I would like to especially thank David Adler, Kristen Altmeyer, Jordan Bastian, Jason Beck, Rhett Bollinger, Mark Bowman, Ian Browne, Anthony Castrovince, Bill Chastain, Gregor Chisholm, Jamal Collier, Anthony DiComo, Mark Feinsand, Joe Frisaro, Brittany Ghiroli, Richard Justice, Jane Lee, Brian

McTaggart, Matt Martell, Scott Merkin, Carrie Muskat, Marty Noble, Arturo Pardavila, Mike Petriello, Grace Raynor, Mike Siano, Nick Suss, T.R. Sullivan, and Todd Zolecki for their contributions to this project and their friendship. Thanks also to Paul Bodi for entrusting a twenty-four-year-old rookie to report on the most decorated franchise in sports, and to the team at MLB Network for making me look relatively good on camera.

From spring training through the end of the season, reporters spend countless hours in taxi cabs, on planes, in the press box (and, of course, at Shaun Clancy's Foley's NY). That time is infinitely more enjoyable when you are surrounded by funny and talented people. I have been fortunate to share the beat with some of the brightest in the industry, many of whom we are blessed to call friends to this day. Special thanks to Peter Abraham, Dom Amore, Marty Appel, Dan Barbarisi, Jerry Beach, Bruce Beck, Erik Boland, Peter Botte, Pete Caldera, Marc Carig, Jack Curry, Ken Davidoff, John Harper, Chad Jennings, Michael Kay, Tyler Kepner, George King, Bob Klapisch, Brendan Kuty, David Lennon, Mike Lupica, Anthony McCarron, Nathan Maciborski, Bill Madden, Meredith Marakovits, Andrew Marchand, Dan Martin, Wallace Matthews, Mike Mazzeo, Randy Miller, Sweeny Murti, Anthony Rieber, Marly Rivera, Al Santasiere, Jon Schwartz, Joel Sherman, Ben Shpigel, Scott Stanford, John Sterling, Tara Sullivan, Mike Vaccaro, Tom Verducci, Suzyn Waldman, David Waldstein, Billy Witz and countless other members of the New York media contingent for the many laughs and being part of our lives. Your coverage, some of which has been referenced in this text, has been top-notch and immensely valuable.

The New York Yankees have great people both on the field and behind the scenes who made this an enjoyable project to work on. In particular, I would like to thank Jason Zillo and his media relations department for their assistance. My wife spent four seasons in the department, earning a World Series ring in 2009, so we can both speak to the intense atmosphere and tireless work that goes on at the Stadium 365 days a year. Marlon Abreu, Kaitlyn Brennan, Ariele Goldman Hecht, Dolores Hernandez, Kenny Leandry, Michael Margolis, Lauren Moran, Rob Morse, Yoshiki Sato, and Alexandra Trochanowski have all been accommodating and helpful.

Many others with connections to the organization have been gracious and generous with their time over the years, including but not limited to: Troy Afenir, Jean Afterman, Tyler Austin, Brian Barber, Dellin Betances, Greg Bird, Aaron Boone, Robinson Cano, Brian Cashman, Starlin Castro,

Joba Chamberlain, Alan Cockrell, David Cone, Lou Cucuzza Jr., Rob Cucuzza, Johnny Damon, Gary Denbo, Billy Eppler, Joe Espada, John Flaherty, Clint Frazier, Todd Frazier, Brett Gardner, Kevin Gausman, Dan Giese, Joe Girardi, Chad Green, Didi Gregorius, Eric Handler, Chase Headley, Jim Hendry, Aaron Hicks, Matt Holliday, Reggie Jackson, Derek Jeter, Aaron Judge, Randy Levine, Jim Leyritz, Kevin Long, Bob Lorenz, Bryan Mitchell, Jordan Montgomery, Tim Naehring, Jeff Nelson, Paul O'Neill, Damon Oppenheimer, Al Pedrique, Tony Pena, Andy Pettitte, Jorge Posada, Darrell Rasner, Kevin Reese, Rob Refsnyder, Mariano Rivera, David Robertson, Alex Rodriguez, Austin Romine, Larry Rothschild, Donny Rowland, James Rowson, CC Sabathia, Gary Sanchez, Luis Severino, Ken Singleton, Hal Steinbrenner, Nick Swisher, Masahiro Tanaka, Rob Thomson, Ronald Torreyes, Debbie Tymon, Tyler Wade, Adam Warren, Chase Whitley, and Bernie Williams. I have great gratitude for your availability and candidness in helping trace of the rise of the "Baby Bombers," and for making it a story worth telling.

Extra special thanks to Mark Teixeira, who was a pleasure to cover during his eight seasons in pinstripes. After hitting 409 homers in the big leagues, I personally feel that Mark should be credited with another after he agreed to write the foreword to this book, responding with an enthusiastic, "Yes!"

I would like to express great appreciation to the staff at Diversion Books in New York, especially Keith Wallman, who gambled that my writing would be able to make the leap from dot-com to the printed page. Keith gathered a selection of terrific photos that added color to the text, nudged back our deadlines while the team battled deep into October, and made many suggestions that improved the final product.

As we wrap the paperback edition of this project, I would like to thank everyone who attended signing events in Tampa, Trenton, Scranton/Wilkes-Barre, and at Foley's NY in Manhattan. It was wonderful to see so many familiar faces and to make new friends. Your support was greatly appreciated. Finally, my thanks to the vast universe of Yankees fans, whose voracious appetite for information challenges us to dig deeper every day. The energy and passion that you consistently bring to the Bronx has created memories that will last a lifetime.

Bryan Hoch
January 2019

INDEX

Italic page numbers indicate illustrations.

ABOUT THE AUTHOR

BRYAN HOCH has written about New York baseball for the past two decades, including covering the New York Yankees as a beat reporter for MLB.com since 2007. A regular contributor to MLB Network, Hoch's work has also been featured in *Yankees Magazine*, *New York Mets Inside Pitch*, and on FOXSports.com. He lives with his wife, Connie, and daughters, Penny and Maddie.

Follow Bryan on Twitter **@bryanhoch** and on
Facebook at **www.facebook.com/bryanhochmlb**.